The Differentiated Math Classroom

The Differentiated Math Classroom

A Guide for Teachers, K–8

Miki Murray
with Jenny Jorgensen

HEINEMANN
Portsmouth, NH

Heinemann
A division of Reed Elsevier Inc.
361 Hanover Street
Portsmouth, NH 03801–3912
www.heinemann.com

Offices and agents throughout the world

The authors and publisher wish to thank those who have generously given permission to reprint borrowed material:

Lyrics from "It's in Every One of Us" by David Pomeranz. Copyright © 1973 by WB Music Corp. and Upward Spiral Music. All rights administered by WB Music Corp. All Rights Reserved. Used by permission of Alfred Publishing Co., Inc.

Figure 1.2a: "Truffles Factory Activity" adapted from *Math Matters,* Second Edition by Suzanne H. Chapin and Art Johnson. Copyright © 2006 by Math Solutions Publications.

Figure 3.7: "Example of a Focal Student Planner" from *Addressing Accessibility in Math.* Courtesy Education Development Center, Inc. For more information, visit www.edc.org/accessmath.

Figure 3.13: "Instructional Matrix for Multiple Intelligences in Mathematics" from "Multiply with MI: Using Multiple Intelligences to Master Multiplication" in *Teaching Children Mathematics*, 2001 (Vol 7, Number 5). Copyright © 2001 by the National Council of Teachers of Mathematics. Reprinted with permission.

Figure 7.6: "Array Game" based on material in *Arrays and Shares* by Karen Economopoulos, Cornelia Tierney, and Susan Jo Russell, part of the *Investigations in Number, Data, and Space Mathematics Program.* Copyright © 2005 by Pearson Education, Inc. Used by permission of Pearson Education, Inc.

Excerpt from "Big Ideas and Understandings as the Foundation for Elementary and Middle School Mathematics" by Randall Charles from *The National Council of Supervisors of Mathematics Journal*, Spring/Summer 2005. Reprinted by permission of the author.

Figure 8.3: Gregorc Mindstyle™ Profiles for Miki Murray and Jenny Jorgensen from the Gregorc Style Delineator™. Used by permission of Anthony Gregorc.

Library of Congress Cataloging-in-Publication Data
Murray, Miki.
    The differentiated math classroom : a guide for teachers, K–8 / Miki Murray with Jenny Jorgensen.
        p. cm.
    Includes bibliographical references and index.
    ISBN-13: 978-0-325-00996-4
    ISBN-10: 0-325-00996-1
    1. Mathematics—Study and teaching—United States. I. Jorgensen, Jenny. II. Title.
    QA11.2.M865 2007
    372.7—dc22   2007027580

Editor: Victoria Merecki
Production editor: Sonja S. Chapman
Cover design: Night & Day Design
Miki Murray author photograph: John Murray/Murray Photography
Compositor: Valerie Levy/Drawing Board Studios
Manufacturing: Steve Bernier

Printed in the United States of America on acid-free paper

11   10   09   08   07   VP   1   2   3   4   5

CONTENTS

PREFACE

IT'S IN EVERY ONE OF US

It's in ev'ry one of us to be wise.
Find your heart, open up both your eyes.
We can all know ev'ry thing without ever knowing why.
It's in ev'ry one of us—by and by.

It's in ev'ry one of us; I just remembered.
It's like I've been sleepin' for years.
I'm not awake as I can be but my seein's better.
I can see through the tears
I've been realizin' that I bought this ticket and watchin' only half of the show
But there is scenery and lights and a cast of thousands who all know what I know
And it's good that it's so.

It's in ev'ry one of us to be wise.
Find your heart, open up both your eyes.
We can all know ev'ry thing without ever knowing why.
      It's in ev'ry one of us—by and by.
      It's in ev'ry one of us—by and by.

Words and Music by David Pomeranz[1]

Like David Pomeranz, we believe "it's in every one of us" and the *it* is mathematics. The last four decades have been witness to a frustrating combination of anxiety and urgency in the struggle to bring all of America's youth into the positive spectrum of mathematical understanding and fluency. Despite the amazing incredible effort of dedicated mathematics educators throughout the country, false beliefs such as "only certain people can learn math" and that "it's OK to not do math" interfere with the potential progress of some if not many of our students.

---

[1]

David's inspirational song speaks to the issue of the capabilities we all have within us as individuals. From the first time I heard it many years ago, it has been a source of energy and continued determination to help children learn and enjoy learning mathematics in meaningful ways. David described for me how he wrote the song after he had a stimulating seminar experience that reached deeply into his soul and helped him understand the depths of the gifts with which we are all endowed when we are unencumbered by emotional difficulties, are self-determined and fully present, and have all abilities in play. David Pomeranz told me he was amazed to realize that he wrote and composed "It's In Every One of Us" in forty-five minutes following his "awakening" while most songs take him weeks, or even months.

The song's message surely convinces us that we have the capacity to meet the math learning needs of all our students. We hope that his song and story along with this book will inspire you to believe that differentiated instruction has the potential to "open the eyes" of all your students and allow the power and beauty of mathematical knowledge to come into their lives.

About This Book

> *Mathematics teaching is a difficult task under any circumstances. It is made even more complicated and challenging when teachers are paying attention simultaneously, as they should, to the manifold paths mathematics learning can take and to the multifaceted nature of mathematics itself.*
> —National Research Council 2001, *Adding It Up*
> Jeremy Kilpatrick, Chair: Mathematics Learning
> Study Committee, Preface xiv

In this book, we present the case and provide support for using differentiated instruction—a purposeful process for adapting the teaching and learning practices of the classroom to accommodate the needs of all learners—in mathematics classrooms as a tool for meeting these complex challenges. We believe deeply that all students can learn mathematics when they have access to quality teaching and learning experiences.

- We summarize the research on teaching and learning mathematics, spell out the issues facing the teaching of mathematics in America, and outline a program for classroom delivery.
- We include many suggestions for creating supportive mathematics learning environments in classrooms across the grade levels.
- We discuss the importance of working with parents as partners, getting to know all about students and their needs, honoring and utilizing the differences to be found within any mathematics classroom, and optimizing deep learning for all students.

- We describe the knowledge and understanding that mathematics teachers require in order to effectively utilize differentiated instruction to accommodate the needs of all learners.
- We promote learner-centered and knowledge-centered mathematics classrooms facilitated by skillful, effective teachers.

Finally, the text is full of lessons and classroom scenarios that exemplify the premise of allowing students to access mathematics through their strengths, learning styles, interests, and levels of readiness.

ACKNOWLEDGMENTS

Jenny and I have been privileged to work with many gifted teachers and mentors throughout two decades of collaboration. Our professional personas are a reflection of the rich professional environments that nourish our growth. We are especially grateful to the entire Connected Mathematics program (CMP) staff at Michigan State University, the EQUALS and FAMILY MATH programs at UCal Berkeley, and the myriad Math Solutions professional development opportunities and materials we've accessed over the past nineteen years. Similarly I want to acknowledge the dedicated teachers and staff at the Center for Teaching and Learning in Edgecomb, Maine, whose ideas we've incorporated in many subtle ways throughout this book: especially Helene Coffin for her amazing work with kindergartners; Jill Cotta for loaning me her class and sharing her insights, opinions, and differentiating tools; and Katie Rittershaus for her inexhaustible creative classroom energy along with her willingness to read and give feedback on portions of the manuscript as it developed. Jenny would also like to thank the teachers with whom she works who have been wonderful about sharing their classrooms with her.

We appreciate Victoria Merecki for asking for a book on differentiated math instruction. Her request made us realize the depth of our passion and thus, she gave us the opportunity to share our professional commitment to math classrooms that work for all students. We also acknowledge the students whose infinite variations of strengths and needs inspire and challenge our classroom work. We are grateful for their willingness to share the mathematical products you see scattered throughout the book. Their often-remarkable work continues to amaze us. We recognize that the efforts of our supportive interim editor, Kerry Herlihy, brought the project to fruition and we appreciate her willingness to sample the vagaries of the mathematics classroom along with her own language arts teaching responsibilities.

Finally, we acknowledge the understanding support of our husbands, Don Murray and John VanOrden. They have been generous with their love, their encouragement, and their patience, enduring the weekly late afternoon meetings that made the collaboration possible and being cheerful during challenging rewrites. In addition, Don brought me bravely through every terrifying technological glitch, especially the major computer crash that without him would have ended the project midstream.

Introduction: A Rationale for Differentiated Instruction in Mathematics

But for a few tiny adjustments, if we knew how to make them, we could release the genius in every child.

—Einstein

Defining Differentiated Instruction

We frequently hear the question, "Differentiated instruction? What's that?" in our various professional encounters.

First and foremost, it is *not* individualized instruction. Differentiated instruction implies a purposeful process for adapting the teaching and learning processes of the classroom to accommodate the needs of all learners. For us, it is an especially useful tool for ensuring that all students have access to and are appropriately supported in their acquisition of important mathematical knowledge. Differentiated instruction encompasses a versatile collection of strategies that have developed over the years including flexible grouping and tiered activities. In the early 1990s, Dr. Carol Ann Tomlinson of the University of Virginia first coined the expression with its current connotation.

However, a touch of history in the annals of educational progress is illuminating regarding the term *differentiation*. In the book *Whatever It Takes*, DuFour (et al. 2004) points out the dramatic educational change that took place in America during the last decade of the nineteenth century. It was at the dawn of the industrial age. Education for all was to extend beyond elementary school with the caveat that all students didn't need the same education. This new "differentiated" schooling would have students sorted into programs designed to meet their different abilities.

The need for a sorting tool was born. By 1916, the Stanford-Binet test with its intelligence quotient (IQ), courtesy of Psychologist Alfred Binet and Stanford University's Lewis Terman, gave schools a single measure to use in the sorting process. For the times, the IQ test was considered remarkably forward looking and was subsequently used by universities to claim that too many students were going to college. The average mental age of Americans was fourteen and universities believed that only students with above average IQs could be educated beyond high school. That's what differentiated schooling was all about (DuFour 2004, 16–19).

What a dramatic shift in the use of terminology! Whereas the earlier differentiated schooling principle was designed to set a limit for what a group of students could learn based primarily on their IQ, *differentiated instruction* is now used to demonstrate that indeed all students can learn at high levels—when the quality of the schooling matches their needs. One of our favorite definitions is that given by Tad Johnston, mathematics consultant for the Maine State Department of Education: "differentiation is reaching common ends through uncommon means in a relatively stable time frame." Variations of the term incorporated into this text include *differentiated curriculum, differentiated classroom, differentiation, diversified instruction,* and *responsive teaching.*

No Child Left Behind

We now appear to be poised at the cusp of a new educational age. The No Child Left Behind Act (NCLB) was signed into law in 2002. NCLB has four basic principles: stronger accountability for results; greater flexibility for the use of federal funds; choice for parents of children with disadvantaged backgrounds; and an emphasis on teaching methods that work. It *is* controversial. The sweeping legislation has changed the educational landscape with dramatic effects on school districts nationwide. In many instances, it is financially troubling because it requires services that are not sufficiently funded.

With its demand for local and state accountability, NCLB impacts mathematics classrooms across America. From our perspective, this is an opportunity to respond to an obvious and critical need, using effectively differentiated instruction in mathematics. We are not arguing the pros or cons of the impact of NCLB but recognizing that the stark reality of the demand for mathematics proficiency for *all* students has opened our eyes more widely than ever to the plight of those children who fall under the umbrella of "partially meeting standards" or below. It is clear to us as math teachers that we need to work together with creative, consistent, and knowledgeable minds to determine how we can move all children into the "meeting or exceeding standards" categories while continuing to challenge the already enthusiastic and successful learners.

As a profession, we are committed to helping children progress as far as they can, but NCLB pushes us further to find ways to give all kids *powerful curriculum, effective teaching,* and the necessary *time and support* to accomplish deep learning. These three essential elements for reaching all students are commented on briefly in the next section. Differentiating mathematics instruction is a strategy teachers can use to accomplish this formidable but critical task.

Powerful Curriculum, Effective Teaching, and Time and Support

Powerful Curriculum

In this book, we describe and illustrate powerful mathematics curriculum through the lenses of problem solving and differentiation. Powerful mathematics is the standard we set for the techniques and strategies used to draw all students into developing a deep understanding of important mathematics. We do so by standing on the shoulders of Carol Ann Tomlinson, Diane Heacox, and others who have developed the primary general theory and guidelines for differentiated instruction. We add our mathematical considerations to these guidelines. It is our way of encouraging math teachers across the country to implement differentiated instruction—an organized yet flexible approach to teaching mathematics.

Effective Teaching

Effective mathematics teachers and teaching provide a natural context for differentiation. But what standard characteristics and/or teaching behaviors describe effective mathematics instruction?

The background work of Ron Ritchhart, Parker Palmer, Liping Ma, and many others in the mathematics community help to clarify the criteria for effective teachers and teaching. In general, effective teachers teach from the heart with a strong sense of identity and integrity (Palmer 1998). They understand the importance of a thinking disposition and model thinking vocabulary (Ritchhart 2002). They have or continuously strive for "profound understanding of fundamental mathematics" (Ma 1999).

Carol Ann Tomlinson summarizes effective teaching in general as responsive teaching where students are highly engaged, contribute actively to the learning, and receive and use quality feedback (Tomlinson 2003). In addition and more specifically, effective math teaching includes the following key behaviors:

- Focusing content on the essential big ideas of mathematics
- Expecting all students can and will understand mathematics
- Continuously assessing student thinking and understanding
- Planning and structuring lessons based on student needs and important content
- Facilitating high-level conversations with appropriate and timely questions

Measuring up to these standards is a tall order for mathematics teachers today, but it is what we need to be doing in our mathematics classrooms. In order to use differentiation effectively, the quality of the instruction must be maintained at this high level. We cannot allow the process to become formulaic and get lost in the details of tiering or some other design. The implementation must always be responsive to student needs and measured against the criteria for quality.

Time and Support

Throughout the book, as we describe various differentiated situations we point out ways to utilize time efficiently and suggest strategies for the extra support some students need in order to learn essential and important mathematics. We do this by paying attention to scheduling details and the numerous mathematics opportunities that occur during math class and throughout the school day. These vary greatly by grade level and situation, but we hope you will find ideas that can be adapted to your needs and efforts.

Differentiated Instruction—The Practice

Carol Ann Tomlinson has written the definitive work on differentiated instruction. During a recent email exchange, I asked Carol about the origins of the term *differentiated instruction*. She indicated that it had come about quite naturally as a way of talking about the work she was doing. In *Fulfilling the Promise of the Differentiated Classroom*, Tomlinson refers to *differentiating instruction* as accommodating the different ways that students learn (2003, 1). In essence, the goal is to plan for the learning needs of all students, providing them with the opportunities they need to reach their full potential and become mathematically proficient.

When reading the literature related to teaching academically diverse learners, Tomlinson noted that others used the term *differentiated instruction* in somewhat different ways from her intended concept (email April 28, 2005). In that regard, it is important to understand Dr. Tomlinson's intention for vigorous, proactive, high-quality differentiation and then work to incorporate those principles into general guidelines for differentiated math classrooms. Tomlinson looks for teachers to create their own responsive classroom environments in ways that align with their own teaching styles as well as the needs of their students. For that reason, there is no one best way to plan for and implement differentiation in mathematics. But there are general principles discussed in Chapter 1 that will support teachers who have the goal of planning differentiated math instruction and who want guidance through the processes that are involved (Tomlinson 1999, 2–3).

Mathematics Classroom Issues

Several issues dominate the challenges of teaching mathematics to the multifaceted, diverse students who are part of all mathematics classrooms. First and foremost is the hierarchical structure of the various strands in mathematics: number and operations, geometry, measurement, data analysis and probability, and algebra. A highly coordinated, well-articulated curriculum is essential. Further complicating the curricular scene is the interplay between the strands that is critical to developing deep understanding and creating a holistic, sense-making picture of what mathematics is and what doing mathematics means. These are good challenges for teachers because it helps us understand our discipline more deeply. The big ideas of mathematics and the National Council of Teachers of Mathematics (NCTM's) recently published *Curriculum Focal Points* (NCTM 2006) help us recognize and organize the intersections of the strands. (See Chapter 9.)

Next are the social and cultural auras that accompany even the mention of the word *mathematics*. Math anxiety and the all too common belief that only certain people do math or that it is OK to say you can't do math, for whatever reason, are prevalent in our social world and can wiggle their way easily into any mathematics classroom. Mathematics is frequently maligned in casual conversation. Similarly, there is the "fear factor" to address.

The biggest fear issues for math teachers are (1) being sensitive to and allaying any fear that might paralyze from within, and (2) learning the subtleties of capitalizing on the "porous" effect—that bit of disequilibrium that creates a "teachable moment." In *Human Brain, Human Learning* (1983), Leslie Hart identified downshifting as the brain's response to threat. Downshifting for students in the mathematics classroom has huge implications. Renate and Geoffrey Caine (1997) explain the effects of downshifting on our responses:

> We are less able to access all that we know or see what is really there. Our ability to consider subtle environmental and internal cues is reduced. . . . We also seem to be less able to engage in complex intellectual tasks, those requiring creativity and the ability to engage in open-ended thinking and questioning. (103)

Simply put, fear-induced downshifting in the classroom virtually blocks a student's opportunity to learn mathematics through problem solving and reasoning—what research tells us must happen in order to generate the deep learning we want. Finding the joy and fun of mathematics and sharing that with students are the seductive sides of this challenge.

Fear behaviors to watch for and allay include silence, withdrawal, and cynicism; they mimic ignorance. We want a safe and pleasurable environment for our students. Because teachers are potential victims as well, we must be aware, make space, pay attention, and listen to students in order to gain insight, alleviate fear, and capitalize on the knowledge that humans can get a real "high" from learning. The positive chemistry of great learning experiences is probably the best antidote.

Consider as well the message of the video documentary, *A Private Universe*, produced by the Harvard-Smithsonian Center for Astrophysics in 1987. It documents how early foundations produce powerful lasting impressions. In some instances, these early experiences create enduring misconceptions that defy correction through traditional methods. The connection to mathematics is all too easy to imagine. The early misconceptions, both attitudinal and conceptual, have been some of the greatest challenges of our collective sixty years of teaching mathematics.

The documentary also demonstrates that children make connections to mathematics learned previously when the lessons are appropriate, engaging, and challenging and can be linked to specific experiences from past math classes. It is our goal to design lessons that engage, challenge, and utilize connections.

And then there is our favorite soap-box issue—the cycle of benign abuse that impacts so many of us who teach mathematics. We tend to teach as we were taught and as in any abusive situation or relationship, if we don't make a serious direct effort to recognize the abuse (meaningless instruction) and change, we innocently and benignly continue to cycle it. This has been a career-long struggle for us because in our most formative years, we were taught only procedures to memorize and practice with little or no understanding of why they worked. We managed to build our own understanding without any discussion, depending totally on "feeling right" about it. In some instances, we came to realize conclusions are flawed—so we must remain cautious and continue to be vigilant, deepening and challenging our understanding. Listening to the reasoning of our students and colleagues is of vital importance to us in this regard.

Additional issues for math teachers today involve the pressure we are under to regain stature in the worldwide arena of mathematics achievement. Media and community concerns reflect misunderstandings about what mathematics is and what it means to do mathematics—our audience is much larger than the students in our classes. Finally, we want to measure up to the well-formulated principles and standards of NCTM and respond responsibly to our individual state and local standards.

In summary, special mathematics issues include the multitudinous diversity of students, the hierarchical interwoven structure of the mathematics, a challenging cultural attitude, fearful downshifting, teachers needing to teach in new and innovative ways that may be outside of their learning experience, and a series of outside pressures that intensify the stakes. Mathematics has its own special difficulties to override in the quest for differentiated classrooms. These are the central issues that challenge and motivate differentiated instruction in mathematics. It is critical that students have robust opportunities to learn mathematics deeply. It is this determination to have a lasting positive impact on our children's mathematical learning that keeps us working toward our goals—one day at a time, overriding the difficulties, and collaborating our way to success. As teachers we can do this if we work together and support each other. The futures of our children are at stake. We must give all students a foothold for reaching their full mathematical potential.

All Students—From Challenge to Change

All students is the hallmark of the gauntlet laid out in today's classrooms. For those of us who have focused our energy in the arena of mathematics, we know only too well the challenges of providing for the broad spectrum of math learners. In most cases, this calls for significant changes in our approach to teaching mathematics. To make these changes reality, we only need to fulfill five conditions:

1. Imagine what we want—a *vision* of classrooms filled with vibrant young mathematicians.
2. Identify and target the new *skills* that we need and find ways to practice and learn them.
3. Realize that the mathematical empowerment of our students is a great *incentive* for focusing our energies on that goal.
4. Identify and obtain the *resources* and support we need.
5. Create *plans* that support and guide the way, collaboratively if possible. (Based on the work of Enterprise Management Ltd. 1987)

Our task is to share with readers our interpretation and implementation of differentiated instruction in mathematics. We share our *vision* in keeping with that of NCTM's Principles and Standards. We offer support for acquiring the essential *skills*, encourage you with the *incentives* of deep mathematical understanding and broad-based student achievement, share our favorite supportive *resources*, and suggest ways for you to *plan*. All this comes from the experiences of our collective work over several decades. Our practice has emerged from a philosophy of reflective and responsive teaching in our own mathematics classrooms, as well as the classrooms of the teachers with whom we collaborate. We support our actions with the research and literature that have guided us over the years as well as the most recent documentations. Our goal is to encourage and support mathematics teachers at all levels through the process of exploring and implementing effective teaching and learning strategies that reach all students.

Who We Are and the Thesis for This Book

Jenny and I have been working together as colleagues in a multitude of settings for two decades. We've taught inservice courses together, provided staff development, presented at national conferences, researched, and generally supported each other through professional growth as mathematics educators and teachers. We understand the challenges facing classroom teachers because we are practitioners and learners. We've faced and continue facing our own demons. High motivation and determination are fairly accurate descriptors for the two of us. We're both willing to try unproven but promising lessons. We observe, take notes, probe for learning effects, reflect, and learn with and from the children. Classroom issue problems inspire us to research, reflect, and find ways to help teachers and kids learn mathematics. We want math teachers to feel comfortable differentiating their programs because they have the knowledge, resources, and support to be successful.

The Work Ahead

In the chapters that follow, we tackle each aspect of the differentiation challenge in mathematics. Section I focuses on clarifying differentiated instruction in mathematics and its preliminary classroom preparations. We begin in Chapter 1 with one teacher's experience differentiating a unit on place value using Tomlinson's guidelines. Each step in the process is detailed with analysis and discussion. Chapter 2 addresses the task of preparing the classroom for an environment that supports this kind of instruction. The Equity, Teaching, and Learning Principles play a key role as well as the Problem Solving Standard (NCTM 2000). We establish guidelines for creating and sustaining the culture for a learning community that is based on thinking and reasoning. Chapter 3 works with coming to know students in ways that build the mathematics learning community from diversity. We consider learning styles, preferences, personal dynamics, and a host of other characteristics including student autobiographies and parental input.

Chapters 4 through 7 of Section II elaborate on each detail of differentiating math instruction including problem solving, flexibility, planning, organizing, and implementing. Through different lenses we illuminate strategies for modifying curricular elements and differentiating instruction. Each lens is supported and clarified with examples of lessons or units across the mathematics content strands and grade levels.

Section III is focused on the "glue" that holds the elements of differentiated instruction together as a viable approach to teaching mathematics. Chapters 8 and 9 discuss teacher knowledge of themselves, mathematics, and mathematics pedagogy. Elements include teaching and learning styles, basic beliefs about learning, and content/pedagogical strengths and limitations. The emphasis is on how teachers can use their strengths to the best advantage, compensate for limitations with positive strength-building actions, and work on continuous growth in content understanding and pedagogical skills.

The chapters that follow round out our differentiated mathematics continuum with a catalog of the lessons described throughout the text, an outline for designing differentiated math experiences, extended descriptions of anchor activities, and a reference guide to the tools for teachers used throughout the book. Principles and guidelines for differentiating mathematics are reviewed, closing with responses to frequently asked questions from a diverse group of classroom practitioners.

SECTION I

The Preliminaries: Developing a Learning Community

The teacher is responsible for creating an intellectual environment where serious mathematical thinking is the norm.

National Council of Teachers of Mathematics,
Principles and Standards for School Mathematics

Four design characteristics from *How People Learn* (National Research Council 2000) are especially useful for thinking about a classroom environment that supports differentiated mathematics instruction:

- the *community-centered lens*—developing a culture of questioning, respect, and risk-taking
- the *learner-centered lens*—beginning instruction with prior knowledge and what students think and know
- the *knowledge-centered lens*—being clear about the mathematics content to be taught, why it is taught, and evidence of its learning
- the *assessment-centered lens*—providing frequent opportunities for students to make their thinking and learning visible as a guide for both teacher and student (Adapted from National Research Council 2005, 12–13.)

Chapter 1

Guidelines and a Differentiated Unit

The beginning is the most important part of the work.

Plato, c. 428–348 B.C.

Guidelines for Differentiating Math Instruction

As a backdrop against which to develop guidelines and principles for differentiating mathematics instruction, let's walk through a beginning process. To start, think about *why* it is necessary to differentiate a specific piece of curriculum. Are modifications needed to make the content more accessible to all students or is the concern student motivation? Maybe the need is for more efficient learning. Selecting the appropriate reason leads to the next consideration, the curriculum portion that is to be adapted.

Any piece of mathematics curriculum has at least three elements: the *content* to be learned; a planned activity or *process* for reaching the content goals; and the *product* expected of students to demonstrate their learning. The environment—the classroom or alternate site—might also be considered as a separate element and a target for differentiation. With learner needs in mind, decide *what* element or elements of curriculum will be adjusted to help students reach their potential.

Next determine *how* the content, process, and/or product will be modified to accommodate the selected student issues. If the selected reason for differentiating is readiness, then the content must be made accessible to all students. If the reason is for interests, groups need to be organized and able to approach the content from their perspectives. If learner styles are the focus, then the content is embedded in processes that match the different styles. Or there could be some combination of all of the above.

A Unit Transformed

Consider the following description of how a traditional unit originally designed for a homogeneous group of accelerated students is transformed into a unit adapted for a multigrade diverse heterogeneous group of children.

Original Plan

The first education course I took at Michigan State University left an indelible impression on me in the realm of intrinsic beliefs. As a committed lifelong learner, I am relieved that even today this belief needs no challenge. It continues to be reinforced in more and more creative ways in today's educational scene. This deep belief is that the major work of my life commitment to teaching is to take students wherever they are and help them move as far forward as possible during our time together, doing whatever it takes. Fortunately, I was blessed with inspired mentors. That, in and of itself, was an important life lesson for me—no matter where I am, there is always more to learn and another pathway to try.

In an early teaching assignment, I was one of three third-grade teachers in the building. The school divided the three classes for mathematics and I was assigned the accelerated students. I remember having more than thirty students in that first class. Knowing the importance of understanding place value as an essential concept for growing mathematically, I designed a unit that was outside the realm of the textbooks of the times (mid-1960s).

The big idea of the unit was to compare number systems and then have students create their own place value number system. The class worked with the Roman system of numeration (Roman numerals) and our own base ten numbers, looking for similarities and differences. Next we worked with Cuisenaire rods and counted in different bases—five, then two, then their choice. I guided them carefully through the counting and recording process. We went so far as to explore the four operations in these different systems using addition/subtraction and multiplication/division tables. Finally, I asked students to imagine a different universe and a different planet—Sputnik and satellites had become familiar conversation in their science work—where inhabitants had different numbers of fingers (digits). They were each to create their own number system for the inhabitants including symbols for the basic digits. They had their choice of which base to use.

It was an exciting and exhausting time for me. Because the class was the best and brightest, no one was challenged beyond his or her readiness and every student was engaged. My problem was the overwhelming task of keeping up with their creations. Nevertheless, each student shared his or her number system by displaying their symbols, their counting numbers to thirty, and a diorama showing how life would be different with the use of their number system. I was exhausted with the evaluation and feedback process but there was never a doubt about the value of the learning experience for the students.

I learned from the students throughout this unit one of the delights of teaching mathematics. From that first experience, the students helped me understand that I could simplify the project options without sacrificing the key conceptual development. The following year I modified the unit considerably by restricting the number of bases students could use for their number system creations. The projects could be either base three or base four place value systems. That made the process more doable for both students and teacher. And that is how I continued to organize the place value number system unit for as long as I taught third grade.

The Transformation

Many years later I am working with a combined classroom of third- and fourth- grade students. I know this amazingly diverse group of students will benefit enormously from a better understanding of our number system. After many years of research and curricular analysis, place value still stands at the top of the "essential mathematics" or "important big ideas" lists. (See Chapter 9.) With such a weighty concept at stake, a differentiated instruction model is my only hope that all the students will have access to understanding this powerful notion. This formal deliberate attempt is new territory even though my philosophy and teaching habits are a comfortable match.

The "truffles factory" activity in Suzanne Chapin and Art Johnson's *Math Matters* opened the way for me to scaffold the major elements of a place value number system: a set number of digits with which to work and the value of the places increasing by powers of that number as they move left—the multiplicative nature of such a system. Pretending to work as packagers in the candy factory provides a real-world context for launching into different base systems (Chapin and Johnson 2006, 26–28).

The following is a description of the planning process and components for the transformed unit.

Unit Design

In designing the unit, my first stop was the *Principles and Standards for School Mathematics* (National Council of Teachers of Mathematics [NCTM] 2000) number and operations standards for grades pre-K–2 and 3–5, where I identified the important concepts to be developed throughout the unit.

- Understand the place value structure of the base ten number system
- Understand the multiplicative nature of the number system
- Understand the meanings of addition and subtraction of whole numbers and the relationship between the two operations
- Understand the various meanings of multiplication and division, the relationship between them, and the relationships to other operations (NCTM 2000, 78, 148)

Next, using Diane Heacox's model from *Differentiating Instruction in the Regular Classroom* (2002), I identified the essential questions and unit questions. Essential questions identify the key understandings you want for students after completing the unit. Unit questions identify specific elements of the essential questions, adding depth and specificity (53–58).

Essential Questions

1. What are the characteristics of a place value number system?
2. How is a place value system different from other number systems?
3. How are the values of the different places determined in a place value system?
4. How are the values of the places in a place value system related to each other?
5. What does the base for the place value system tell you about the system?
6. What and how many symbols are used to record numbers in our base ten place value system (Hindu-Arabic decimal system)?

Unit Questions

1. What place value number system do we use every day?
2. What symbols and words do we use to count with in our number system?
3. How many different number symbols are there?
4. How does our system compare to the Roman system of numeration?
5. How can we design another place value system for counting, recording, and keeping track of the numbers of objects we work and live with?
6. How can we create addition/subtraction and multiplication/division tables to support our newly designed system?
7. What everyday elements of our lives will be changed if our number system is adopted?

Finally, thinking about all the characteristics of the students, a plan emerged for the implementation of the unit. The plan included working in groups of various sizes—whole class and partners are the most common arrangements, although pairs of partners (groups of fours) sometimes work. In many instances, a teacher may carefully choose partners. For this unit, students chose their own partners because these students were accustomed to doing this and it was appropriate to the unit design. The students worked individually or used their partners to talk about the work and check with each other before consulting the teacher. I also decided that most assignments would have open-ended challenges to accommodate the readiness levels.

Activities

1. Talk about two familiar number systems: our base ten number system and Roman numerals [whole class—with partners in semicircle]. Compare the patterns for using them: place value and addition/subtraction (additive/subtractive) [same as above].

2. Write about how the systems are alike and how the systems are different [individual]. (See student work in Figure 1.1.)

3. Work for the truffles candy packaging factory that packages only in units (box), threes (three-pack), nines (tray), and twenty-sevens (carton). The packaging is recorded in a chart that essentially becomes a place value chart for truffle numbers. Orders are filled and recorded for up to thirty truffles. Figure 1.2a shows the package sizes and lists the factory rules for packaging the candies. In addition, Figure 1.2b shows the record for sample orders of fourteen and fifteen truffles and the truffle numbers that emerge [whole group, then individual with partner, then back to whole group].

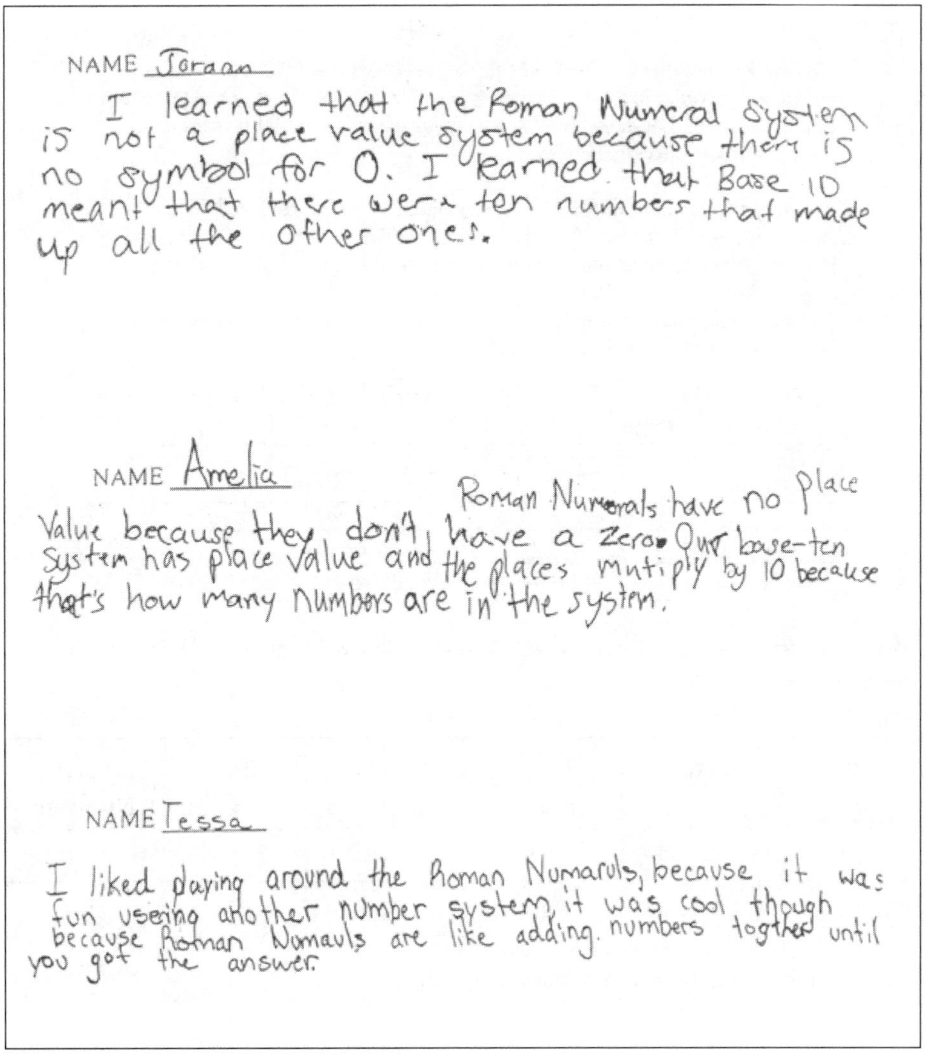

NAME Joraan

I learned that the Roman Numeral System is not a place value system because there is no symbol for 0. I learned that Base 10 meant that there were ten numbers that made up all the other ones.

NAME Amelia

Roman Numerals have no place Value because they don't have a Zero. Our base-ten System has place Value and the places mutiply by 10 because that's how many numbers are in the system.

NAME Tessa

I liked playing around the Roman Numaruls, because it was fun useing another number system, it was cool though because Roman Numauls are like adding numbers togther until you got the answer.

FIGURE 1.1—Student comparisons of Roman numeral and base ten number systems.

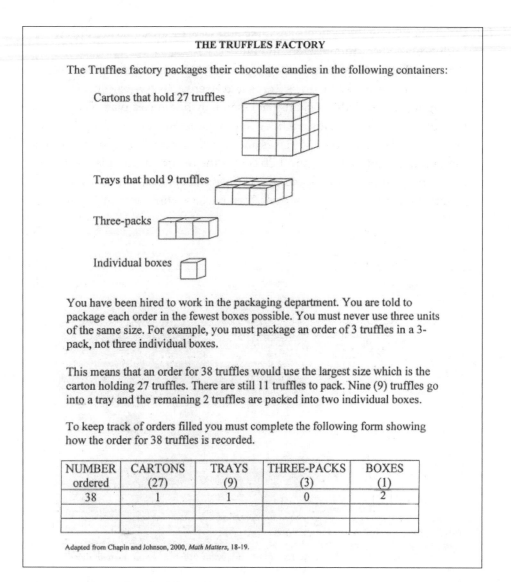

FIGURE 1.2a—Truffles factory packaging rules. (Adapted from *Math Matters* [Chapin and Johnson 2006], 26–28)

Order size	Cartons 27	Trays 9	3-packs 3	Box 1	Truffle Number
14	0	1	1	2	0112
15	0	1	2	0	0120

FIGURE 1.2b—Sample record of packaging work.

In addition, Figure 1.3 shows fourth-grader Maura's record of her packaging work.

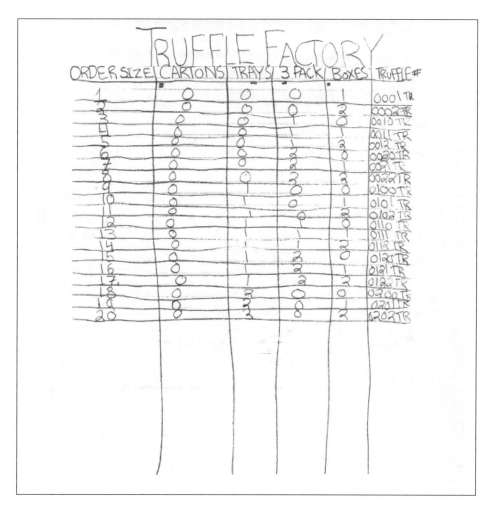

FIGURE 1.3—Maura's record of truffle factory packaging.

4. Find patterns within the truffles packaging chart: think-pair-share.
5. Compare truffles chart to the base ten number system we use every day. How many symbols are used? What are the values of the places? How do the values of the places relate to each other? How do they change as you move from right to left? How do they change as you move from left to right [whole group]?
6. Writing—describe how the truffles system is similar to and different from our base ten system of numeration [whole group, then partners, then homework]. Figure 1.4 is a student response to the assignment.
7. Vocabulary—a word list is posted throughout the number system unit. All terms used related to the work with number systems are recorded on it.

Project

During your intergalactic exploration you happen upon a new planet, which you subsequently name *Quarto*. A friendly group of highly intelligent beings

> Our number system is like the truffle Factory
>
> System they both have Patterns (Patters are when
> Things repeat) 😊 Our number system Pattern is 123456789
> 10 and repeats 12345678910 when it Goes in to double
> digits.
>
> The truffle factory Pattern is 012 and then repeats
> 012 when it Goes to double digits and they
> Share the same numbers which are; 012.
> Our number system is different from the truffle
> factory system because our system has 10
> numbers and the truffle system has only 3
> numbers.

FIGURE 1.4—Comparing truffle numbers to base ten numbers.

welcomes you. You are immediately struck by their strange appearance but disarmed by their warmth and charm. You notice that they have two fingers on each of their two hands for a total of four fingers.

As you get acquainted, you realize that these otherwise brilliant creatures have not yet developed a number system. It is your task to help them create a place value number system that they can use to keep track of themselves and the myriad visitors who will surely be joining them. You understand immediately that you need to design a number system that coordinates well with Quarto finger counting. Remember the importance of zero in a place value number system. In many ways, "zero is a hero"!

The following project was to be completed by individuals or partners. (They all worked with partners but kept a folder record of their individual work.)

Students were to create a place value number system for planet Quarto. They could create a "math book" for their project, a poster, or a cardboard cube display. They could also create a "diorama" or poster to show how the world would be different if we adopted their number system.

Following are steps that were to be completed as the project developed:

1. Design or select symbols.
2. Define the meaning for each symbol (illustration and words).
3. Name each symbol.
4. Use the symbols to count at least thirty objects. Display with a four-column table (our base ten number, the set of objects it represents using *X*'s, the planet Quarto counting number, and the planet Quarto word name for the number).
5. Describe what each place value in the number system is worth. Explain how each place value is related to the place values next to it.

Following are additional project elements as agreed upon by student(s) and teacher. (An asterisk denotes elements required for all students.)

1. *Create an addition and subtraction table (chart) for the number system.
2. *Write three addition/subtraction fact families that can be justified by the table (chart).
3. Create a multiplication and division table (chart) for the number system.
4. Write three multiplication/division fact families that can be justified by the table (chart).
5. Create a diorama or mural to show how daily life would change if we had to convert to your planet Quarto number system.
6. Explore what "fractions" might mean in your number system. Illustrations and models would be very important if you choose this activity.

FIGURE 1.5a—Planet Quarto number system—student work.

FIGURE 1.5b—Planet Quarto number system—student work.

7. Imagine another planet with a different number of fingers for each inhabitant. How would they count in their place value number system? Give enough examples to be convincing.

8. *Design something of your choice related to the Quarto number system (clock, calendar, and so on).

9. *All students need to be prepared to explain their number systems to classmates and other interested groups and individuals.

See Figure 1.5 for a sampling of the student project displays.

Unit Analysis—What, How, and Why?

As mentioned earlier, accommodating instruction involves consideration of content, process, product, and/or environment. Student characteristics such as readiness, interest, and/or learning styles determine how and why the unit is altered: Do I need more accessibility? Am I looking for a more motivating situation? Or is efficiency of learning the concern?

What was differentiated?

In the place value unit, the process and product were both varied in order to accommodate the needs of my students. A series of activities were designed to build up to the big content ideas. Each of the activities had open-ended elements so that both the students and teacher could differentiate on demand, sometimes expanding or contracting depth, sometimes breadth. Because the teacher was continuously assessing, suggestions and questions could easily direct the next steps for students as they worked. For example, some students translated Roman numerals in the thousands and millions while others felt good about working in the tens. (See Figure 1.6 for the range of responses possible.) The major product for the unit—the creation of a base four place value number system—is differentiated both by level of difficulty and choice (see project description above).

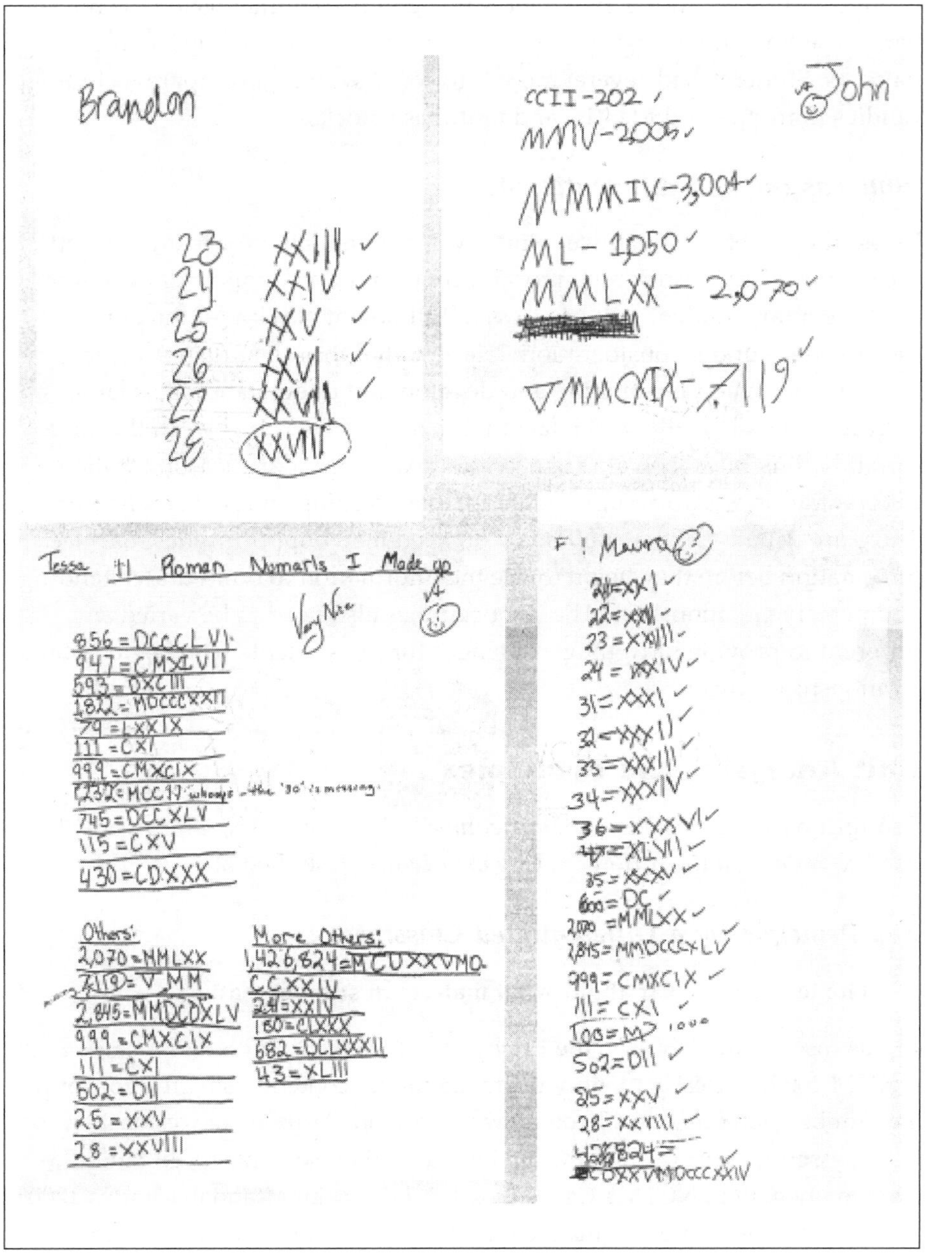

FIGURE 1.6—Four student responses to open-ended Roman numeral homework assignment, showing a range of desired responses.

How was the unit differentiated?

The unit was differentiated for readiness by selecting activities that allowed students access to the key concepts. The activities were designed so that growth could occur at any level. For example, as students worked with the truffle packaging problem, some struggled with packaging ten candies while others went on to challenge themselves with packaging forty candies. Several even attempted to package one hundred; they found they couldn't follow all the rules and needed to create a new package design. Scaffolding experiences included varied counting experiences using Roman numerals, truffle numbers (base three numbers), and base ten numbers, all the while looking for patterns. Students had several models to count with and compare including candies (Smarties and M&Ms) and multibase blocks.

Why was the unit differentiated?

Without a doubt, the place value unit was differentiated for readiness and accessibility. This is such an important concept for students to understand. No elementary student will progress to full potential without the power of the key ideas under consideration. It is essential that all students are able to participate with understanding and develop that understanding as far as their readiness will allow. The fact that motivation was high with this unit certainly illustrates the value of accessibility. A secondary reason for the differentiation was to accommodate various learning styles. (See Chapter 3.) There are usually several students who need many opportunities to collect information before they begin to use the information to build understanding and perceive relationships. The opportunities also need to be varied and different to provide intriguing challenges for the students who begin to build relationships quickly.

Unit Analysis—the Principles

Tomlinson's *Key Principles of a Differentiated Classroom* (1999, 48) can now be used to reflect on the differentiating experience described above.

Key Principles of a Differentiated Classroom

1. The teacher is clear about what matters in subject matter.

In this case the teacher used the *Principles and Standards for School Mathematics* (NCTM 2000) to clearly identify the mathematics content, using the appropriate number standards. In Chapter 9 we share and clarify what we consider to be the essential learning and the big ideas for all of elementary- and middle-level mathematics. NCTM's *Curriculum Focal Points* and Randall Charles' (2005) "Big Ideas" link numerous math concepts central to math learning. Understanding place value is one of those big ideas. The unit questions and essential questions further clarified the content and pinpointed learning expectations.

2. **The teacher understands, appreciates, and builds upon student differences.**

Differences among the students were identified and targeted for accommodation. Readiness was a primary concern. Motivation and learning styles were secondary but significant. Previous scattered student knowledge was incorporated into introducing Roman numerals and comparing number systems. There were multiple opportunities to count truffle numbers (whole group, partners, and individually using the candy factory setting, place value metric blocks, and candies for consumption), so that the students who processed ideas and data over time had the opportunity and motivation they needed for their ideas to gel. At the same time, the activities challenged and fascinated the students who were eager to move ahead. They were able to make conjectures from the patterns they perceived and try out their ideas to share with the group.

3. **Assessment and instruction are inseparable.**

Throughout the unit, the teacher was constantly assessing students through observations of their processing and their written work. Feedback was provided throughout the instructional process. For example, I noticed that Ben struggled to write down the truffle numbers on the chart he created. He most likely lacked the small muscle skills. There were charts available if he needed them, but I encouraged him to continue with his own as long as it didn't trip him up. He needed to check with his partner, who was doing fine. Also, when several students wrote about the comparison of the base ten and truffle (base three) number systems, they talked about the truffle numbers skipping eight because they go from two to ten. This led to clarification in the beginning math circle the next day.

4. **The teacher adjusts content, process, and product in response to student readiness, interests, and learning profile.**

The unit activities and assignments were designed exactly for these purposes. The truffle factory packaging activity was incorporated into the unit in response to student readiness. Planet Quarto captured the interest and imagination of otherwise resistant students who not only created Quarterian images but wonderful number systems as well (Figure 1.6, p. 21). In addition, daily plans were adjusted to accommodate student needs as they arose. Some of these adjustments took place during the daily whole class sessions (usually beginning and end of class) or as the partners worked on their tasks, as noted in the anecdote above.

5. **All students participate in respectful work.**

All students were able to work at their comfort level because of the open-endedness of the tasks. The whole class processing at the beginning and end of each class period gave everyone the opportunity to share his or her individual contributions.

6. **Students and teachers are collaborators in learning.**

In this regard, the teacher recognized the importance of being aware and noting unique ideas that emerged during individual and small group work time so that these students were called upon to add to the discussion. In the beginning of the unit, the students were the major resource for information about the Roman numerals. Although they had never formally studied the Roman system of numeration, the class was able to collect and display all of the necessary background information from their collective informal experiences. Only then did the teacher use formal resources to validate their collective knowledge, add to it, and give students hard copy to support their work with the Roman numerals and the comparison with the place value number system.

7. **Goals of a differentiated classroom are maximum growth and individual success.**

It is difficult to measure maximum growth, but it was a realistic goal for this situation. All students presented their number systems for the class to analyze, question, and comment upon. Each set of partners had something unique to add, and in one instance, the students were able to question a misunderstanding in symbol representation that had eluded the teacher. It was clearly a positive experience for everyone—the students who questioned the confusing data, the students who had made the error and were relieved to have the presentation clarified, and this teacher who was delighted to feel the power in the students.

8. **Flexibility is the hallmark of a differentiated classroom.**

The open-endedness of the activities provided the basic flexibility, which was supported by various group sizes and interactions. Student ideas were incorporated into the instruction. Rubrics were designed to guide the work, feedback was continuous, and adjustments were made throughout the activities and the creative process.

Summary and the Work Ahead

In summary, this example of differentiated math instruction grew out of the generalized guidelines and suggestions for differentiation in any content area. There are some special mathematical concerns that have emerged for us.

In the *Principles and Standards for School Mathematics* (NCTM 2000), the first process standard for teaching and learning mathematics is the problem-solving standard. It states "Instructional programs from prekindergarten through grade 12 should enable all students to build new mathematical knowledge through problem solving. . . ." (52) It seems appropriate therefore to add this ideal context for math learning into the guiding process. There are many layers to the differentiating process, but we find it helpful to keep good problem-solving tasks at the forefront of the lesson-design routine.

Consequently, we consider engaging problems with embedded worthwhile mathematical tasks to be the starting point for many powerful differentiation experiences that can help all students reach their full potential in mathematics. The place value unit described previously was a series of engaging problems for the children to solve and in the process discover important mathematical patterns and relationships. It began with comparing and contrasting the Roman system of numeration with our base ten number system, moved on to the truffle factory packaging challenge and search for patterns, applied those patterns to new situations, and finally challenged students to create a number system for a new planet of four-fingered creatures. In Chapter 4, we expand on the character and function of problem solving in a differentiated environment.

Now that we've established basic principles and guidelines for differentiating mathematics instruction, in Chapter 2 we move on to address the development of a mathematics learning community in the classroom.

Chapter 2

Preparing the Classroom: Establishing a Mathematics Learning Community

Students' learning of mathematics is enhanced in a learning environment that is built as a community of people collaborating to make sense of mathematical ideas.

Professional Standards for Teaching Mathematics, NCTM

Scenario

Heather greets students as they enter, telling them they need their pre-assessment results, which are in their notebooks. The students proceed to their tables where they are seated in groups of three or four. They retrieve their assessment results in a relaxed, comfortable, nonthreatening environment. Eric and Tami leave the class quietly to retrieve their notebooks from their lockers. Within two or three minutes, all are ready.

Heather describes the options she has organized for today's lesson, which are based on the errors and misconceptions highlighted by the preassessment: for example, subtraction of mixed numbers with regrouping, addition of fractions with unlike denominators, multiplication of mixed numbers, and division of fractions. The activities are: a teacher minilesson on subtraction with regrouping; a handout review of practice problems with answer keys posted; a fraction game to reinforce the addition and subtraction of fractions with unlike denominators; cooperative group problems focused on fractions, decimals, and percents from *United We Solve* (Erickson 1996, 151–57); a design task to create a round-robin I Have—Who Has? fraction game for the entire class.

The activities are available in different locations in the classroom. In their notebooks, students have Heather's feedback about their assessment. It includes a list of the general concepts the students are to be working on during this lesson (Figure 2.1). Students received this list during the previous class.

General Concepts You Should Know

Operations with fractions:

      Addition and subtraction of fractions with like and unlike
          denominators

      Addition and subtraction of mixed numbers with like and unlike
          denominators

      Multiplication and division of fractions

      Multiplication and division of mixed numbers

How to find equivalent fractions

How to write fractions as decimals and decimals as fractions

FIGURE 2.1

As Heather describes each activity (Figure 2.2), she connects it to the highlighted concepts on the students' papers. In this way, each student knows which activities he or she is expected to do. For example, when addition and subtraction of unlike denominators is indicated for a student, there is a review handout to complete and the fraction game to play with other class-mates who have the same need.

Fraction Activity Choices

Practice Problems:

      Subtraction of mixed numbers

      Addition of mixed numbers

      Multiplication of mixed numbers

      Division of mixed numbers

Action Fraction Game

United We Solve Activity Cards

Design a round-robin I Have—Who Has? activity

FIGURE 2.2

As class begins, Heather asks the students who need regrouping work to join her at the work table; today there are six students. She directs the rest of the class to select the concept on which they will work and to get started on that activity. As Heather begins with her small group, the other students also get started. Some check their lists with each other in order to find someone to work with, while some move immediately to a particular activity. For example, those students who did really well on the preassessment go to the cooperative group problem-solving center because they love to do those types of challenging problems. After several minutes, Heather glances around the room to confirm that everyone has begun working. She checks in with a couple of students briefly because she knows they need this confirmation.

Some students talk quietly about their work while others move purposefully around the room gathering materials and bringing them back to where they are going to work. Ten minutes into the work time, Joan and Samantha go to the answer key posted to check their work. The following conversation is heard:

> **J.** Did you get number six right?
>
> **S.** Yes, did you?
>
> **J.** No, let me see what you did.
>
> **S.** Remember you have to multiply both parts of the mixed number by the whole number.
>
>> In $2\frac{1}{2} \times 3$, you only multiplied the whole number and that gave you $6\frac{1}{2}$ and it should be $7\frac{1}{2}$.
>
> **J.** Why is it 7 instead of 6?
>
> **S.** Because $3 \times \frac{1}{2}$ is $1\frac{1}{2}$ and that is added to the 6 from 3 times 2.
>
> **J.** Ohhhh, I always forget that part—now I get it.

Heather leaves her small group working on some problems together and checks in on other students. She talks with the three students using the cooperative problems, complimenting them for adapting the four-person activity for their group of three. She asks them to tell her how each person is contributing to solving the problem and reminds them to summarize their problem-solving work on their exit slips before they leave class, highlighting their contributions, and briefly evaluating their group work.

Heather watches the students playing the fraction game and notices that they need a reminder to verbalize the trades that they are making. She demonstrates by using the action that Adam just completed: Adam had a yellow hexagon and blue rhombus at the beginning of his turn. He rolled a one-sixth and took a green triangle from the pattern block pile and passed the fraction cube to the next player. Heather demonstrates the language she wants Adam to use prior to passing on the fraction cube: "Besides my one whole, I have one-third and one-sixth and I am going to trade them for one-half; my total is now one and one-half."

As she leaves the game-playing group, Heather notices a hand raised and moves to that student. Toby has a question about the handout he is completing related to dividing fractions. She asks him if he has used manipulatives and suggests he try that and raise his hand again if that doesn't help. Before returning to her small group, Heather checks in with the students who are using their computer to create the round-robin I Have—Who Has? game for the class.

Before class ends for the day, students complete an exit slip that gives Heather information on what they've completed. (See Figure 2.3.) They are to staple any completed worksheets to the exit slip. Those working on the round-robin are to print what is completed so far and attach that to their exit slip. She reminds the class to return supplies, put their exit slips in the work tray, and set up for the next class. The lesson will continue tomorrow with a different minilesson depending on the class needs.

Exit Slip   Name _____

What activity did you do today?

_____

_____

_____

If you had a chance to correct your work and you had mistakes, what types of mistakes were they?

_____

_____

_____

Do you need help with this concept during tomorrow's class? If yes, attach your work to the exit slip and describe what you think would help.

_____

_____

_____

What are you going to work on tomorrow?

_____

FIGURE 2.3

Reflection on Scenario

This 'well-oiled' differentiated math class is not happenstance. Heather has established a learning environment in her classroom where respectful attention is paid to the needs of all her students. The academic needs are determined by her observations and the preassessment that students completed for the unit. Students enter and get to work quickly because they know what is expected of them. Heather counts on students to bring the necessary materials to class even though she understands they are middle school students and need to be gently reminded occasionally. Students understand that they each have different needs and that it's OK to be working on different activities. Heather is well prepared. She organized a set of activities that match the results from the preassessment, but long before that she has established an autonomous work ethic. For example, she has confidence that a student will not copy answers onto a worksheet and pass it in as his own work. She is also careful to give students enough feedback along with their preassessment to understand what they need to learn and where they need to improve or stretch their understanding. The students have obviously learned to work productively without constant direction. They move about the classroom quietly to retrieve the materials they need: no one directed the students to use their laptops to create the game—they knew enough to make that decision on their own.

Heather is confident about what she wants students to learn, gives clear directions, and provides time for questions. Once students begin their work, they are able to work with relative independence for the remainder of the class period. They know it's OK to ask their classmates for help, especially while a minilesson is in progress. Throughout the class period, Heather tracks the students' progress in subtle and unobtrusive ways. She uses her observations of the class and the collected exit slips to plan for the continuation of the lesson the next day.

Preparing for Differentiation—What and How

We can learn about the essential expectations, norms, and management techniques needed for differentiating a mathematics class by analyzing what we have just seen. Heather's mathematics classroom culture easily incorporates differentiated instruction. In the scenario, children come to class matter-of-factly, listen to directions, and ease into action. Although they are working in various configurations throughout the class, they know where to go to begin class and they are confident with regard to where specific materials are located throughout the room. Although there are five activities happening at any moment, the class appears to have a single purpose. The room is not quiet; neither is it noisy. These adolescents are using quiet, considerate voices. This classroom aura doesn't happen by chance—it is carefully and deliberately developed early in the academic year.

The classroom structures listed here follow directly from Heather's class scenario and are among those critical to differentiation. The label in parentheses is an attempt to loosely categorize the structures as expectations, norms, and management practices.

1. The class attends to the general and mathematical needs of all students with consideration and respect. (norms)
2. Students know routines and expectations: assignment posting; entering and moving about the room; getting to work; acceptable voice and noise levels; asking for help; minilesson rules; and so on. (management)
3. Students are clear about the location, use, and care of materials. (management)
4. Students have different work assignments because of interests, skill levels, and learning styles. (expectations)
5. All persons in the room are teachers and learners so thinking is made transparent—think-alouds are modeled by the teacher and practiced with partners, small groups, and the whole class. (expectations)
6. Students are expected to stretch their thinking for all assignments: lessons, projects, activities, and skill practice. (expectations)
7. Independence and self-starting is nurtured and valued. (expectations and norms)
8. Respectful listening skills are critical; paraphrasing is a frequent part of group processing. (norms)
9. All work is documented. (management)

From Heather's classroom we can move to a general comprehensive set of expectations, norms, and management techniques. These can be exceedingly helpful to a mathematics teacher who is just beginning to differentiate instruction. We expect that for many teachers, what follows is familiar territory— descriptions of what good teachers already do. What is key here is that a well-conceived, business-like intellectual culture is sacrosanct for effective differentiation—prepared, planned, and initiated in a timely manner.

Before continuing, create for yourself a mental image or frame for differentiation as "the practice of varying teaching and learning strategies so that all students can reach high standards of achievement and become independent learners" (Appelbaum 2005, 2). Then you can begin to paint your own classroom culture within the framework using expectations, norms, and management strategies that make such differentiation possible in your math class. The *expectations* are what you believe and want to occur. Some are stated explicitly at the beginning of the school term or unit, while others are delivered implicitly through the modeling and teacher behaviors. *Norms* are the values, customs, and habits for how things are done in a group structure. In math class, they refer specifically to the formal (and informal) code of conduct about what is acceptable behavior. *Management* refers to organizing the elements of the math class: students, materials, time, and space. It also refers to how instruction and learning interact with those elements.

Expectations, Norms, and Management—What

The elements that follow don't always fall neatly into a single category, which is unimportant. What is important is that each element needs your attention and consideration if you hope to sustain a successful differentiated mathematics program.

Setting Expectations

Target high expectations for all students. Establish an intellectual culture rich with discussion, questions, conjectures, mistakes, and justifications. State all expectations positively, including at least the following ideas and adding your own.

- Expect students to work toward independence; take responsibility for their own learning; stretch their thinking; reflect and practice metacognition (think about how they think and learn) regularly.
- Clarify performance standards for groups and individuals: use exemplars.
- Prepare students to expect different assignments because of interests, skill levels, and learning styles.
- Expect students to think about how they learn and work in order to expand their learning styles for added learning opportunities.
- Expect students to understand that all members of the learning community are teachers and learners; everyone explains their thinking—orally and in writing—and makes their thinking transparent.
- Expect all members of the community to know, understand, and respect each other and value their differences.

Norms for Classroom Conduct

Students need to understand rules and norms; they should be reviewed frequently and prominently displayed. The following categories with examples will get you started.

- *Behavior for individuals and groups:* class time focused on mathematics; work quietly with eight-inch voices; accept roles responsibly; ask for help when needed; use time efficiently; make good choices when options are available; have a serious purpose
- *Discussion/discourse:* respectful interactions; listen attentively; safe environment; wait time; students formulate and answer questions; everyone contributes; share talk time; build student capacity for discourse through practice
- *Content and process:* read and follow directions; compute accurately; make appropriate choices for computation; listen and take notes; explain thinking; find and describe patterns; complete and hand in assignments

- *Minilessons:* set other work aside; move quickly and quietly into groups; come prepared with folder and tools; listen carefully; contribute or ask for help; other noninvolved class members work quietly with consideration.
- *Use of anchor activities:* assigned work completed; work quietly without distracting; be alert to signals for return to group; log time and concepts covered

A Management Mosaic

- Establish routines for: coming to class, beginning class, and ending class; collecting and returning student work; changing work stations; weekly and biweekly activities
- Define student responsibilities: folders, moving furniture quickly and quietly for useful configurations, use and care of resources, peer conferencing, work logs, goal setting, self-assessment, setting standards, suggestions
- Give clear directions for auditory, visual, and kinesthetic learners— utilize task cards, peer helpers, study-buddies, chalkboards or white boards, and charts
- Set parameters for use of space and time: home base to begin class; clear expectations for orderly movement; time on task; specified time limits; stray movement controlled
- Establish indicators of quality: share exemplars; create rubrics
- Establish acceptable noise levels: small group and conference eight-inch voices; create signal for silence
- Create signals to ask for help: visual signal; use peers; within group or when all group members need help
- Define record keeping: short term and long term; logs, notebooks, folders, archives
- Establish lines of communication: share rationale for differentiating instruction with both students and caregivers; establish regular lines of communication—newsletter, email, as needed

A Note About Routines

Establishing routines is critical for the kind of responsive teaching we're after. Knowing when the seating will be changed, how to submit papers, how work will be returned, the kind of feedback to expect, where the work is to be stored, where homework assignments can be confirmed, the school-home communication network, and so on—every one of these details can be established to save countless hours and precious minutes throughout the school year. None of the routines preclude changing a routine from time to time, but the routines are always there for stability. This frees up the teacher and the schedule for instruction that is responsive to student needs. Important elements of differentiated instruction such as minilessons, flexible groups, anchor activities, and a dependable daily class schedule complete the management mosaic. (For a recommended daily math class format see Chapter 6.)

Getting Started—How

Once you have determined the guidelines to use for developing your mathematics classroom culture, you need to decide *how* to introduce these critical ideas to students in compelling ways. It's best for students to feel involved and understand how they will personally benefit from the rules for their mathematical journey ahead. Whenever possible, use tactics that engage students in the process of setting the expectations. They will then become your best monitors. Above all, plan to reinforce and revisit key elements frequently and vigorously. It is helpful to have exemplars to share with students or an activity to clarify particular expectations. For example, when we discuss the following bullets from our expectations, we play a game for clarification.

- Making errors is an important tool in learning mathematics.
- Explaining our work in mathematics is of great importance to our mathematics learning.

I tell students that I am thinking of a three-digit number and I want them to tell me what it is. Once someone has made a guess, it is recorded and I respond with the number of correct digits and the number of correct places. We talk about what we now know that we didn't know before and why, emphasizing that it is by making an error and sharing our thinking aloud that we are able to learn more and get closer to a solution.

In a similar manner, we have diverse student work samples to share with students to highlight our expectations. We use exemplars from students with different visual and literary strengths.

- Every day that we have mathematics, we are expected to reflect upon the work that we do and write about it in our math journals.
- Writing about the math we do is a way to think about it and develop deeper understanding.

Putting a variety of great student work in students' hands makes expectations concrete. In addition, explaining how this work contributes to satisfying different individual student needs builds respect and strengthens the differentiated classroom culture.

An Example of Establishing the Mathematics Learning Environment

Earlier you had a chance to peek inside a seventh-grade class. Now let's see how third- and fourth-grade teacher Jill Cotta sets the stage for differentiating during the first days and weeks of the school year: the physical arrangement, performance standards, beginning lessons, and expectations.

Multigrade Level 3–4

Jill is a multigrade teacher at the Center for Teaching and Learning in Edgecomb, Maine. Her classroom is a delight to visit during math time. She differentiates her instruction systematically (pretty much consistently throughout the year), although students' designated grade levels are not necessarily the criteria for doing so.

The Physical Setup

Before school, Jill inventories and organizes supplies, manipulatives, and other tools mathematicians use so that they are accessible to students when they need them. The manipulatives are stored in removable trays on shelves and the math picture books are categorized and stored by the math curriculum strands. A space is cleared for the meeting area, where kids "group up" on the floor in front of the easel to begin and end class.

Standards for Performance and Interaction

Before school starts Jill reviews her teaching materials, the printed Expectations for Mathematics (see Figure 2.4), and the goals to refresh her thoughts and make changes. The expectations are shared with the children; the goals are for parents at Open House. She uses the Expectations for Mathematics sheet as a platform for discussions and activities that establish the classroom routines and norms. These are critical to the smooth functioning of the differentiated teaching and learning that are critical parts of her mathematics program.

Special Lessons for the Beginning of the Year

Jill spends the first several weeks on procedural minilessons: how to keep folders and journals, rules for math workshop, how to care for manipulatives, tools mathematicians use, a definition and overview of the math strands, extension activities, daily math circle warm-ups, and a few more. The class talks a great deal about how they can approach a task in different ways. Jill shows them that with every lesson, there is a way for them to adapt it to make it harder or easier; she always gives them several options. They also talk about the procedures and rules for group work: everyone must participate and try his or her best; everyone listens; and you must check with everyone in your group before seeking the teacher's help. For any task, Jill sets the minimum expectations that everyone must complete. She then gives them several ways to adapt or extend the challenge.

> ## EXPECTATIONS FOR MATHEMATICS
>
> - Know and understand concepts under the five math strands: number and operations, measurement, probability and statistics, geometry, and algebra (patterns and functions).
> - Understand the purpose of mathematical concepts (by participating in many different experiences) and how they help us solve problems in everyday life.
> - Use math concepts you have learned to solve problems in all parts of your lives.
> - Be an active problem solver: analyze, predict, make decisions, and evaluate your solutions and mathematical thinking.· Understand the vocabulary of mathematics throughout the five strands.
> - Participate in whole class and small group math lessons.
> - During small group and individual mathematical tasks:
>   - ✑ Listen to others' ideas.
>   - ✑ Be willing to help any group member who asks.
>   - ✑ Seek help from group members.
>   - ✑ Small group tasks: make sure that everyone has an equal chance to speak and contribute to some part of the solution.
> - Explain your mathematical thinking and ideas both orally and in writing (during large and small group discussions).
> - Use your math journal to write about mathematical ideas and thinking, solve problems, explain how you solved a problem, gather and organize data, and set goals.
> - Try some extension activities for small group and individual math tasks.
> - Take care of math manipulatives and tools. Keep manipulatives sorted and in good condition. Return all math tools to their appropriate place.
> - Work hard, challenge yourself, try new problem-solving strategies, and become an independent mathematical thinker and problem solver as well as a group problem solver.
>
> Jill Cotta
> Center for Teaching and Learning

FIGURE 2.4

More Preparation Work

Anchor Activities

Anchor activities are tasks that become options for students when they have completed their assigned tasks. Since a differentiated math class is a place where time needed to complete tasks is one of the targeted diversities, anchoring becomes a major management strategy. Remember, an essential characteristic of differentiated activities is that they be important, challenging, big idea mathematics for all learners at all times. This carries over to the anchor activities as well. An anchor activity might well be a game but it will be a game that has important mathematics embedded in it (most games do!), and the caveat for using the game includes a recorded reflection on the perception of the embedded mathematics. One technique for accomplishing this task is the initial class expectation and agreement that all mathematics activities will be documented throughout the year.

Anchor activities are also useful when students are waiting for help and the teacher or peer tutor is busy with other students. The anchor options are safe places for students—they will not get in trouble by making an anchor choice during their free time. Activities selected for anchoring can be general for the entire class or they can be individualized in response to needs and/or interests. They can encompass enrichment work, extensions for current or past curricular units, or skills practice. Again, clarity is the key. Students need to be introduced to the activities and the directions and use made clear.

It is a good idea to introduce the notion of anchoring by using some general anchor tasks at the beginning of the school year along with the procedures for using them. For example, we use the menu of problems from the National Council of Teachers of Mathematics (NCTM) monthly *Mathematics Teaching in the Middle School* or problems from the MATHCOUNTS program. The MATHCOUNTS program is an annual nationwide problem-solving program for grades six through eight. At the beginning of each school year, a manual containing sets of intriguing and challenging problems and support materials is distributed free of charge to all United States middle schools. (See www.mathcounts.org for more information.)

Once we introduce how the anchor activities are to be utilized, we practice using them in alternating time periods for different readiness groups. Half of the class works on the anchor task or tasks while the other half of the class takes part in a minilesson. Then the groups are reversed. Between sessions and after both groups have experienced the process, we do a critique with the class and clairify any elements of the process that are not clear. The goal is to have students understand how to move to the anchor activity at appropriate times and work carefully and diligently within the agreed-upon guidelines. More ideas for anchor activities are located throughout the book and indexed in Chapter 10.

Math Survey

An effective differentiated learning community holds high expectations for all students at the same time that it gives students the support they need to measure up to those expectations. The teacher as leader of the learning community probes current student knowledge at the starting gate, targets the essential knowledge to be learned, and designs the challenges and supports that enable powerful mathematics learning to happen consistently.

Because it is important to determine where students are relative to basic mathematical readiness early in the academic year, I give students a math survey during the first week of school. It is predominantly skill based and includes items that sample an overview of what I want them to know at the end of the year. I also include items to explore their process levels in communicating, problem solving, representing, reasoning, and connecting—the NCTM process standards. Students are informed that they are not expected to know this mathematics but if they do, I need to know. I also tell them that they will repeat the survey in June, analyze their progress for the year, and submit this as part of their portfolio. In some schools, it is repeated midyear as well.

The information provided by this tool is critical to my work for the year; planning for readiness differentiation is a direct result of the data. The surveys are kept in a handy file folder and checked frequently for specific information to alert me at the beginning of each unit. I set up a series of minilessons for flexible groups immediately. "Review" data are included in the survey so that I am able to identify individual gaps and areas where extensive scaffolding will be necessary. For example, I need to know seventh graders' level of comfort with fractions and fraction operations. I need to know if they can perform problem-based multiplication and division, if they can determine the necessary operation in a contextual situation, and their knowledge and skill with number theory.

Tuning Up the Orchestra—Jenny's First Day

One of Jenny's primary classroom culture concerns for differentiating is that students learn how to share the learning process respectfully. Productive, independent, small group work is critical to having multiple activities within a single class period. In order to establish norms for a small group in which all students have the opportunity to learn and express their thoughts, Jenny starts the year by immersing students in cooperative learning activities from *Get It Together* (Erickson 1989.) Students arranged in groups of four are given a problem to solve as a group. The problems in the *Get It Together* book are designed for the students to each have one clue for solving the four-clue puzzle. The students take turns reading their clue to the group and then work together to solve the problem. There are always two extra clues that students can use to confirm their answer or use as additional information if they are having trouble solving the problem with just the four essential clues. This cooperative process gives Jenny a chance to see how the students work together and what she needs to do in order to establish the type of differentiated mathematics environment in which students will be expected to work throughout the year. During the students' first few experiences with this type of learning, Jenny is providing them with feedback about how they are functioning within their group and as a whole class of learners. For example, Jenny:

- makes sure all students have a chance to talk
- points out when a student is not being listened to

- asks the group to lower their voices for the class work environment
- reminds students that they may only read their clue; they need to ask to have the other clues reread if needed

After all the groups have solved at least one problem, Jenny brings the class together to talk about the process. She asks students to think about their role in the group. Were they the leader? Were they the person who used the manipulatives (if there were any)? Were they the quiet participant? In this way, the students are encouraged to think about who they are as learners and what their needs are when they are working in groups – an expectation for the year. Jenny also asks the students to think about and describe how they worked together as a group; she strives to have the students be more descriptive than just saying "good." She probes to find out what it means for a group to work well together. For example:

- We took turns.
- Everyone agreed on the answer.
- We decided how we wanted to work before we started reading our clues.
- We listened to each other.

This then becomes part of the expected learning environment for math class for the year. Once the year is underway and Jenny knows the students better, she then keys in on who the students are as learners and as people who have individual sensitivities (being middle school kids). If a student tends to be domineering, Jenny might quietly tell that student to make sure everyone in the group talks before he or she talks again. If the groups are sharing their work with the rest of the class, Jenny might tell the vocal student that he or she can't share for the group. This requires another student from the group to speak for them. It also alleviates the burden of always being the person voted to share for the group from the vocal or more confident student.

Promoting On-task Behavior—Miki's Domino Metaphor

I needed to impress kids with the value of time in the classroom other than telling them and talking about how precious little time we had to do all the work expected of us. I thought about how long it takes to build a house and how quickly it can be destroyed by fire or natural disaster as being similar to how much time and effort goes into creating a positive, productive, interactive classroom culture that can be destroyed in an instant by one careless or thoughtless comment. I needed a way to concretely model this concept in the classroom, so I decided to use all the color tiles we had available (*a lot!*). I gave each table a large pile and explained to students that we were going to collect data. I would time them while they stood all of the tiles on end domino style in a line so that if one tile fell all would fall. I demonstrated with several. The timing would be recorded only after *all* the tiles on all the tables in the room were in a standing position at one time. Students were to work together on the task. It took close to five minutes because some would accidentally fall over from time to time and they learned in the process to move cautiously as they worked (peer pressure helped). Next, I told them I would time them on another task. One person at each table was to tilt the end tile at their table when I gave the signal, and I would time how long it took for all tiles in the room to fall over. It took less than 10 seconds. It was an impressive "wow!" moment for the class.

We then formed a semicircle discussion group to think-pair-share the similarities between (1) our experience with the tiles and (2) turning a good learning experience into time spent on discipline or non-math-learning issues. We also brought into play the mathematical ratio involved in the timing: the ratio of the time it takes to build—five minutes—to the time it takes to destroy—ten seconds. The discussion was positive; students were engaged, analyzing and comparing the two types of situations. From then on, if anyone in the class threatened to disturb the work of the class or any individual's "different" type of work, someone would call out, "Remember the domino metaphor." This tactic also addresses the wise use of time class-room management issue.

Getting Students to Listen and Respond to Each Other

Sixth-grade math teacher Teri Keusch describes her deliberate work to engage all learners in classroom discourse. She invites students to post different solutions and steps back so that students can talk to each other about their thinking. They are instructed to ask other students for help in sharing their reasoning. She almost always defers questions to other students. She has evolved a classroom environment where explanations of inaccurate reasoning are valued as highly as explanations of correct reasoning. Students come to recognize the value of being involved and watching learning happen, their own as well as others. They do this by having the class work through the thinking. This classroom is a safe place for students.

Teri describes preparing her classroom as "a collection of subtle things starting when students walk in the door." She reinforces behaviors such as "look at the speaker," "ask questions appropriately," "talk about what you think," and "listen." She pushes student thinking, remains neutral in expression and body language, and deals with unhelpful behaviors quietly and immediately. She sets the tone early and models her expectations throughout the year. She provides scaffolding devices for students such as "ask a partner to help you" when they have difficulty expressing their thinking. She defers questions put to her by students, encouraging students to question one another directly and see each other as resources for learning (Johanning 2004). I've had Teri as an instructor in professional development situations. Her manner and methods are inspirational.

Making Thinking Transparent

Another challenging classroom cultural element in mathematics is making student thinking transparent. To make progress on this front we, as teachers, need to model and make our thinking transparent. Consider the teacher who demonstrates her own processing by saying, "I know this isn't the solution but this is where I am in my thinking." Posting her result so far, she continues, "Can you help me work through this?" When teachers demonstrate their own thinking processes and treat incorrect responses with respect, students can gain substantial understanding over time. Because there is the potential for a variety of different mathematical events happening in the differentiated classroom, structures and norms need to be in place in order for all the good stuff to be shared. We must expend great effort to constantly monitor the classroom for student self-assured safety and respect—students have to feel comfortable in order to learn how to contribute respectfully and acknowledge their own level of understanding.

Getting to Know Each Other

Graphing Interests, Needs, and Strengths

The effectively differentiated mathematics classroom uses the interests and strengths of individuals within the learning community. Finding interesting and engaging ways for everyone to get to know each other is part of the challenge. Chapter 3 is devoted to the details of learning all about students; our purpose here is to have students and teachers get to know each other and develop positive interactive relationships.

Each year, I try to involve students with their interests and strengths in some beginning activities that will naturally bring about the opportunity for everyone to know each other better. It is also a way to personally connect students to the expectation that they will at times be doing different assignments because of their interests and strengths. We don't focus just on mathematics because we want to broaden the connections for mathematics and get a holistic view of the gifts individuals bring to the group.

Try the following as a way to get started. You will be making graphs to picture both the general and mathematical strengths and interests of individual students. Have students respond to the following three prompts:

1. What are your greatest interests (hobbies) and what do you think you are really good at? List up to three.
2. What are your greatest strengths in math? List up to three.
3. What do you want or need to learn or get better at in mathematics this year?

From student responses list a broad spectrum of choices—at least ten—for each question. On overhead transparencies, create a first quadrant graph template with an *x*-axis (horizontal) and a *y*-axis (vertical). Begin with the responses to the first question. Label the vertical axis with a scale to indicate interest. With the class, determine descriptors for the scale to express low to high interest—think in terms of ten intervals as you plan your spacing. The labels might simply be High, Medium, and Low. However, students might enjoy labels such as Intense, So-So, and Dull.

Place the High interest label at the tenth interval, the Medium interest label at the fifth interval, and the Low interest label at the first interval. Along the horizontal axis, evenly space the items from your interest list, leaving space for students to enter at least one more of their own choice. Before

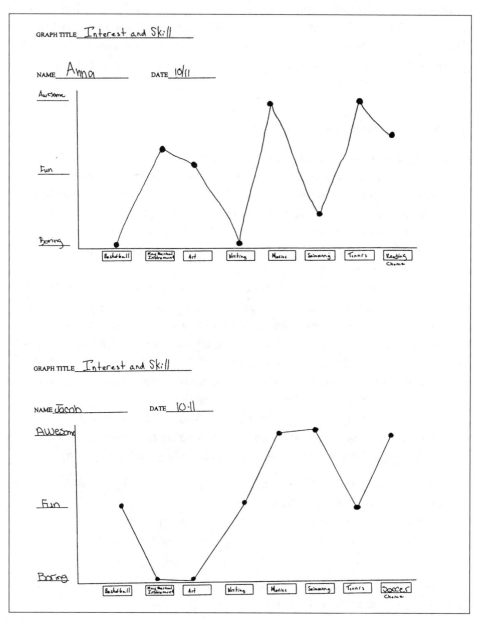

FIGURE 2.5—Personal interest graphs.

continuing, make a clean master copy of the graph you have outlined. Make enough copies so that each student has one and you maintain the master.

As students watch, demonstrate at the overhead how to complete the graph by plotting your own interest level for each item, placing a dot above the item and across from the appropriate level on the vertical scale. Remember to add at least one choice item on the horizontal scale. Connect the points on your graph with line segments (so that a profile is created) and ask students to describe what the graph shows: how do they know your greatest interest? your least interest? See Figure 2.5.

Have other graph templates prepared for the second and third questions. The graph for the second question will be labeled Mathematical Strengths. The vertical axis needs appropriate scale labels to indicate level of expertise, such as 'awesome,' 'maybe,' and 'disaster.' Let students help you select labels. Again, make copies for each student. The graph for the third question will be labeled, Mathematical Needs. The vertical axis of this graph needs labels that correspond to great need, more work helpful, and complete mastery.

Have the graphs completed for homework over a period of time; perhaps students could complete graphs for the first question for homework the first or second day. Spread the processing of the graphs over several days, with five or six students sharing their interests each day. Culminate with a class display of the graphs. With class discussion, compare the graphs, look for patterns, and acknowledge, respect, and celebrate the different interests and talents within the group. Talk about how these differences are important to the math class. Ask if they have suggestions for using the interests. (They will!)

Next repeat the process for the second question—mathematical strengths. Again, talk about how the diverse strengths need to be a factor in how the math class operates. Elements might include the following (from one of my seventh-grade classes):

computation	substituting for X
fractions, decimals, and percents	working with variables
solving word problems	working with exponents
geometry—shapes and angles	graphing on paper and with calculator
linear equations and	using Pythagorean theorem
solving equations	working in different
logic problem solving	number base systems
order of operations	graphs, tables, and equations
probability	

Complete the graphs for the third question after students have finished their preliminary math survey for the year. This will help them identify their greatest needs. The culminating question for this set is "How should the teacher respond to those needs over the year?" The ultimate acknowledgement is that different students have different needs and that differentiated instructional strategies will be important to everyone if all the needs are to be met. Suggestions from students are welcomed and utilized. This is invaluable preparation for the work ahead and a good time to reiterate that "We are all teachers and learners in this room." If you need to modify the presentation of the graphs for questions two and three to protect student sensitivities, that is easy to accomplish. You can select several of the graphs in each category that will show the diversity of talent and need and use those *by permission only* to share with the class in order to make the point. In the meantime, you have valuable information for your teaching files that will support your instructional decisions throughout the year.

Math Autobiography (Mathography)

Having students write their mathematical autobiography at the beginning of the year fills several needs. Students have a chance to think about their history with mathematics, even in first grade, and it gets them used to writing in math class. It can be completely open-ended, but we find that prompts such as the following are extremely helpful in reminding students of influences that might otherwise be overlooked.

- Write about your earliest memories of learning math.
- Tell me about your school experiences with math.
- How do you use math in your everyday world outside of school?
- Tell me about your mathematical triumphs.
- Who has helped you most to learn mathematics? How has this person or persons helped you?
- How do you best learn mathematics (alone, in a group, using manipulatives, discussion, reading, writing)?
- What is one concept you know really well and one concept you would like to know more about?
- Is there something you don't like about math? Explain.

The information collected in the math biography helps teachers know about their students from the beginning. We also know where to go for more information or how to interact with students in safe, respectful ways early in the year. We learn about the range of all sorts of needs that wouldn't likely surface any other way and we know where we must tread lightly until rapport is established. Figure 2.6 shows examples of student autobiographies. Notice how well you feel you know seventh-grader Nathanial and his attitude toward mathematics after reading through his responses. In the fifth-grade example Nina clearly shows her feelings as well as her ability with written communication.

The Parent Connection

It is critical for parents and caregivers to be well informed about the goals and expectations you have for their children. To this end, develop a comprehensive plan to keep families informed and, if possible, involved.

First, a letter to parents before the beginning of the school year is highly recommended. Keep it friendly and upbeat while stating your plans for the

9/6

Prompts for Mathematical Autobiography

1. Once I had to draw out a 50 x 50 box of X's and O's to try and find a pattern within them. I miscounted once, and I had to redo the entire grid. It was extremely disheartening.

Andrew Weles

2. I like math, because I enjoy discovering new ways to accomplish tasks that normally would have taken longer. I find when I have worked a while on one math problem and still cant find the answer, I became frusterated and my mind blocks up. *Take Breaks*

3. I like learning new and different ways to do things and the joy when I finish learning a problem. NB

4. I remember doing work sheets in the First grade, like "Mad Minutes". I did not enjoy them. I thought they were very restricting.

5. I was especially proud of my math performence when I solved my first Math counts problem in the sixth grade. *ME too*

6. I like pre-algebra and learning about variables because it gives me a completely new way of thinking about math. I dislike word problem because they mix up the sentences and all and all the are not very straigh forward.

7. My brother. He showed me the joy in math and that it wasxt all just boring problems with no point.

8. I feel that If you come to math unwilling to learn it will completey effect the outcome of your learning experence.

9. ③ I am almost completely comfortable working with a partner; but I find it very irritating when they dont try as hard as me.

10. ④ I am confident with my learning skills and rarely ask a peer questions.

11. I am not nervous to stand up in front of the class and do not really get discouraged when my ideas are wrong.

12. Pre-Algebra and Algebra.

FIGURE 2.6a—Nathanial's responses to prompts for mathematical autobiography.

1/10
Name <u>Nina</u>

Class Profile

Math is <u>fun and interesting half of</u>
<u>the time, and not as fun, and</u>
<u>a little depressing at other times.</u>

When I think about math I <u>can feel my brain</u>
<u>squirm, with uneasyness sometimes,</u>
<u>and happiness other times.</u>

Three ways math is used are:

1. <u>to learn mathematics</u>

2. <u>to use money and other everyday things</u>

3. <u>how to learn to use fractions and numbers</u>
etc.

What I like about learning math is
<u>fractions. I love fractions so much because</u>
<u>I have always been good at them, and</u>
<u>they are so fun to do. Also, I know that</u>
<u>I am always getting smarter.</u>

There is something I do not like about math. <u>✓</u> yes __ no   If yes,
what is it and why?
<u>I really dislike speedtests. All of the</u>
<u>problems I solve, I get right, but it</u>
<u>is too stressful. My mind turns off, and</u>
<u>all the problems I just studied last</u>
<u>night leave my head.</u>

On a scale of 1 to 4 with 4 being "very" and 1 being "not at all," how
comfortable are you working with partners? Explain your rating.

1------------------2--------------③--------------4
Not at all comfortable   Very comfortable
Explanation <u>Most of the time I am fine, but</u>
<u>sometimes I am the one getting all the wrong answers</u>

On a scale of 1 to 4 with 4 being "very" and 1 being "not at all", how
comfortable are you working alone? Explain your rating.

1------------------②--------------3--------------4
Not at all comfortable   Very comfortable
Explanation <u>What if I can't find the answer and I</u>
<u>need to talk to someone? Usually, I can do it</u>
myself, but sometimes I get confused.

If you are working on a math problem and you get "stuck" what do you
do?
<u>Mostly, I skip it and go back to it</u>
<u>later, and if that doesn't work, I ask</u>
<u>someone at my table, a teacher, or</u>
<u>anyone else who might be of help.</u>
If that doesn't work, I will just have to
tell the teacher the truth, "I couldn't do
it."

FIGURE 2.6b

mathematical year ahead. Include an overview of the content and your rationale for a student-centered differentiated classroom. Use language that is comfortable for parents, such as "There are a variety of ways for children to learn math; therefore, different students may use different materials and activities designed to match their needs and strengths." Ask for parents' help in getting to know their children: interests, ways of learning, special needs, extracurricular commitments, social issues, and so on. Let the parents know you look forward to meeting them at parents' night and tell them the best time and manner to contact you.

At parents' night be prepared to suggest concrete approaches for working together to help their children learn, succeed, feel good about themselves, and grow mathematically. Give the parents copies of your goals and expectations. Discuss the kinds of differences that influence the flexible strategies you use to help students learn. If possible, have a brief activity planned that lends itself to different approaches or different responses. But, a warning: be certain it is a nonthreatening type of activity such as collecting data or playing a simple open-ended game such as Double Digit from the FAMILY MATH program, played with partners.

Reflection Guide

We close Chapter 2 with a reflection guide for teachers (Figure 2.7) to oversee their work at the beginning of the academic year and to reflect upon as they move through their differentiated mathematics agenda. The eight questions are based upon the work of Ron Ritchhart. In his book *Intellectual Character: What It Is, Why It Matters and How to Get It*, he lists the key factors that influence the culture of a learning community. They are the foundation for establishing a classroom culture in support of responsive mathematics instruction. They offer finite concrete elements upon which to focus (Ritchhart 2002).

Summary

Throughout this chapter, we have emphasized the critical role of the mathematics learning community and the importance of its establishment in the beginning of the school year. We have shared possible tools and techniques from the field for establishing expectations and creating an intellectual interactive environment, and we've provided examples of management tools for all of the elements necessary to create a learning community that supports differentiated instruction in mathematics. We also shared how effective mathematics teachers use their content and pedagogical knowledge to enhance the learning environment to better serve all students.

Planning for a Mathematics Classroom
A Reflection Guide
(*based upon Ron Ritchhart's Cultural Forces*)

- What are your expectations for student learning and thinking with regard to mathematics?
- What routines and structures will you employ to guide the class?
- How will you use the language of mathematics and encourage conversation and discussion?
- What different kinds of learning opportunities will you create to ensure mathematical learning for all your students?
- How will you model using and learning mathematics?
- What are the attitudes you want to convey to your students about learning mathematics?
- What relationships and interactions do you want to foster within your classroom between and among students and between you and your students?
- What are the important physical elements of the classroom, and how will you organize them to maximize student opportunities to learn mathematics?

FIGURE 2.7

Recommended Reading

Emmer, E. T, C. Evertson, and M. E.Worsham. 2006. *Classroom Management for Middle and High School Teachers*. Boston: Pearson Education.

Wong, H. K. and R. T. Wong. 2005. *The First Days of School*. Mountain View, CA: Harry K. Wong Publications, Inc.

It doesn't matter how long you've taught, these publications are full of practical advice and sound ideas for preparing your classroom and your students for differentiated instruction.

Chapter 3

Knowing and Understanding Students as Learners

Teachers who differentiate accept the responsibility of knowing students well enough to offer choice and variety when it helps them achieve the learning goals. Ultimately, however, it is the teacher's role to help students see their own learning differences and similarities . . . Students who possess self-knowledge make wiser decisions within and beyond the classroom.

Leslie Applebaum
Instructional Differentiation for Student Independence

Introduction: Differences in Student Math Learning

By its very nature, a differentiated mathematics classroom is learner-centered. Each child's social experiences and expectations are different; their concepts of intelligence and how they have experienced learning mathematics are different; and their background and cultural values are likely different as well. Within this pool of diversity, a significant strategy for differentiating mathematics is to tap into individual student strengths and styles. Getting to know these student characteristics takes specific planning and purposeful inquiry.

As teachers work with students early in the year, both teachers and students are gathering information on how students learn mathematics best. Because the focus of this chapter is on learning about the students we teach, it includes the consideration of learning styles and a review of how the interplay of individual characteristics and brain function can impact or enhance the learning of mathematics.

The beginning of the year is a time of anticipation and discovery, and a potentially rewarding and enjoyable exploration for both teacher and students. Thinking about, probing, revealing, and sharing the heterogeneity within a group of students are among the more delightful and energizing parts of planning for and implementing differentiation. The knowledge and understanding that come from these probes are the foundation for responsive mathematics instruction, the earmark of differentiation. The more teachers know about the disparate characteristics of students, the more choices teachers have available for designing effective learning options.

A Lesson for Learning about Students

Most teachers plan something special for the beginning of the school year to engage and energize students. Remembering that this is a great opportunity to observe individual characteristics and begin to develop a class learning profile, a line design lesson is used by a cadre of sixth-grade teachers at Harrison Middle School. They designed it specifically to reveal student characteristics including mathematical dispositions, work habits (see Figure 3.1), and learning styles.

Habits of Work

The following is a comprehensive list of the ideal habits of work the mathematics teachers keep in mind as they observe students at work.

1. Comes to class prepared to learn, with book, notebook, writing implement, calculator, and homework.
2. Engages in class activities in a positive and productive manner, listens when others speak, and follows classroom norms.
3. Works well in a group (offers and accepts help) and varies group roles (not always the reader, material gatherer, or time keeper).
4. Uses peers, math tools, notebook, calculator, and resources appropriately.
5. Volunteers to answer questions in small or large group settings.
6. Uses teacher feedback to improve math performance (multiple opportunities, pays attention to comments on papers, asks questions, and so on).
7. Makes a genuine effort to complete all assignments within the allotted time frame with a reasonable effort to meet the criteria especially after being absent.
8. Seeks extra help, if needed, and seeks work missed when absent.
9. Returns borrowed materials, treats resources with care, respects school property, and cleans up.
10. Respects visitors and substitute teachers.
11. Recognizes consequences of actions; doesn't blame others or whine.

List adapted from Science Habits of Work (HOW) Rubric, Poland High School, Poland ME

FIGURE 3.1

The line design lesson engages students in a series of minilessons that lead to the creation of a product. They first learn a process for creating paper-and-pencil drawings using straight lines that give the illusion of a curve. After analyzing the mathematics (impact of angle size, segment length, and precision) in a series of designs, they create their own designs, which are then transferred to cardboard to be stitched in color. (See Figure 3.2.)

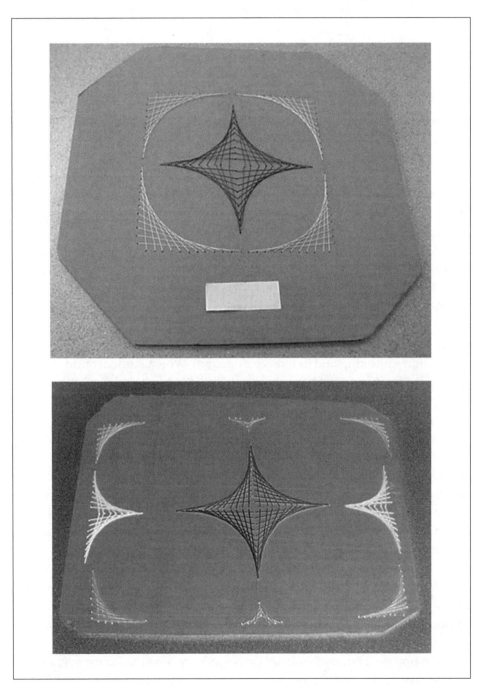

FIGURE 3.2

This lesson is chosen because it has the potential to reveal the desired characteristics. All students can complete the project, and yet the range of products indicates the range of learners in the classroom and how they approach mathematics work. There is sound mathematics embedded in the exploration and development of the product as well as opportunities for a full spectrum of interaction. In addition, students can and do experience success with this project at the beginning of the school year.

Teacher Observations

While the project provides students with the opportunity to review and apply their knowledge of geometric concepts, use geometric tools, and appreciate mathematics as the study of patterns, teachers use the time to support, observe, and record information about their students. They note how students approach the overall project—some work methodically, others need constant support, and still others make little progress during each class. They observe how students deal with making mistakes. The teachers look for interactions among the students—who readily asks for or offers assistance, who prefers to work alone, who is distracted easily, who purposefully pulls others off task, and so on. These observations and notes are valuable information for the teachers to keep in mind as they begin the school year with their students.

Teachers also learn about student dispositions toward mathematics—which students use their time well, seek out resources to complete the assignments, are on task or not? Which students are self-starters and which ones require nudging and extensive direction? Which students find the work purposeful and try to do their best? Who is eager to learn? What motivates individual students? Who is willing to work hard? Is there evidence of resistance or withdrawal? Who responds thoughtfully to questions about patterns and the challenges of creating a specific design? Teachers note students who spend a long time thinking about their design and looking through design resource books while others quickly settle on a design and begin making the template. Some students are motivated to create their own design using compass, ruler, and protractor. Teachers also watch for the quality of the individual work—the execution of design as well as the final products. See sample observations in Figure 3.3.

While teachers get to know students, their habits of work, and how they learn best, students get to know about themselves and each other as learners. By doing so, students can begin to make more informed choices and move responsibly toward becoming independent mathematics learners. For we are not only concerned with teaching mathematics, we also strive to teach children how to learn mathematics and especially how they learn mathematics best. This work also serves to clarify for students what it means to be responsible for their own learning, an expectation for students in a differentiated mathematics classroom.

Sample Teacher Observations	Sample Teacher Notes
Jamie struggles with holding a ruler to draw a straight line.	In this instance Mrs. Ellis helps him with a demonstration and makes note of the coordination challenge Jamie has.
Mr. Morse notices Ben is using the inch side of the ruler to measure off segments when he needs to be using the centimeter units. He then sees Nick reach over and turn Ben's ruler to the metric side.	He notes the helpfulness of the student as well as Ben's need to understand American standard vs. metric attributes.
Jenny is fascinated seeing that Hector is zooming ahead in a different direction from everyone else by creating a complex design using a compass and protractor.	She notes that Hector is a self-starter high in independence and creativity.
Mr. Morse observes Tammy making her third attempt at creating her template. She crumples yet another paper.	He notes that Tammy has not asked for help, is impatient with herself, and will need subtle support.

FIGURE 3.3

The Brain and Individuality

As teachers continue their probes they need to be mindful of several aspects of what is known today about brain function. The kind of deep mathematical learning we want for all students is innately connected to how an individual's brain operates. Among other things we know that (1) brain functions are significantly affected by social relationships and emotional responses; (2) the brain responds with positive intensity to appropriate challenge but shuts down when threatened; and (3) like fingerprints and DNA, the subtle organizational workings of each and every individual brain are different (Caine and Caine 1997; Jensen 1998).

Mathematics teachers must walk a fine line between providing captivating challenges for students and avoiding any sense of threat to students. For this reason, it is imperative for math teachers to be alert to the sensitivities of students and use students' natural interests and inclinations as entry points for mathematical challenges.

Student Curiosity About the Brain

My own experience with middle schoolers opened my eyes to their innate fascination with how their brains work. On one occasion, I read excerpts to them from my favorite "brain" resource, a heavily highlighted, sticky-noted volume of *Teaching with the Brain in Mind* (Jensen 1998). The content focus at the time was large numbers, and this book provided an interesting practical use of large numbers when discussing numbers of brain cells and their various functions. The next day, one student asked if I would read them more from the brain book! I probed their interest and continued to share bits from the book as appropriate. (They especially loved the connection of Mozart music to geometry learning and talked me into purchasing the music to play for them before geometry explorations. I am definitely an indulgent teacher when it comes to capturing their interest!) I shared excerpts from other brain resources as well, particularly in regard to keeping the brain healthy for learning mathematics—keeping the brain hydrated and the effects of anxiety and fear—as well as the uniqueness of each individual brain. All of this appeared to help students understand and work more effectively as individuals and with each other. This is just one suggestion for avoiding the negative effects of downshifting that is easily triggered by threats, usually imagined or related to anxiety about unknown or unfamiliar circumstances.

Student Characteristics: What and Why

We began to address the issue of learning about students in Chapter 2 (see "Getting to Know Each Other") with three different strategies: administering a math survey early in the year; creating personal graphs on interests, needs, and strengths; and having students write their mathematical autobiographies. We also suggested that teachers reach out to parents for important and helpful information about their children.

The chart in Figure 3.4 lists student characteristics that differentiating teachers find useful for both instructional decisions and lesson designs. Sources for how to obtain information on these characteristics are also suggested.

The value in knowing these student characteristics is at least twofold. The first is being readily able to adapt lesson elements to accommodate the needs of individual students. The second is in knowing how to plan more effectively for the entire class. As informal and formal student profiles develop, a class profile emerges, which can be used to guide overall design features for the year. For example, when it is clear that many of my students are kinesthetic learners, I am mindful of their need for physical movement and active involvement whenever possible and appropriate. A specific instance is during a statistics unit when the class uses the Median March, a highly interactive move-about activity, to determine the range, median, and mode for a particular set of data. (See Figure 3.5.) At the same time I support auditory and visual learners with clear directions, task cards, diagrams, and/or reporting opportunities. The knowledge and understanding I have of students translates into powerful management tools for keeping students focused and

Student Characteristics	Source(s) of Information
Talents, interests, ways of learning, strengths, goals	Student self-reporting, parents, records, former teachers, inventory, observation, math autobiography, professional reading

Cognitive profile
    Language: oral, written, and mathematical
    Thinking and reasoning
    Content strand skills: number, geometry, measurement, etc.
    Conceptual needs and strengths
    Estimation and problem-solving skills
	Records, former teachers, mathematics survey, math autobiography, observations, preassessments

Emotional characteristics: Motivation, responsibility, persistence, anxieties Physical conditions: preferences and needs Social relationships: peer and adult Work environment preferences and needs: distractibility, individual/group, competitive/collaborative Language, cultural background, worldview	Parents, former teachers, observation, records
Intellectual issues and exceptional needs Math experiences, attitudes, and learning dispositions	Records, former teachers Math autobiography, former teachers, observation

Learning preferences
    Auditory, visual, and/or kinesthetic
    Silver and Strong mathematics learning styles
    Human Dynamics
    Gardner: multiple intelligences
	Professional reading, inventories, former teachers, observation

FIGURE 3.4

engaged. Active involvement gives all students a higher probability of understanding more deeply the mathematics they are doing. In addition, students gain more control of and become more responsible for their own mathematics learning.

In this example, a characteristic (kinesthetic learners) from a general class profile was the major motivation for using the Median March while alternate

---

The Median March

Students collect a set of data—the estimations for the number of jellybeans in a jar. They write their estimate on a small slip of paper along with their initials and place it in a collection container. The estimations are then randomly redistributed to the students. (This is done in order to remove personal ownership while working with the data, making it *safe* for those students who are self-conscious about estimating.)

Students organize themselves in a line from least to greatest according to the random estimate on their slip of paper. The students then call out the estimate they are holding from least to greatest and everyone can check to see that the lineup is in order. Once complete, they can identify the range of the data (the smallest and the largest estimates) and the mode or modes if there are any. The call out can be repeated to check the mode.

The teacher then announces that they will maintain their order in line by marching single file behind the teacher (as leader) until she or he calls stop. The teacher carefully turns and leads the highest estimate holder, followed by the ordered lineup, along the line of students to the point where the highest estimate holder is next to the holder of the lowest estimate. They become partners as do each subsequent pair of high-low estimate holders. The single student at the end of this double line becomes the median, or if there is an even number of estimates, the last pair of partners will find the number that is exactly between their estimates and that becomes the median.

P.S. Don't forget to share some of the estimation strategies as well as reveal the actual number of jellybeans.

FIGURE 3.5

style approaches were folded into the overall lesson. Knowledge about specific students influences the entire math program—curriculum, instruction, and assessment—guiding instructional responses to support individual student learning. For example, contexts for problems can be tailored to a student or class profile, and activities and processes can be flexibly designed to match student readiness, interests, and learning styles. Indeed, tiered assignments, menus, centers, and open-ended challenges should be grounded in the teacher's understanding of student learning styles and needs.

In addition, early planning decisions should be based upon knowledge of the potential barriers to learning that a particular concept presents. Armed with enough background knowledge, teachers can transform barriers into stepping-stones using scaffolding techniques as described in Figure 3.6.

Turn Symmetry

When the mathematics textbook introduces students to turn [rotational] symmetry, it suggests that the teacher make several transparencies of the pictured regular pentagon and actually demonstrate the rotation on the overhead. Because of what I know about my students' learning styles, I know that half of my students will not grasp the subtleties of rotational symmetry, especially finding the center point and turning around that center point, by simply watching me demonstrate and explain.

Therefore, I made paper copies large enough so that students could cut out their own pentagons, label the vertices, find the center point by folding, and have a second copy to use as a "frame." They can now follow along with the overhead demonstration in a way that allows them to experience the concept kinesthetically. During the entire scaffold experience, we used the mathematical language over and over as a way to support the linguistic and auditory learners as well.

FIGURE 3.6

To accomplish similar transformations, teachers need to absorb a good deal of information about their student population. It is a daunting task but the Addressing Accessibility in Mathematics (AAM) project of the Educational Development Center Inc. (EDC) proposes a more doable process. They suggest the teacher select three students who represent the range of learners within the class. The teacher creates a profile of these focal students, analyzing their strengths and weaknesses across six areas involved in learning mathematics: conceptual, language, visual-spatial, organization, memory, and attention. A sample profile is shown in Figure 3.7.

These profiles give the teacher a ready source for identifying and subsequently accommodating potential barriers. Planning with these focal students in mind helps teachers choose instructional strategies that meet the needs of most learners in the class. Teachers may also need to make additional accommodations for individual students, particularly those with more significant disabilities (Brodesky, Gross, McTigue, and Zorfass 2004).

Other class profiles might be created, as Jenny does, by using the inside of a file folder divided into four sections labeled with the learning styles you'll read about later in this chapter. She uses student names on sticky notes that she places in the appropriate learning style section. It's quick, handy, and easy to refer to as she plans differentiated lessons throughout the year. The sticky-note names can be moved about as new observations dictate. Teaching mathematics is, after all, a responsive art that reflects student growth and understanding.

Example of a Focal Student Planner		
	STUDENT'S STRENGTHS	**STUDENT'S DIFFICULTIES**
Conceptual	• Able to visualize and extend patterns • Good number sense and estimation skills	• Very concrete • Difficulty making generalizations and coming up with rules
Language	• Comfortable expressing ideas in pairs and small groups	• Difficulties with writing explanations • Weak vocabulary • Nervous about speaking in front of class
Visual-Spatial	• Strong drawing skills; creates diagrams to solve problems • Able to interpret and create 2-D and 3-D representations	
Organization		• Binder is disorganized, making it hard to find prior work • Loses homework
Memory		• Major area of weakness • Makes frequent errors when retrieving math facts • Forgets formulas and procedures
Attention	• Able to sustain attention when drawing and when working with a focused partner	• Has difficulties focusing • Short attention span • Easily distracted
Other	• Works well in pairs • Strong fine motor skills	• Feels discouraged about learning math

Helpful Strategies for this Student

• Provide visuals and manipulatives to build conceptual understanding
• Sequence activities to move from the concrete to the representational to the abstract
• Have student create a resource section in her binder so that she can look up information that she tends to forget. Have her create resources on computer so she has a back-up on file.
• Teach organizational strategies and set up a binder organizational system with frequent checks
• Use a non-verbal cue to direct her to focus her attention

FIGURE 3.7 (*Used with permission of Education Development Center, Inc.*)

Ways of Knowing Students

Determining Dispositions: Observing and Reflecting

Among the subtler points to understand about students are the *dispositions* they bring with them with regard to productivity and thinking. That is, what are their inclinations and tendencies toward understanding that learning mathematics requires thoughtful, intentional work? It's another way of thinking about students' attitudes toward mathematics and their readiness to work toward mathematical goals. Teacher observation is key as pointed out in the sample lesson on line designs described earlier in this chapter. Reflecting on the observations is indispensable. Here are some guiding questions along with examples of what you are likely to observe in the classroom, possible interpretations, and potential responses:

- *What kind of internal motivations are at work and how are they reflected in classroom actions and responses?* Alison attracts my attention because she is quiet, with withdrawn body language. My interpretation is lack of confidence, math weakness, or social dynamics or a combination of the three. I'll find an opportunity to build rapport and look for interests or strengths in any area. Suzie, on the other hand is loud, outspoken, and impatient with just about everyone. She is quick to point out any potential error. My interpretation is that she is ready for challenging mathematics, with a need to learn about her impact on and role in the learning of others. I'll direct her toward challenging opportunities while helping the class understand and support the math learning needs of all.

- *Do student actions and responses reflect what is possible and maximize potential?* First-grader Eric has the "Eeyore" complex. He whines, "This is hard . . . I can't do this." He requires many miniscaffolds to move him gradually toward independence. He needs to be "caught" having fun and doing math. Second-grader Darrell loves math time; he is excited, compliant, and nondemanding with great number sense. He will help the entire class improve their mathematical dispositions.

- *Which students are ready to tackle the math work and eager to learn?* Both Suzie and Darrell fall under this descriptor even though Darrell is more pleasant and supportive.

- *What is the range of willingness and resistance?* Sixth-grader Tonya is unhappy and oozes anger. She either withdraws into the corner or attempts to distract a classmate with off-task conversation. Tonya needs one-on-one time to establish rapport along with math help, possibly work with the counselor, and some agreed-upon clues to redirect negative behaviors. Seventh-grader Neal is quiet, shares when asked, pays attention to feedback, wants to know how to do better, is confident and likely to challenge a teacher's indication of error because he is always careful in thinking through the work.

- *What are the various levels of motivation for thinking?* Effective mathematics learning requires thinking, which in turn depends on thinking dispositions that are enculturated over time. Seventh-grader Kristin wants to get the right answer. She is likely to say, "Don't ask me to think, just show me how to do it!" Fourth-grader Hope has to understand "Why? Why? Why?"—an answer is appropriate or inappropriate, a particular strategy is likely to produce a solution, or a piece of information is useful. Hope insists on making sense of everything she does in math. Emily thoroughly enjoys explaining her work to others in great detail; she also invites questions so she can think about the situation even more. Alexis listens very carefully to others and evaluates their responses; she loves paraphrasing practice when she gets to summarize and evaluate before she adds her own thoughts to the mathematical discourse. These students represent the full range of thinking dispositions. Probing questions will help to bring students along—questions that ask for clarification, further thinking, or redirection.
- *What are the values and belief systems held by individuals that impact the ability to develop mathematical skills and abilities?* Once again there is a broad range: Claire wants to please, sometimes in distracting ways; Breanna seems unwilling to contribute to discussions but does quiet, quality work; Fritz works hard to manipulate any situation for personal satisfaction; Colby sees no value in school but has great street smarts; Su Jong works hard and has good family support; and Andy reports that his parents "were never good at math either!" Goal setting and having students understand what and why they're supposed to be learning help students develop the values and beliefs they need to achieve mathematically.

Leaders in mathematics education believe that productive mathematical dispositions are developed in concert as students develop mathematical proficiency. Teachers need to know where students are in the beginning of their time together in order to foster and enhance positive attitudes toward mathematics as a thinking, sense-making, useful, and doable discipline.

One of the most daunting challenges faced when working with students having extraordinary learning difficulties in mathematics is tapping into the sense making and usefulness of mathematics. By probing, I often find gaping holes in conceptual development. For example, consider students who have been pushed to memorize number facts (usually unsuccessfully!) before connecting to the concrete, real-world instances of their applications and what they represent. A startling illustration occurred with a fifth-grade student I was diagnosing. She had successfully memorized (with immediate recall) all of the multiplication facts but could not connect a single fact to a real world example that it might represent, such as $3 \times 7 = 21$ representing the number of days in three weeks. Continued probing revealed an absence of any conceptual under-standing of multiplication—only rote memorized abstract symbols. This student was totally lacking a productive disposition and this reality impacted all aspects of her mathematics learning. Developing productive dispositions and having students make sense of the mathematics they are learning is the backbone of differentiated mathematics instruction—diverse learning opportunities that bring out the practical and important aspects of mathematics.

General information about student readiness, prior experience, preferences, interests, and goals is key to critical aspects of the differentiation process. Yet, still more pertinent information about student diversity and how to use it effectively comes from scanning the work of learning theorists such as Howard Gardner (multiple intelligences) and Sandra Seagal and David Horne (Human Dynamics). Knowledge of the research and development associated with their work adds a high degree of pedagogical power to the teacher's arsenal for adjusting the learning environment and accommodating the learning needs of all students.

Learning Styles

Learning about learning styles has been a great professional gift! In this instance, the diversity that motivates us to differentiate math instruction is also a wonderful tool for expanding the mathematics-learning repertoire of all students. While a plethora of approaches to learning styles have been researched and developed over the past thirty years, our interest stems from the consequential impact that learning styles have on the overall teaching-learning landscape of a mathematics classroom. Knowing the range of student preferences and the contexts that clearly connect to them can smooth many mathematics-learning pathways. Yes, differentiating teachers need to know about learning styles, intelligences, and strengths, but it is not necessary to know the precise descriptors for each individual student unless there is a significant or puzzling learning issue.

Visual, Auditory, or Kinesthetic

First and foremost are the learning style referents that have been around for years and referenced as *visual*, *auditory*, and *kinesthetic*. They are summarized in the Figure 3.8. I think we have all been fascinated with the discovery of our own particular preferences. I was amazed to discover that I don't hear well if I'm not seeing at the same time I'm listening. No wonder I never enjoyed using the phone (except as a dating teenager!). Once I recognized this visual preference in myself, it was intriguing to measure the effects of deliberately working to learn through both auditory and kinesthetic experiences as well. I did this to better understand my students and walk in their shoes. I find my learning is greatly enhanced using all three types of learning activities. An important role for the teacher with regard to these styles is to help students recognize their preferences and work to embrace elements from all three learning style characteristics.

Learning Style	Needs, Characteristics, and Challenges
Visual learners	Need to see what they're learning, are often artistic, doodle, have strong sense of color; need to read, write, and observe; use graphics, diagrams, and written directions; may find lectures confusing.
Auditory learners	Need to hear information, participate in discussion; need oral presentations and explanations; may have difficulty reading, writing, and following written directions.
Kinesthetic learners	Need to manipulate objects and move; well-coordinated athletic ability; need to make models, do lab work, experiential learning; trace letters and facts, memorize while exercising.

FIGURE 3.8

Common Threads

For over twenty years, Jenny and I have explored and utilized the learning style work of significant researchers. Over time we found key common threads among the various approaches that allowed us to simplify the analysis of our classes and enhance the use of learning style preferences in the classroom. In essence, we collapsed the different learning styles programs important to our mathematics instruction into one. At the same time, we excluded Howard Gardner's multiple intelligences from the compacting process and continue to find multiple intelligences useful in concert with various learning styles.

The table in Figure 3.9 is designed to highlight the attributes of learners in each common thread, their preferences for getting information, how they tend to work with and organize data, and their learning needs. The descriptions are a compilation of key attributes from various learning styles programs.

The Learners

In the paragraphs that follow, we briefly describe each type of common thread learner and present an example for that learning style. Keep in mind that no individual student would exactly match a learning style. Students will most always share characteristics from more than one style.

Typical style I learners are visual and focused. They gather information best in structured formats that they can see or read. They appreciate carefully sequenced modeling, uninterrupted practice, and a quiet work space.

Matt comes to class and pulls out his notes. He rewrote them last night in outline form after finishing his homework. His tablemates join him but they

Style	Attributes	Input—Getting Information	Processing Data	Learning Needs
I	Logical, linear, focused, highly principled, verbally skilled. Connect math to skilled calculation.	Use five senses, see, read, want structure, prefer context with concrete and real instances.	Sequential, step-by-step, orderly, logical, dichotomize into black/white.	Sequential demonstrations, reading, practice, work alone, cannot tolerate distractions.
II	Risk-takers, intense, verbally skilled, evaluative, single focused, theoretical, leaders. Connect math to reasoning and proof.	Intuitively link connected organized resources, experiment, like novel innovative resources.	Conceptual understanding, forward moving, reasoning and proof, experiment, create images and pictures, creative approaches.	Combination of resources, organization, structure, briskness, discussion, graphic organizers, no repetition.
III	Multifocused, multi-sensory, sensitive, flexible, creative, adaptable, divergent. Connect math to solving nonroutine problems.	Intuitive combining of resources, see the whole, then gather parts.	Visualize, absorb the environment, explore, search for pattern and meaning, generate new ideas, see grays.	Flexibility within structured busy environment, drama, time parameters, group work.
IV	Flexible, holistic, quiet observers, less verbal, street smarts, excellent memory, pragmatic. Connect math to its real-world applications.	Use five senses, concrete objects, real events, context, seeing the whole with parts.	Gather massive data, detailed, sort and organize, make connections, intuitive leaps.	Stimulating rich environment, work both alone and cooperatively, hands-on, time, be able to shape environment.

Influenced by Gregorc (1980–2006), Strong, Thomas, Perini and Silver (2004), Seagal and Horne (1997), Sternberg (1997).

FIGURE 3.9—Table of Common Thread learning styles.

do not draw him into a conversation. He listens as they talk, but does not engage with them. He focuses on the teacher as questions are asked about the homework. Matt feels that the most important aspect of mathematics is good computation skills.

Style II learners are bold and brisk. They move easily into leadership positions with no time to waste. They set a goal and begin moving toward it almost simultaneously, being focused and evaluative of everything and everyone. They love innovation, experimentation, and discussion as long as they don't have to do it again.

> Jenny charges into the classroom ready to work. Her homework complete, she gets her group started by comparing answers with tablemates. She discusses correctness and comes to agreed-upon answers by offering and asking for proof and justification—that's what mathematics means to her. She turns to the next lesson in the book. She is ready to move on to another task.

Style III learners are sensitive and multifocused, absorbing information of which they're not even aware. They are flexible, dramatic, and highly intuitive, spotting patterns, demanding meaning, and generating new ideas. Although they love a busy environment, it needs to be structured.

> Marisol comes into the classroom wide-eyed, scanning the room for information to direct what she should be doing (board work) and notices Haislip's sketching. She quickly and accurately copies and completes the board work on addition and subtraction of fractions, which she loves, and begins sketching. Then, changing her mind, she creates some challenging fraction problems of her own and asks Mrs. Green if it's all right to help a classmate with the board work. Marisol believes that solving unique challenging problems is the most important part of mathematics.

Learners in the style IV category are the quiet ones, although not necessarily shy. They will be absorbing all kinds of data, observing the big picture and the details at the same time. They don't want to miss anything. They like to take their time preparing for and completing tasks and will have practical suggestions for the usefulness of the math they are learning.

> Fred is attentive and quiet. He prefers to work alone until he has a lot of information. He rarely volunteers during whole group discussion. He often appears to not be engaged. However, when queried privately he is working on developing his ideas about the current topic and can readily relate it to a model he's building at home.

These four styles present a simplified knowledge base for:

1. observing, assessing, and reflecting on student learning styles;
2. designing accessible mathematics lessons that accommodate the needs indicated by those styles;
3. providing students with developmental opportunities to expand their mathematics learning styles as they develop mathematical proficiency.

Contributing Program

Human Dynamics™ is a personality analysis program that has contributed significant elements to our broad-based palette for observing learners and

Learning Style	Human Dynamics—Dr. Sandra Seagal
Style I	Mentally centered personality dynamic
Style II	Emotional objective personality dynamic
Style III	Emotional subjective personality dynamic
Style IV	Physically centered personality dynamic

FIGURE 3.10—Learning style alignments with personality dynamics.

better understanding their needs. The Human Dynamics program and learning style alignments are represented in the table in Figure 3.10. Dr. Sandra Seagal's research and subsequent development of the Human Dynamics program has been critical to my practice and the determination to differentiate mathematics instruction. The primary contribution of Human Dynamics comes from the altered perceptions of teachers who, like myself, have completed a training session. When teachers learn to recognize the different personality dynamics at work in their classrooms, they discard negative labels. They understand that the previously considered slow learner is in reality a style IV or physically centered learner who needs (1) more time to assimilate, (2) considerable context, and (3) hands-on concrete experiential opportunities. The behavior problem is perhaps an insufficiently challenged style II or emotional objective learner who needs the opportunity to experiment. The child with attention deficit disorder may be a style III or emotional subjective learner who needs ways to detach from emotional overload, both from within and outside, as well as support in order to maintain focus (Seagal and Horne 1997, 298–305).

When I was preparing the place value unit described in Chapter 1, I considered everything I knew about the children. A comment from the teacher about "the quiet cooperative boy who just doesn't get it" prompted me to ask about what he likes and does best in math—drawing. I also suspected his learning style might match those who need a lot of data and time—style IV. I planned the lessons with flexible time, plenty of information, and opportunities for him to illustrate his work. I subtly watched and supported him and by the fourth class period he began to contribute on his own and greatly surprised us with his insights. Without knowing about these learning style characteristics, we never would have planned for or appreciated the moment.

Another contribution from Human Dynamics comes from understanding that style II and style III (emotional objective and emotional subjective) individuals have difficulty working with each other until they come to understand each other's needs. They are inexplicably irritated with each other because their communication patterns are conflicting and confusing to each other. It is helpful to acknowledge and incorporate this information into interactive group skills work such as Jenny's cooperative problem-solving lesson in Chapter 2. It is also useful when forming small groups.

A third Human Dynamics contribution is understanding the data-processing "activity rhythms" exhibited by different personality dynamics as revealed by the research, and consequently those of the associated learning styles. They are pictured in the chart in Figure 3.11 as they relate to mathematical problem solving.

Let A represent reading, articulating, and understanding the problem (*launch*).

Let B represent exploring how to use the available information to solve the problem (*explore*).

Let C represent presenting the solution to the problem and applying the results (*summary*).

Each style and personality dynamic is indicated in the first column. Imagine the problem-solving begins there and moves to the right across the row for each dynamic. For example, style I students will collect all of the information and define the problem in an even step-by-step manner and only then move on to explore possible solutions, giving each process about the same amount of time and effort. They then organize their results for presentation, all very straight forward.

[Begin Problem Solving] ⟶

Style I— mentally centered	A A A A A A	B B B B B B	C C C C C C
Style II— emotional objective	A A C C B A	C C A A A C	B B B B A C
Style III— emotional subjective	B B A A B A B B A	C B A B B B B B C	A B C B C B C C C C
Style IV— physically centered	A A A A A A	A A A A B B	B C C C C C

Adaptation, Seagal and Horne (1997, 231)

FIGURE 3.11—Problem-solving activity rhythms for the four learning styles.

However, according to Seagal and Horne, about 55 percent of Western populations are emotional subjective or style III (1997, 32). Note that style III learners have a significantly different activity rhythm compared to all other styles. They begin exploring solutions before they have data or a problem interpretation! In summary, styles I and IV collect all their data before they begin processing, while styles II and III tend to begin with the end— proposing an organizational scheme or a potential solution before they have much if any data. Seagal and Horne found similar differences in communication styles (Seagal and Horne, 213). It makes us realize that the teacher is in essence conducting a complex multirhythmic symphony while striving for a harmonious environment—not an easy task to be sure. It does help to know the score! This research into human interactive behaviors was a breakthrough for me both as a teacher and a colleague of other teachers.

Implications for Lesson Planning

To plan a differentiated lesson with the four learning styles in mind, notice that they all need structure and motivation. Begin with a logical systematic launch, set clear parameters, and answer the questions *what, why, where, when, how.* Paint the big picture for the lesson, add a dramatic element with a heavy dose of context, and provide a familiar comfortable environment that allows each student to process their work according to their natural rhythms with the understanding that others will do their work differently and can learn from each other.

Multiple Intelligences

Multiple intelligences and learning styles are complementary. Consider individuals as having natural rhythms for using their intellectual gifts. The multiple intelligences of Howard Gardner are a centerpiece for understanding the potential perspectives from which students work and learn, and subsequently for diversifying instruction. Gardner has identified eight ways to think and learn so far. The descriptions below have been adapted to emphasize their implications for learning mathematics.

- *Verbal/linguistic*—enjoy language and are sensitive to subtle meanings and context; learn mathematics best through verbal tasks, writing about and describing their thinking
- *Logical/mathematical*—classify, compare, reason, and love numbers and patterns; learn best by developing understanding of and analyzing numbers and patterns
- *Visual/spatial*—perceive the visual world accurately and create images; learn mathematics best by creating multiple representations, visualizing, and recording work graphically
- *Bodily/kinesthetic*—use their bodies in creative and differentiated ways and express themselves through movement; learn mathematics best with action, manipulatives, and hands-on opportunities
- *Musical*—respond to pitch, rhythm, tonal quality, and emotional expression (all mathematically based); learn mathematics best when connected to musical attributes and rhythm (patterns)
- *Interpersonal*—understand and communicate sensitively; learn mathematics best collaboratively and thrive on cooperative problem solving
- *Intrapersonal*—the ability to understand oneself and enjoy a metacognitive perspective; learn mathematics best from personalized experimentation, reflection, and goal setting

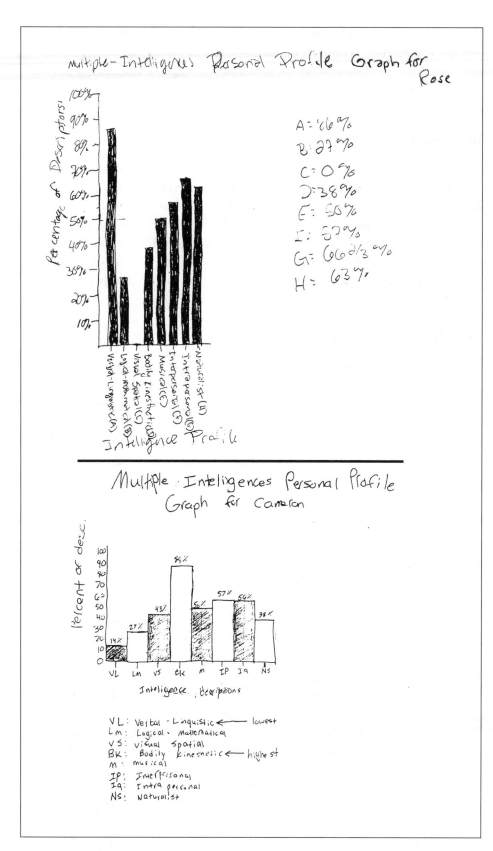

Multiple-Intelligences Personal Profile Graph for Rose

A = 86%
B = 27%
C = 0%
D = 38%
E = 50%
F = 57%
G = 66 2/3%
H = 63%

Multiple-Intelligences Personal Profile Graph for Cameron

VL: Verbal-Linguistic ← lowest
Lm: Logical-Mathematical
VS: Visual Spatial
BK: Bodily Kinesthetic ← highest
M: Musical
IP: Interpersonal
Iq: Intrapersonal
Ns: Naturalist

FIGURE 3.12

■ *Naturalist*—sensitive to the natural world, recognizing and classifying from nature's patterns; learn best by observing and figuring out how things work; will recognize mathematical patterns and examples in nature

(Gardner 1993, 1999; Willis and Johnson 2001; Heacox 2002)

A number of inventories have been developed over the years for identifying your own significant intelligences, and we can tell you that middle school students love doing just that for themselves. We are careful to explain that their intelligence preferences are a work in progress, constantly changing and developing, especially at their age. We attend to multiple intelligences because they connect to metacognitive thinking (students thinking about how they think and reason) and high student interest. Diane Heacox has a checklist style inventory designed for parents to use with their children in *Differentiating Instruction in the Regular Classroom: How to Reach and Teach All Learners, Grades 3–12* (2002, 38–39).

We adapted her multiple intelligences checklist this past year for use with seventh and eighth graders. After completing the inventory, each student created a bar graph to compare the level of strengths for the eight intelligences and highlighted his or her three strongest preferences. (See Figure 3.12) This was a mathematics activity for them as well because they needed to determine the percent of descriptors checked for each intelligence subset. I was then able to use their results to create a class profile revealing overall strengths of bodily/kinesthetic, verbal/linguistic, and naturalist.

Jody Kenny Willis and Aostre N. Johnson used Gardner's multiple intelligences theory to frame out a program for studying multiplication. In a January 2001 *Teaching Children Mathematics* article, they describe numerous strategies for each intelligence preference. They suggest using the elements in a variety of instructional settings ranging from direct instruction to centers that are visited throughout the day. Any third- through fifth-grade teacher will be able to differentiate their study of multiplication (and division!) using this amazing resource. The basis of their differentiated multiple intelligence study of multiplication is summarized in the practical, easy-to-use instructional matrix shown in Figure 3.13.

General Information: Students, Parents, Records, And So On

As you can see in Figure 3.4, a good place to begin gathering information about students is with the students themselves, their math autobiographies, their caregivers, school records, former teachers, and the mathematics survey. These sources supply basic information including academic histories, interests, talents, strengths, prior mathematics experiences, and family and cultural backgrounds. Refer to Chapter 2 for details on mathematical autobiographies, math surveys, and connecting with parents and families.

Additional useful information can be gathered using parent and student inventories. Figure 3.14 is an example of such an inventory. The data obtained

Instructional matrix for multiple intelligences in mathematics

Intelligence	Materials	Learning Activities	Teaching Strategies

Logical-mathematical	calculators
	manipulatives
	games
	number lines
	Venn diagrams
		creating or solving:
		  brain teasers
		  problems
		  logic puzzles
		  equations
		  algorithms
		  justifying thinking
			worthwhile tasks
			connections with previous
			  concepts
			variety of representations
			inquiry methods

Naturalistic	natural objects models observation notebooks magnifying glasses	using nature classifying objects observing patterns	demonstrations outdoor activities naturalistic investigations
Bodily kinesthetic	manipulatives models individual children or groups	sequencing movements exploring tactile models dramatizing clapping, tapping, hopping using concrete materials	gestures dramatizations hands-on examples physical models

Linguistic	children's books
	textbooks
	audiotapes
	activity sheets
	journals
		reading word problems
		writing mathematics stories
		  listening to explanations
		  talking about strategies
			storytelling
			book corners
			humor and jokes
			questions
			assessment tasks
			lectures
			written or oral explanations

Spatial	computers
	graphs
	charts
	playing cards
	manipulatives
	dominoes
	bulletin boards
	overheads
		decorating flash cards
		drawing diagrams
		creating pictures or
		  other representations
		looking at illustrations
			mental models
			visual cues; e.g., color,
			  circles, boxes, arrows
			guided imagery
			graphic organizers
			concept maps or webs

Interpersonal	games shared manipulatives	working cooperatively participating in simulations interviewing others engaging in role playing sharing strategies assessing peers' work	discussions people-based problems peer tutoring group activities guest speakers
Intrapersonal	self-checking materials diaries or journals	writing in journals addressing values and attitudes reflecting on connections with students' lives conducting self-assessment	private spaces choice time empowerment
Musical	tape recorders CDs instruments	composing, performing, or listening to raps, songs, chants using musical notation creating rhythmic patterns	listening corners rhythmical activities background music

FIGURE 3.13—Instructional matrix for multiple intelligences in mathematics.*

from this instrument can enhance the teacher's ability to keep students engaged and motivated.

It is so important to learn from the families of your students that we revisit this important source of information. One of the ways this can happen is to have parents or caregivers use the multiple intelligences checklist, either with their child if age appropriate or as observers of their child for the

*Reprinted with permission from *Teaching Children Mathematics*, copyright 2001 by the National Council of Teachers of Mathematics. All rights reserved. This table was adapted from a model by Thomas Armstrong in *Multiple Intelligences in the Classroom*, Alexandria, VA: Association for Supervision and Curriculum Development, 1994.

Student Motivation Inventory

The following inventory is modeled after a form developed by Raymond Wlodkowski, University of Wisconsin–Milwaukee, in 1978. He created it to help teachers plan lessons related to student needs by learning about the interests, values, and desires of their students. His inventory centered on four basic clusters: (1) interests, concerns, and desires; (2) satisfactions, accomplishments, and strengths; (3) valued rewards; and (4) curiosity.

1. I am proud of _____
2. My favorite reward for good deeds or good work is _____
3. A beautiful thing I have seen is _____
4. Something I do very well is _____
5. Something very mysterious to me is _____
6. I like to read stories about _____
7. One of my finest accomplishments is _____
8. This is how I would spend $25 _____
9. I wonder about _____
10. I like to spend my free time _____
11. I know that I am able to _____
12. I enjoy _____
13. What I like best about myself is _____
14. A nice thing my teacher could do for me is _____
15. In math my greatest strength is _____
16. Something I really want is _____
17. What really makes me think is _____
18. An important goal for me is _____
19. I know a great deal about _____
20. Sometimes I worry about _____
21. When I grow up I want to _____
22. What I want to know more about is _____
23. What I like to do with my friends is _____

Adapted from Raymond Wlodkowski (1978) Student Motivation Information Form

FIGURE 3.14

younger set. Diane Heacox (2002) provides ample support and explanations for parent participation. There is an important public relations aspect to using this type of parent connection: parents will truly sense that they are partners in providing the type of mathematics instruction that will serve their children best. And, as always, be open to the questions parents have about your mathematics program, what differentiating means, and how they can be of most help—it might actually be an extra pair of hands as with my daughter-in-law Amy.

Currently, Amy goes into her son's classroom every week for an hour to work with a small group of children on math skills, as determined by the teacher. It's a win-win relationship for their entire mathematics learning community. Amy even purchased and uses the NCTM *Principles and Standards* (2000) so that she can be consistent with the teacher.

A Note About Special Needs

We define students with special needs to include both the gifted and those with individual education plans. When gathering information about students, be sure to have conversations with the resource teachers who work with these children. These teachers have volumes of information about the students with whom they work, and they know how to address specific learning needs. If possible, develop a collaborative relationship with them for planning and implementing differentiated mathematics instruction.

Summary

After considering the range of characteristics and learning styles that differentiating teachers face, the bottom line is in implementing general practices that have the potential to embrace all learners. Many years ago the It's Elementary Task Force of the San Diego County Office of Education created the following list of opportunities that teachers could offer students as a teacher self-assessment of their classrooms. We pass on the modified list in Figure 3.15 as a reflection tool for planning to accommodate various learning styles and use student characteristics to expand learning possibilities. Folding these strategies into the overall math instruction program helps assure a diversified platform that supports more complex accommodations for all your students as needed.

Give students opportunities to:

Make choices	Study independently
Use visual materials	Listen to audio materials
Listen to lectures	Work at his or her own level
Study quietly	Work at his or her own speed
Study in groups	Correct failures/errors
Present oral responses	Learn by doing
Present written responses	Clarify information
Create projects	Take oral assessments
Engage in discussion	Take written assessments
Share in the planning	Be creative

FIGURE 3.15

SECTION II

The Essentials: The Lenses of Differentiating Mathematics

We cannot see what is "out there" merely by looking around. Everything depends on the lenses through which we view the world. By putting on new lenses, we can see things that would otherwise remain invisible.

The Courage to Teach, Parker Palmer (1998, 26)

Optical instruments from powerful telescopes to exotic microscopes are used to explore the world and our universe, all of them dependent on the concept of the lens: bending light that we might see more clearly. Even the simple water drop lens is a jaw-dropping, mind-grabbing event for fifth graders learning about microscopic science. Engagement, fascination, and intellectual stimulation are appropriate descriptors of the memorable experiences that emerge from their initial lens experiment.

And so we choose a lens metaphor to explore the essentials of differentiated mathematics instruction.

Chapter 4

A *Problem-Solving* Platform

Problem solving should be the central focus of the mathematics curriculum. As such, it is a primary goal of all mathematics instruction and an integral part of all mathematical activity. Problem solving is not a distinct topic but a process that should permeate the entire program and provide the context in which concepts and skills can be learned.

National Council of Teachers of Mathematics,
Curriculum and Evaluation Standards for School Mathematics

Problem Solving

In 1997 I went back to the classroom to experience using the problem-based curriculum, *Connected Mathematics*, in a multigrade 7–8 program. My biggest worry was two grade levels in the same class period. I had experienced twenty-five years of challenging and often frustrating work with one grade level at a time. What really worked for the seventh- and eighth-grade combined group were the engaging problems that allowed students to differentiate for readiness—the biggest issue—for themselves! Every problem was accessible and the students took it from there.

When students are engaged in the exploration and solution of a problem that "grabs them," they will go as far as they can, or as far as their readiness takes them. Some will attain only part of the solution and some will go well beyond and make important connections and hypotheses for themselves. Those who might be considered "below grade level" are not shut out of the closing discussion, which is an additional opportunity for conceptual development while considering the thinking of contributing classmates.

I worked hard to facilitate an environment to support and maximize their learning. I was very much the reflective/responsive teacher. I tweaked and planned for every available moment and each student need, but the key was the *problem-solving platform*. How powerful that was and is!

A problem-solving platform is a mathematics curriculum that consistently draws students into mathematical inquiry through stories, situations, or scenarios that challenge students with intriguing problems. The problems are embedded with rich content waiting to be uncovered. The revelation of the mathematics takes place in an atmosphere of shared strategies at an individually determined pace. By that we mean that each child grapples with the mathematics at her or his readiness level while operating in a collaborative environment where support comes from the perspectives of other students as well as the teacher.

Good Problems

Good problems are essential to this process. They are irresistible and open, come in a variety of forms including games and puzzles, can emerge from a teachable moment, and invite persistence. The contexts vary and shift with the needs and interests of the children. Good problems also allow the teacher access to student thinking as the work (exploration) progresses.

Here are two of my favorite problems to begin the year.

1. I hold up a classroom chessboard and ask, "How many squares do you see?" Hands are raised. Wait time is honored. Suz is called on and responds with "sixty-four." Asked how she knows it is sixty four, she explains that there are eight squares on each edge so she multiplied 8 × 8. There is a pause before several tentative hands are raised. Jonathan sees the single large square outline of the chessboard. Kristin then eagerly comes to the chessboard to outline a 2 × 2 square with her finger. Soon the issue of all the different size squares is raised and the exploration begins, individually or with a partner. Figure 4.1 shows Nick's explanation for his solution.

The chessboard problem differentiates itself because it is open to different processes for solving. All students have access; they need only understand squares and be able to count. The idea of different-size squares can be scaffolded if necessary. Students can use different strategies, such as make a simpler version, look for patterns, sketch with different colors on grid paper, and so on. Because students are required to write about their solution processes, there are multiple opportunities to observe student understanding—during the exploration and by reading the students' explanations. A great deal of mathematics is explored during both the solution process and the summary of shared solutions and discoveries.

2. Petals Around the Rose is a casual challenge that intrigues students. I read about it in an article written by Marie Appleby, a middle school math teacher from South Hadley, Massachusetts (Appleby 1999). The game begins by rolling five dice while circling the room and chanting: "The name of the game is Petals Around the Rose. The name is very important. For each roll of the dice, there is one answer, and I will tell you the answer." Continue

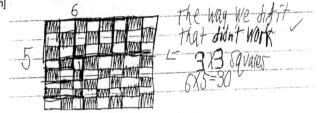
FIGURE 4.1—Nick's problem-solving.

rolling and give only answers (for example one, one, three, four, and six have an answer of "two"), presenting the students with data without questions or conditions. The students are drawn in, trying to figure out a connection between the dice they are seeing and the answers being given, as you should be. See Anna's conjecture in Figure 4.2 for an explanation of how answers are determined.

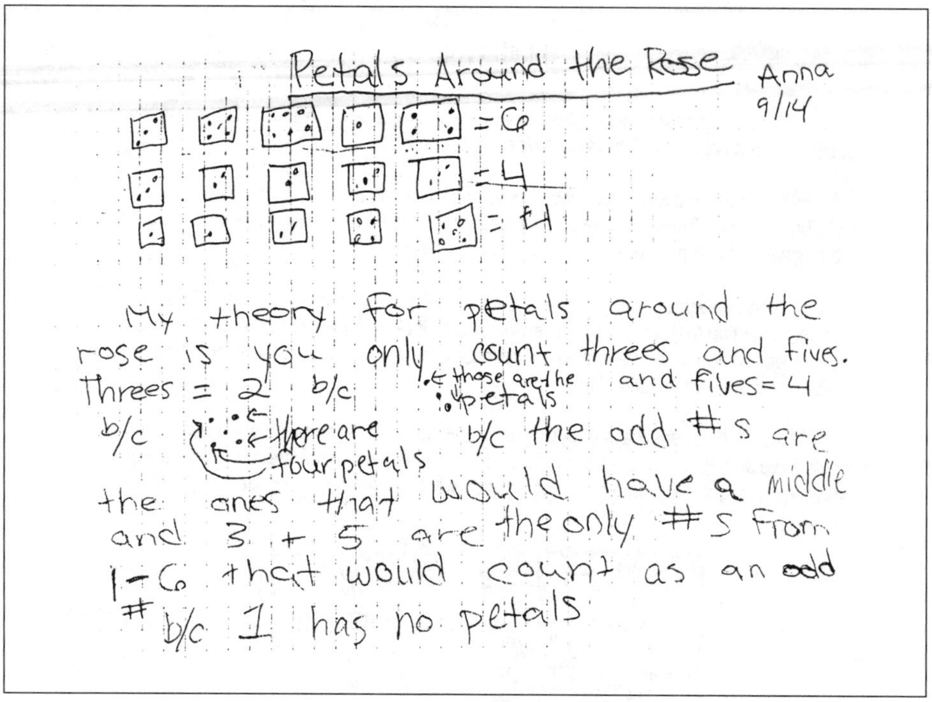

FIGURE 4.2—Anna's solution for, *Petals Around the Rose*.

The stage is set for students to begin verifying their ideas without teacher input. Give no feedback. They now "need to know." Continue the game over several days in short bursts as a sponge activity with intermittent group processing and data collecting prompted by questions such as "What do we know about Petals Around the Rose?" Ask students to write their thoughts about the game in their journals. Establish the rule that the only way a conjecture is considered is with a roll of the five dice and a correct response from the conjecturing student. Swear students to secrecy once their solution is confirmed. Institute this constraint early so that all students have the opportunity to eventually discover the pattern for themselves. Once a student is able to crack the code, that is "see the rose and its petals," that student can run the game for others.

Glenn, a fifth- and sixth-grade teacher, used the game this year and enhanced its benefits by establishing the knights of the order of the Rose. A ceremony knighted each solver who was then certified to run the game for classmates.

This casual informal game for all ages makes several statements about problem solving and differentiation. First of all, it's fun. It is challenging and engaging at various levels for all students. They can use a number of strategies such as guess and check, list known facts, draw diagrams and samples, write about it in a journal, and make the problem simpler by rolling fewer dice.

Such experiences led us to use engaging problems embedded with worthwhile mathematical tasks as the centerpiece or platform for differentiating instruction in mathematics. For three years I watched *all* of my students grow in their mathematical knowledge and understanding (some exponentially), from the most challenged or disengaged to the most gifted—all in the context of problem solving. I was amazed to realize, after twenty-five years of grouping with basal texts, individualized programs, creating units and math labs, using cooperative learning and homogeneous grouping, that the problem-based curriculum was the format that empowered me most as a teacher of mathematics and empowered students the most as learners of mathematics.

So how does this work for an overarching plan? Start the study of each major concept or fundamental math idea with a juicy problem in which the content is embedded. For example, in the February 2006 issue of *Mathematics Teaching in the Middle School*, a group of middle school teachers share the problem they use to introduce their algebra units for grades 5–8 that have the following range of conceptual goals: to represent real-world situations with tables and graphs, to introduce linear equations, and to bridge linear equations and systems of equations.

> If you have $10 to spend on $2 Hershey's bars and $1 Tootsie Rolls, how many ways can you spend all your money without receiving change? All chocolate, no change! (Hyde et al. 2006, 262–63)

Although simple, the level of difficulty is easily increased by changing the dollar amounts. The task is simplified for younger or special needs students by giving them play money. The teachers spend from two to five class periods uncovering the rich connections and unlimited extensions. Students are absolutely engaged when the problem is introduced in the presence of a giant chocolate bar and a basket of Tootsie Rolls!

Criteria for a Good Problem

Teachers are constantly challenged to select or create suitable problems even if they work with problem-based curricula. They sometimes want or need to adapt a lesson to match student interests, readiness, or sensitive issues.

For example, in the February 2006 issue of *Teaching Children Mathematics*, Christina Nugent, a fifth-grade teacher in Dubuque, Iowa, describes a problem she created for her at-risk school classroom. She posed the question, "How many blades of grass do you think are on a football field?" and a powerful differentiated unit of work ensued that included number sense, estimation, measurement, area, computation practice, and communication (writing is used in all aspects of her mathematics class). The work also foreshadows and prepares for more in-depth development of proportional reasoning. She calls this a high-quality problem for many reasons. Football is of high interest, the context is meaningful and real world, it piques students' curiosity, and there is no obvious way to solve the problem (Nugent 2006).

The following criteria can be used as guidelines for developing or evaluating good problems. The list represents the thinking of several major curriculum researchers and developers. A problem does not need to address all of the issues but should fall within these guidelines to meet standards of worthiness, what Christina Nugent refers to as "high quality."

- Solving the problem leads to significant mathematics.
- The process leads to (foreshadows) important mathematical ideas for future work.
- The problem is open-ended; it can be approached in multiple ways using various strategies.
- There are different ways into the problem: it is accessible to students with different strengths, needs, and experience.
- The problem is interesting and engaging to a wide range of students.
- The problem has various solutions that encourage justification or comparison.
- The problem leads to higher-level thinking and discourse.
- The constraints provide direction without limiting thinking and exploration.
- The problem strengthens conceptual development related to important mathematical ideas.
- The problem provides the opportunity to practice key skills.
- The problem allows teachers to assess how and what students are learning and to identify needs. (Mokros, Russell, and Economopoulos 1995; Lappan and Phillips 1998)

The Chessboard, Petals Around the Rose, and All Chocolate, No Change problems fall within the guidelines for high-quality problems. In addition, they seamlessly lend themselves to differentiating for readiness and learning styles. Here are more examples.

1. Basic multiplication facts are used constantly in our math work. How many *different* products result from multiplying the whole numbers one through nine, two at a time including factors that are the same such as 2×2? Record your thinking. (Posed before introducing the Product Game, a game used for practicing basic facts that has a matrix of products as a game board with the factors below. The products are exactly those needed for all possible combinations of any two of the factors—none are repeated as they would be in a multiplication table.)
2. How many ways can you stack six boxes? Which requires the least floor space? (Ask your own questions and create different constraints.)
3. The dimensions of a typical cereal box are about two inches wide by six inches long by twelve inches high. The shape and size of cereal boxes haven't changed much over the years. Each cereal box creates waste to recycle. Find a way to help the environment by designing a cereal box with the same volume that uses less material for the package.

4. Jenna was visiting her cousin and the weather turned really cold. Aunt Anne went to the closet and returned with a jacket that was now too small for her cousin and told Jenna she could keep the jacket and anything she found in the pockets. She reached into her pocket and found sixty-seven cents. What possible coins might have been in the pocket?

5. Use four 4's to generate equations that equal 0, 1, 2, ... For example:
$$(4 + 4) \times (4 - 4) = 0 \qquad 4(4 - \sqrt{4}) + 4 = 12$$

A good problem can emerge in various formats. It may be a question; it may be a situation; it may be the challenge in a game. Students might formulate a problem as the result of a puzzling context, or a problem might seemingly pop up out of nowhere—a teachable moment. The criteria for high-quality problems listed above give guidance for the design and selection of appropriate problems for accomplishing your curricular goals. In the following scenario, Glenn uses a carefully designed problem to help all his students develop a deep understanding of a key mathematical idea, the mean of a set of data.

Scenario

The fifth-grade students in Glenn's class measured and recorded their heights during a unit on data. The heights were recorded on a class chart. Each student also recorded his or her name and height on a 3×5 index card along with other personal data to be used in the unit. The day they began the study of the mean as one kind of average, Glenn took out the class data deck of cards, shuffled them, and drew five cards from the deck at random. Without revealing the names he had drawn, Glenn performed a mysterious calculation on a hidden pad of paper and announced that he had the mean height of the five students whose cards he had drawn. The challenge for the class was to identify five students in the class who have that mean height. (Not necessarily the ones drawn!)

First, Glenn explored what students thought the *mean* meant! A sound understanding of the mathematical concept of mean was critical to their investigation, so Glenn asked for volunteers for a demonstration. He selected students of obviously different heights and cut strips of gridded chart paper (with convenient one-inch markings) to match their heights. These were taped to the chalkboard, and with the students seated in their math circle, he instructed them to talk to each other about how the three paper strips representing the student heights could be made the same length without losing *any portion* of the paper strips. Using student suggestions and discussing options, a strategy was devised. The students collaboratively advised, cut, and taped the strips until they were exactly the same length. (They giggled a little about why it's advisable to use paper strips instead of the actual children for the demonstration.) In this way, the class was able to experience what it means to "even out" the data in order to determine the mean height for the three students.

Then it was time to tackle the problem. All the students set to work with their partners or groups of four, armed with the class table of heights and whatever tools they considered necessary. They were directed to find at least one set of five classmates (themselves included) who could be evened out to the given mean height. They were instructed to record their work and prepare to justify their choice of five students and prove that the mean for those students matched the given mean. Glenn circulated among the groups, listened to and noted how different groups approached the problem, supported struggling groups, and planned for the lesson summary, next steps, and extensions. There would be something fun and interesting for any group that was able to identify the exact group associated with the given mean—to be revealed after all possible sets had been proposed and justified.

In this session, Glenn differentiated by scaffolding the concrete meaning behind *mean* and making the problem accessible to all students. He also differentiated by allowing students to attack the problem their own way, choosing whether to work with partners or a group of four, and inviting multiple solutions. Glenn's problem was open-ended, interesting, engaging, accessible to all students, and packed with mathematical concepts and processes. It was about the students (always seductive to kids), could be approached systematically or creatively, and had the possibility for multiple solutions. It clearly matched the criteria for a good problem and was an especially good match for the kinesthetic learning style described in Chapter 3.

Timing

It is important to understand that attaching an expected time to any particular problem belies the variable nature of how that problem might serve the differentiation process. The timing depends not so much on the problem as on the students, the time available, and how the teacher is using the problem—is it a daily warm-up or an introduction or the substance of a unit? What is the time available to the class? Some problems are presented at the beginning of a unit only to pique interest and won't be tackled by the class until somewhere midway through a four-week series of investigations. This is true of all of the *Connected Mathematics* units. Also, a problem that takes one day for one student might take a week for another, as is the intended case for Petals Around the Rose.

Problem-Posing Support

Sullivan and Lilburn in *Good Questions for Math Teaching* (2002) offer wonderfully simple three-step processes for creating a good question for any math area. One process involves working backward from a closed question and the other adapts a standard "what" question to a broader context.

Step 1:	Identify a topic.
Step 2:	Think of a closed question or a standard question.
Step 3:	Open the closed question by including the answer and working backward to situations that might elicit such an answer as in the above scenario.

Or adapt a standard question:

| Example 1. | "What is a rectangle?" to "What can you tell me about this rectangle?" |
| Example 2. | A completed addition or subtraction problem with digits from both addends and the sum replaced with question marks: |

$$
\begin{array}{r}
2?9 \\
+ \ ??8 \\
\hline
67?
\end{array}
$$

Example 3.	"What is the volume of a 2 inch by 3 inch by 4 inch box?" to "The capacity of a box of caramels needs to be twenty four cubic inches. What are possible dimensions for such a box?"
Example 4.	"What is the median of the set of data {2, 10, 15, 5, 7, 9}?" to "A set of data has six scores and a median of eight. Three of the scores are two, nine, and ten. What might the other three scores be?"
Example 5.	"Draw pictures of the first five square numbers" to "How does the area of a square change as its side grows?"
Example 6.	The answer to the given fraction multiplication is 2¾. A good question is: The product of two numbers is 2¾. What might the two numbers be? (Sullivan and Lilburn 2002, 7–9)

Try several of these for yourself. You'll be amazed—it really works!

When you pose such problems with differentiating in mind, the open-endedness accommodates for readiness and indeed informs the teacher of student levels of understanding. In some cases, this may indicate minilessons with various groups emerging. These problems also invite students to use their own styles in the solving process and to pose similar problems of their own to challenge others. Along with multiple solutions, products can be varied as well: some students will explain their work effectively in narrative; others need to draw pictures or want to demonstrate how they know they have a solution. In all these ways, differentiation is embedded in the problems and only has to be enhanced by how the teacher directs the work.

Summary

In this chapter, we looked at differentiating mathematics through a problem-solving lens in order to capture the essence of the critical role that problem solving plays. Problem solving offers a sturdy platform for striking out and trying your hand at differentiating a mathematics program. Make use of Sullivan and Lilburn's suggestions for turning any simple exercise into an engaging problem or different levels of problems to suit your classroom needs. Within each part of the problem-solving process, there are opportunities for differentiation. Keep in mind that learning happens most effectively with moderate challenge. Adaptations and scaffolding can occur at the beginning when the problem is posed, in the middle while the exploration is taking place and you are working with individuals or groups, and at the end when the class is summarizing the work and you are assessing their understanding.

Chapter 5

The Flexibility Lens

We will either find a way, or make one.

Hannibal, 247–183 B.C.

Flexibility is an attribute generally associated with differentiated classrooms. It's a fuzzy idea so we take a closer look through a clarifying lens. What might flexibility signify for an effectively differentiated mathematics classroom? From its Latin origin, *flexibilis,* and the dictionary definition, it's about bending without breaking or being pliant, supple, and malleable. For purposes of differentiating mathematics instruction, translate that as being adaptable and able to be modified. However, "bending without breaking" is an important message for maintaining the integrity of the mathematics content standards.

Nonnegotiables (or What's Not Flexible)

In the National Research Council's publication, *Adding It Up* (2001), the term *mathematical proficiency* was coined to encapsulate the essential qualities necessary for successful mathematics learning. The five completely integrated and interwoven strands described below—none of which can exist alone— define the term. Now we use the five strands of mathematical proficiency as standards for what is not flexible when considering adaptations for differentiating purposes, be it a lesson, a unit, or an exercise.

1. *Understanding.* Learning activities target significant mathematics with understanding—concepts, operations, relationships, symbols, diagrams, and procedures.
2. *Computing.* Computation and mathematical procedures (e.g., addition, subtraction, multiplication, and division) are flexible, accurate, efficient, and appropriate whether done mentally, by paper and pencil, or with technology (calculator/computer).

3. *Applying*. Problem-posing and -solving skills are continuously developing, applying concepts, logic, and learned procedures appropriately.
4. *Reasoning*. Thinking and reasoning, explaining and justifying are basic processes and what is known is used to connect and extend to what is not yet known.
5. *Engaging*. Learning activities are engaging and students see mathematics as useful, sensible, and doable; learning takes work and students have the will to do the work.

(National Research Council 2001,2002)

So, if *flexibility* implies "bending without breaking," then modifications used for differentiating need to honor these five parameters. This means the various levels of activities must be engaging and appropriately challenging; they should also require persistence, sense making, and diligence. Sound essential mathematics drives instructional decisions. Teachers select and design contexts that demand thinking and reasoning, depend upon good choices for computation, develop computational fluency, build understanding, and construct new learning on the firm foundation of past experience. Above all, there are high expectations for all learners. All these elements are *not* flexible.

What Is Flexible?

When Carol Ann Tomlinson talks about elements of flexibility, she summarizes them as content, process, and product. We are more specific in our discussion of flexibility, which includes grouping, learning processes, timing related to content depth and breadth, time as a resource, product outcomes, ways of assessing learning, and lesson design.

Flexible Grouping

Grouping for instructional purposes is a major strategy for differentiating instruction. Aside from the extremes of whole class lesson launches, minilessons, and summaries and the individual work students need to do, there are myriad opportunities to form small groups within the math workshop. Flexible group structures are best planned for early in the academic year when establishing the culture of the class. Once a routine is instituted, groups can easily change in response to readiness, interests, learning styles, and occasionally choice. Jennifer Taylor-Cox uses the terms *fluid* and *purposeful* to aptly give sense to the concept of flexible grouping practice (Taylor-Cox 2005). Sometimes groups are homogeneous relative to achievement or interest, at other times heterogeneous to access a variety of strengths. Because student readiness and needs are in a constant change of flux, easy "fluid" grouping practices can respond readily to evolving needs.

Random Groups

Sometimes small groups are completely random and are changed simply to create a new interactive environment. Our basic strategy is to institute partner seating (two at a table) at the beginning of the school year. Each student then has easy access to a think-pair-share partner—a format used frequently for lesson launches and minilessons. Partnering is an important feature of the differentiated math class because when students are given the opportunity to share and clarify their ideas with a classmate first, they are more willing to share with a group or the class. These partnerships are selected randomly and usually change every two weeks. The partnering processes are frequently done with random card draws. The following are examples used throughout the year.

- Selected portions of a deck of playing cards
- Fractions and decimals or percents to be matched
- Vocabulary and illustrations or examples to be matched (Figure 5.1a)
- Vocabulary and definitions to be matched (Figure 5.1b)
- Simple computations and their answers to be matched
- Mixed numbers and improper fractions to be matched

The possibilities are endless and interesting and students offer suggestions that add to the fun. We establish early on that we can change any partnership on the spot to serve the greater good of the class and our mathematical learning purposes.

In addition to the basic partner structure, the tables of two are organized in pairs so that there is a heterogeneous group of four good to go at any moment. This same structure is accomplished with four students at a table or similar arrangements of single student flattop desks. The setup is especially handy for lesson or unit launches that involve cooperative problem solving such as the problem collections from *Get It Together* and *United We Solve* (Erickson, 1989, 1996). These groups of four are also useful for the efficient processing of homework. In Glenn's classroom in the earlier scenario (Chapter 4), students are given the option of working with their partner or the group of four at their two tables.

Readiness Groups

Readiness groups are important for meeting the needs of all students. In the individual classroom, they can be used to provide appropriate challenge and support. For example, a readiness group can be called in the middle of an exploration when the teacher notes a subset of students needs a minilesson to refresh a forgotten or rusty but essential skill. These students are quietly asked to meet at the white board or chart stand. The teacher also offers an open but optional invitation to others for, let's say, a refresher on subtracting mixed numbers. It may last only ten minutes but it is critical support at a teachable

Even numbers	0, 2, 4, 6
Odd numbers	1, 3, 5, 7
One fourth	$\frac{1}{4}$
Number sentence	$3 + 4 = 7$
Tens	10, 20, 30
Cube	
Circle	
Square	
Triangle	
One half	$\frac{1}{2}$

FIGURE 5.1a—Primary version for choosing partners.

moment. In this way, the teacher is able to readily provide the scaffolding that some students need in order to access the mathematics. In yet another instance, Jenny and two of her colleagues have instituted the practice of meeting briefly with individuals or small groups who are not meeting the current content standard while the class works on additional practice challenges. This ongoing practice keeps all students challenged and supported at appropriate levels.

Scaffolding is the use of a variety of strategies to support learning that asks students to extend their thinking. Scaffolding clearly connects to readiness groups. For example, a teacher determines that an individual or small group needs to use a particular strategy to get a deeper understanding of a concept. This could be for remediation as noted above or for a learning extension as with Jill's third graders. The class has been using a variety of manipulatives to represent multiplication in real contexts. Jill decides that some of the students could build deeper conceptual understanding by using the Cuisenaire rods in trains alongside meter sticks (or rod tracks if they are

Extending the Use of Readiness Groups

In my last full year teaching, I was able to take advantage of a parent volunteer who consistently came in for forty-five minutes once a week. Matthew (the parent) was an enthusiastic supporter of the MATHCOUNTS program. Since the warm-ups and work-outs from the national competitive program were a major "anchor activity" for my math classes, Matthew worked with students who spent time with those materials during the week. He and his group used one side of the classroom with chart pad and easel. I was then free to concentrate on students who needed support in a particular area during that week. The groups were determined from notes I made throughout the week as I observed the work of students. They changed easily to accommodate the current needs of students. It was a highly productive collaboration.

In Jenny's school, they use some similar strategies. They have an "extended learning after-school program" where teachers take turns and students come for specific skills work at the suggestion of their teachers. Before or during regular school hours including lunchtime, skills groups work with the math lead teachers. During study period when four teachers are available, three teachers cover study hall while the fourth teacher

Array	An arrangement of objects in a rectangular pattern with rows and columns.	
Congruent	Figures that are the same size and shape.	
Hexagon	A six-sided polygon	
Polygons	A two-dimensional closed figure made of line segments that meet only at their endpoints.	
Quadrilateral	A polygon with four sides.	
Tangram	A seven-piece puzzle made from a square. It has 5 triangles, 1 parallelogram, and 1 square.	
Acute angle	An angle that measures less than ninety degrees.	
Right triangle	A triangle that contains a right angle.	
Obtuse angle	An angle that measures more than ninety degrees.	

FIGURE 5.1b—Intermediate version for partners or groups of three.

available) in addition to the rectangular arrays they've been using as models. This will help this group of students build an understanding of the relationship between the linear and area models for multiplication. After working with the group, these students will have an opportunity to share what they learned with the rest of the class.

Heterogeneous Groups

In some instances random groups are heterogeneous but that is not always true. A group may easily be tilted toward interests, readiness, or specific styles because of the chance involved in the selection process. Here we talk about groups specifically designed to be heterogeneous in that they represent a broad range of styles, intelligences, and abilities. For example, in the Blades of Grass problem described in Chapter 4, Christina Nugent uses heterogeneous groups. Within those small groups, she assigns special jobs that match student readiness or challenge those with special talents to apply them in ways that enhance the group's work. She knows that students can get excited about each other's ideas and check with each other for what has potential as a solution strategy.

Time

Time is a flexible resource as well as a precious commodity. Students need various amounts of time to process new ideas. Some students naturally work slowly; others process information quietly over time as a function of personality. (See Chapter 3.) Some work quickly and are ready for new challenges. Anchor activities (introduced in Chapter 2) are a major strategy for accommodating this difference and maintaining the flexible use of class time. Anchor activities are mathematical challenges, activities, games, centers, or books that are introduced to the class as opportunities and options to be done when assigned tasks are completed but the class is not yet ready to summarize the work or begin the next lesson (Figure 5.2). Anchor activities can also be used when other class members are attending a minilesson on concepts already mastered. They may include extensions and enrichments related to current work, individual assignments, or practice with specific skills. It is important that the activities be purposeful, challenging, and engaging as well as build mathematical knowledge.

Jenny's Crate Work as Anchor Activities

Students who complete class work early are expected to keep their focus on mathematics learning and applications. I provide them with a variety of engaging options that can be worked on individually. Activity folders in the "anchor crate" include:

- the NCTM menu of the month from the *Mathematics Teaching in the Middle School* Journal (ten monthly problems sometimes classified as appetizers, main courses, and desserts)
- MATHCOUNTS problems
- sudoku puzzles
- logic puzzles

I try to make sure at some point during each two-week period that all children have time to work on one of these activities. It's also important for children to have time to work together on these problems so that they are not always done in isolation. Part of differentiation is recognizing that students' needs include working together and sharing strategies for solving problems. The crate work also gives students an opportunity to challenge themselves beyond the regular required class work.

FIGURE 5.2

---

works with specifically identified students on their needs. The Title I teacher, the learning centers (special ed), and any available staff work in this way to respond to the needs of small readiness groups, again identified by their teachers. Although the before-school, lunchtime, and after-school sessions are voluntary, they are well used, and the flexible readiness groups are essential to the school's determined efforts to support and nurture the mathematical proficiency of all their students.

Jenny's Awareness of Respectful Group Work

As I move from groups of two to groups of four students working together, I recognize the importance of doing an activity to help students know how to work and respect each other. I start by describing a situation I'd seen the year before with a group of seventh graders. As a small group was working on a problem, one student shared her ideas about what she thought the solution was to the problem. Her contribution was ignored. It appeared that the other group members had the preconception that this student was a "low" math student with nothing to contribute to the group. When it was the group's turn to respond to the problem, their solution was incorrect. As it turned out, the correct answer was what their group member had tried to tell them.

Complex Instruction and Its Grouping Strategy

Nugent's use of heterogeneous groups is similar to the grouping technique used for Complex Instruction (CI). CI utilizes heterogeneous groups that are carefully formed to represent the multiple abilities required to complete group-worthy tasks or problems. The central premise of complex instruction is that each individual brings valuable and different abilities to the task. All contributions are needed for success. Elizabeth Cohen developed CI at Stanford University in 1979 to address the many inequities found in classrooms. Implementing authentic CI requires professional development centered on developing or selecting multiple ability curricula, training students in the use of cooperative norms, and learning how to recognize and treat status problems. Think of CI as framed by the following criteria:

- *Multiple-ability heterogeneous groups use multiple intelligences, interests, and special talents with specific role assignments.*

The timing for introducing a particular concept to individual students can also be an element of flexibility. Timing is related to readiness: some students are ready for or need work with a concept well before others. This often happens when using the MATHCOUNTS materials as an anchor because the problems introduce students to more sophisticated mathematics. In another instance, a major curriculum element may be introduced to one small group within the classroom at different times of the year, again dictated by the needs of individual students. For example, third-grade students are working on problems related to multiplication and division. Some students understand and are ready and eager to work with long division while the teacher knows that introducing it to the class would interfere with the conceptual development of many. Therefore, part of a menu plan (introduced in Chapter 7) includes the teacher option of convening a special group. The rest of the class will be introduced to the procedure at a later time, after they have developed a more robust understanding of division and its applications.

Content Flexibility

Ted's second graders are working on a measurement unit, finding the weight or mass of different real-world objects. Through a preliminary launch and assessment activity, he finds that five students are exceptionally comfortable using nonstandard and standard units of weight to determine the relative mass or weight of a variety of objects. An even larger group of students is at the very beginning stages of using instruments to weigh objects other than themselves. So Ted has three centers for the students to explore. One introduces students to different kinds of scales with a variety of objects to weigh as well as a range of standard and nonstandard units to use. The task cards are designed for students to work independently in teams of two or three choosing objects, selecting weighing instruments and units, recording their results, and justifying their choices and results. Extensions are included. A second center has simple balance beams for pairs of students to use to rank sets of objects from lightest in weight to heaviest in weight. The third center is for introducing students to balance beams and using nonstandard units, such as one-inch cubes, to weigh simple objects from the home and classroom. In this way, Ted is using the content flexibly to meet the needs of his students.

Effective content modifications are highly dependent on teachers having deep knowledge of mathematics and how students learn it. The content may be adapted in the way it is presented for different groups of students, maybe to develop deeper understanding or to give a broader application of a concept, but all students need access to that content. Jeanne Purcell created a graphic organizer to help teachers think about and plan for curriculum modifications and decide whether to go for depth and/or breadth adaptations (Figure 5.3). Going for depth means using readiness as a guide for organizing the learning activities, while going for breadth is more focused on learning

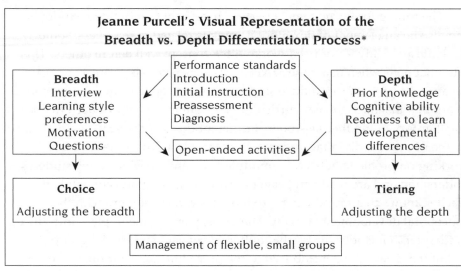

FIGURE 5.3

*J. H. Purcell (personal communication, January 18, 2007)

styles and motivation. Notice that open-ended activities can serve both intentions and in all cases small flexible grouping is the class configuration. Central to the tool is the content objective, preassessment, and diagnosis.

An example of a depth adaptation for developing conceptual under- standing and skill with multiplication is a minilesson that extends the rectangular array multiplication model as an introduction to determining the area of a rectangle, developing a key connection between number and geometry. An example of a breadth adaptation for the same objective is a game for partners called How Long? How Many? using dice and Cuisenaire rods. The first roll of a die indicates the length of the rod (from one to six) to use and the second roll indicates how many of those rods to use to make an array that is then colored on a paper grid. The goal is to fill in as many parts of the grid as possible. This gives students a chance to model and practice their multiplication facts (Burns 1992, 201).

Student readiness and content flexibility are closely related differentia- tion elements. The structure of the content often dictates the direction of a teacher's decisions. For example, the kindergarteners are learning about coins and making exchanges. It is important that their teacher, Helene, understands the sequencing that helps them learn with confidence. (See Chapter 9 for the importance of teacher knowledge.) She begins with pennies and lots of counting experience before she introduces dimes. After studying all of the characteristics of dimes, they do some exchanging together. Finally, carefully organized partners work with varying amounts of pennies and dimes to make exchanges. Helene knows that only now can she effectively introduce the nickel, which is much more challenging for most of the students. This transition requires visual scaffolding, what Helene refers to as crutches: trading sheets designed with coin stamps representing pennies, nickels, and

- Multiple-ability treatment where teacher and students review an extensive list of competencies required for completing a task or solving a problem; no one has all the compe- tencies but everyone has some.

- Group-worthy problems and open-ended tasks that are embedded with important mathematical concepts, invite multiple representa- tions, and offer several solution paths.

- Status treatment, where the teacher assigns competence to low status students by praising something done or said that has intellectual value; teachers train to learn how to do this authenti- cally and inclusively.

This more intense form of differentiated instruction is inextricably keyed to heterogeneous groups. It is a powerful program worthy of exploration once you are comfortable with less intense formats for differentiating mathematics instruction. The jigsaw strategy used for the lesson on linear relationships in Chapter 7 is an example of a differentiating strategy sometimes employed in CI; this is especially true of the jigsaw quiz described there. (For details on the substantial positive impact that CI has had on student mathematics achievement in challenging urban environments, see the work of Jo Boaler: Boaler and Staples 2005, Boaler 2006.)

dimes to give the children a one-to-one model for their exchanges. Gradually the crutches are withdrawn as the students build skill playing the trading games. This teacher understands the sequencing and complexity of the concepts and organizes the groups and materials in order to match the content challenges to student readiness and needs.

The levels of complexity related to a particular concept offer a convenient platform for the tiering technique of differentiating. Ted's lesson on measuring weight is an example of the tiered approach, as is the fourth-grade lesson on two- and three-dimensional shapes in Chapter 7. Tiered lessons have a specific conceptual end point in mind but offer different small group pathways for students to follow to reach the goal. The tiers or layers usually respond to prior knowledge, readiness, developmental differences, and cognitive ability but can also be designed to accommodate interests and learning styles as well. Varying the level of the complexity of the mathematics content is the major goal for tiered lessons. (See Chapter 7 for details on developing tiered lessons.)

Process Flexibility

The students in Ms. McAllister' fourth grade are working on the relationships between addition and subtraction in various real-world situations such as:

> In the newly renovated local theatre, a children's theatre production of *Cinderella* is coming to benefit the PTA. The theatre seats 350 and more than half of the tickets are sold. Prices for tickets are $10 for adults and $5 for children under twelve. Add information so that you can ask questions about this situation that require addition or subtraction to answer. For example, "If there are 129 tickets left how many tickets have been sold?"

Students are asked to work with their partner to write questions and then work in their groups of four to solve the problems they created. Each group is to use three different processes for solving a problem: at least one member should use paper and pencil showing all work; another member uses base ten blocks and sketches the work; another uses a calculator and records the buttons they push to get their solution; and for bonus points, the group can describe a mental math way to answer their questions and describe it.

Following this experience, students are given the following multiple-solution subtraction problem to solve using any process they choose. They may work with their partner.

$$
\begin{array}{r}
5\,3\,\_\\
-\,\_\,4\,\_\\
\hline
1\,\_\,5
\end{array}
$$

Each student must record and describe the solution process, which should be different for the second solution they find.

By definition, the process portion of a mathematics lesson refers to the ways students work through a lesson to make sense of the concepts involved. Process flexibility comes from the many ways to represent and make sense of mathematical situations. We believe that process options are exciting and rewarding ways of differentiating mathematics because there are so many ways to develop conceptual understanding. Manipulatives, games, and creative contexts lend themselves to engaging opportunities for all learners.

Process options include alternatives like those used in the above lesson. They also range through the various strategies for problem solving such as using models, guess and check, solving a simpler problem, and looking for patterns, and include games. They accommodate different interests, readiness, or learning styles. The options may be designed and assigned to specific learners or available by choice. One of my great "aha's" as a teacher was realizing the motivational reward of having a choice. I began immediately to find myriad opportunities for choice—within manageable constraints, of course. The teacher also needs to encourage or require learners to expand their process choices over time because that is also an important goal in learning mathematics. Ms. McAllister did that when she required students to use a different process for their second solution in the open-ended subtraction problem.

Product Flexibility

In Justine's eighth-grade pre-algebra class, students are each assigned a famous mathematician to research and share with the class. Students create their own product for "introducing" their mathematician to the class. Some students dress up as their mathematician and give a mock lecture on the mathematician's life and contributions; others collect objects in a box that are metaphors or symbols of their mathematician; some create time lines that relate the life and contribution of the mathematician to other historical events; and yet others create posters or PowerPoint presentations.

The product for a unit or lesson is the end result or outcome expected on completion of the work. Justine's assignment offers a range that illustrates flexible product options for differentiating. Along similar lines, when I give a mathematics vocabulary writing assignment, students are offered a broad range of outcomes from which to choose. They may write a song, a letter to a relative or a friend, a descriptive paragraph, a poem, a commercial, an imaginative story—or any other written genre of their choice. However, they must attend to the constraints and requirements indicated by the assignment, for example, appropriate use and convincing evidence of understanding for the chosen mathematics vocabulary terms.

It is also possible for students to design their own product for a project, especially if the student is writing a contract for a special assignment. It may be done collaboratively or individually in response to student preferences, offering an additional element for differentiation.

Assessment Flexibility

The Faces of Assessment

Assessment and instruction are so inextricably bound together in a differentiated math program that the boundaries between them are virtually invisible. The demands on the teacher to continually assess the status of students and provide feedback are major components of differentiated practice. Challenging, observing, questioning, and listening are constantly recycling and feeding data into the reflection, decision, design, and implementation cycle that rules our classroom lives. The key to flexible assessment is the choices teachers have for responding to those demands.

The assessment formats may be formal or informal, but from my thirty-plus years in the classroom, the majority of assessment happens in the informal realm—casually but consciously. It becomes second nature for a math teacher to look for clues to levels of understanding and to mine for specific clarification because of our need for a steady stream of information and the students' need for feedback. At the same time, specific tools are essential for more formal assessments. The partial litany below (Figure 5.4) serves as a reminder of the potential for bending without breaking that permeates the assessment world.

Using the list in Figure 5.4 as a starting point, it is easy to see that the preassessments used to guide preliminary instructional decisions can be as flexible as they need be to pinpoint where students can best begin their work on a particular topic. Figure 5.5 shows a teacher-created preassessment for a fraction unit. Then throughout the teaching/learning routine, a differentiating teacher has many options for assessing progress and accommodating student needs—the ultimate flexible approach to teaching mathematics.

Partial List of Assessment Tools

*Graphic organizers	*Reports	*Demonstrations
* Journals	*Writing prompts	*Skill performances
*Portfolios	*Projects	*Tests
*Pop quizzes	*Checklists	*Rubrics
*Likert scales[1]	*Response cards[2]	*Exit slips
*Hand signals	*Observations	*Interviews
*Manipulatives	*Student choice	* Inventories
*Sketches	*Puzzles	*Simulations
*Posters	*Role-playing and drama	*Diaries
*Logs	*Contracts	*Partner quizzes
*Jigsaw quizzes[3]		

1. Students rate themselves on a scale for level of performance or agreement with a statement, i.e. 1—2—3—4.
2. Students respond to a query on cards that are submitted to the teacher.
3. See Chapter 7, page 123

FIGURE 5.4

Fraction Unit **Name** _____

Grades Three and Four **Date** _____

In this unit you will learn how to:

- Compare and order fractional parts (from one whole to $\frac{1}{16}$), from largest to smallest or smallest to largest.
- Demonstrate the meaning of the numerator and denominator of a fraction.
- Use fractions to describe parts of wholes and parts of groups.
- Find and describe equivalent fractions.
- Convert mixed numbers to fractions.
- Add and subtract fractions with like denominators.

We will be investigating a number of situations in which fractions are used. Rank the following in order of interest to you with (1) being the most interesting and (7) being the least interesting.

_____ making fraction kits using construction paper
_____ solving problems with a partner or a group
_____ writing number sentences to describe your work with manipulatives and games
_____ writing about what you are learning about fractions
_____ playing fraction games
_____ using manipulatives (pattern blocks, Cuisenaire rods, tangrams) to explore patterns in fractions
_____ drawing and labeling sketches as a record of your work

What do you already know about fractions?

1. What does *fraction* mean? How would you explain it to someone younger?

2. Show some examples of what you know how to do with fractions.

3. How are fractions used in your world, at home, and at school? Why are fractions useful?

4. Give examples of how you have used fractions in your life.

FIGURE 5.5—Preassessment for fraction unit.

Rubrics

Rubrics came into my life in the late 1980s while working with the EQUALS program at the Lawrence Hall of Science UCAL–Berkeley. I just didn't get it! *Rubric* was a strange word to incorporate into my practice. (Actually, I didn't even know how to spell it—I only heard it used.) It took time for me to realize that by looking into the history of the word itself, I could make the connections to understand why this word had come into the classroom scene.

The etymological dictionary saved me. Rubric of course means *red*—so? My first thought was this is someone's idea of a better method for giving students feedback than the red correcting pencil/pen that I grew up with as a student and beginning teacher. (And that may well be the case!) But a deeper look at the history restored my equilibrium. Red was used in early manuscripts for titles and headings as well as early church ritual guides to highlight how things should be done. Now I understand the rubric to be a guide for various purposes: to objectify an assessment, guide an assignment and its evaluation, or clarify an instructional/learning process. This is an ideal match for a differentiated environment.

Incidentally, although I never heard the word *rubric* until the late 1980s, once I understood its reference and meaning, I realized I had been using detailed rubrics with my students since 1965. However, I made up my own term—working guidelines. Always, when an assignment was complete, both the students and I would evaluate the products by comparing them to those very guidelines.

Heidi Goodrich Andrade aptly describes the potential power of the rubric as follows: "Rubrics, at their very best, are teaching tools that support student learning and encourage the development of sophisticated thinking skills" (Andrade 1999, 1). As such, rubrics play multiple roles. By defining expectations, rubrics improve the quality of student work and learning, provide excellent scaffolds and work guides for students, and help students become more responsible and independent as mathematics learners.

Primarily, there is flexibility in the variety of rubrics that can be used to support students: scoring rubrics, instructional rubrics, and student self-evaluation rubrics are some that we talk about here. On another level, students can help design their own rubrics when their work is outside the range of an existing rubric. On these two levels, rubrics offer the flexibility of personalized assessment while supporting instructional diversity.

An instructional rubric simply means that a rubric is used for more than the assessment purpose usually connected to rubrics. Flexible use of assessment rubrics turns them into tools for tracking and supporting learning: when presented before learning, they set expectations; during learning, they independently guide task completion; and after learning, they help to assess products and evaluate knowledge gained. In these ways, instructional rubrics and differentiated mathematics are perfect partners: the rubrics set clear expectations for all levels, provide a scaffold for students who are more tentative, and furnish a flexible assessment instrument and guide for various avenues of exploration. These roles are clearly seen in the pool table rubric from the *Connected Mathematics* Comparing and Scaling unit (Lappan et al. 2006) shown in an abbreviated version in Figure 5.6.

The unit project directs students to play Paper Pool on grid paper rectangles of various sizes with the corners labeled *A*, *B*, *C*, and *D* counterclockwise. The corners are the pockets. The ball starts with a hit at *A* and travels only on 45° diagonals even after it hits a side and bounces. A particular sized rectangle's game is over when the ball hits a corner and thus falls in a pocket. The challenge is to predict the pocket the ball will drop into and how many hits it takes to get there for any size rectangle. An extension is for students to predict the number of diagonal units a ball will pass over in its travels. Students must then write a report including rules, drawings, tables, charts, and patterns. In general, rubrics usually list the criteria for a product and then describe at least three levels of quality performance with regard to each criterion. Only the highest-level performance descriptor is included here as an illustration of how a rubric guides and clarifies individual work. This rubric is not only used for scoring but also as a guide during the completion of the project. See Figures 5.7a and b for a portion of Audrey's write-up.

Teachers usually design rubrics, but we've found that student/teacher-designed rubrics can be even more effective. The rubric development procedure delivers a "buy in" for students—a motivation that is hard to engage any other way.

Suggested Scoring Rubric

- **Mathematics:** Rules for predicting *the dropping pocket*. Student states at least one correct sophisticated rule and addresses all possible situations for which pocket the ball will drop. (4 points possible)
- **Mathematics:** Rules for predicting *the total number of hits*. Student states at least one correct sophisticated rule and addresses all possible situations for the number of hits. (4 points possible)
- **Problem Solving and Reasoning**: Student shows complete reasoning to support at least one sophisticated rule for both situations. (4 points possible)
- **Communication:** Report is clearly presented and easy to follow. (4 points possible)
- **Checklist** (5 points possible)

  1. Student completes labsheets.
  2. Student gives a correct new table for each rule and gives at least two rules.
  3. Student uses organizational tools to search for patterns and rules.

Extension: Student shows complete reasoning to support a sophisticated rule for determining the diagonal length traveled. (4 points possible)

(Adapted from Lappan et al. 2006, 96)

FIGURE 5.6

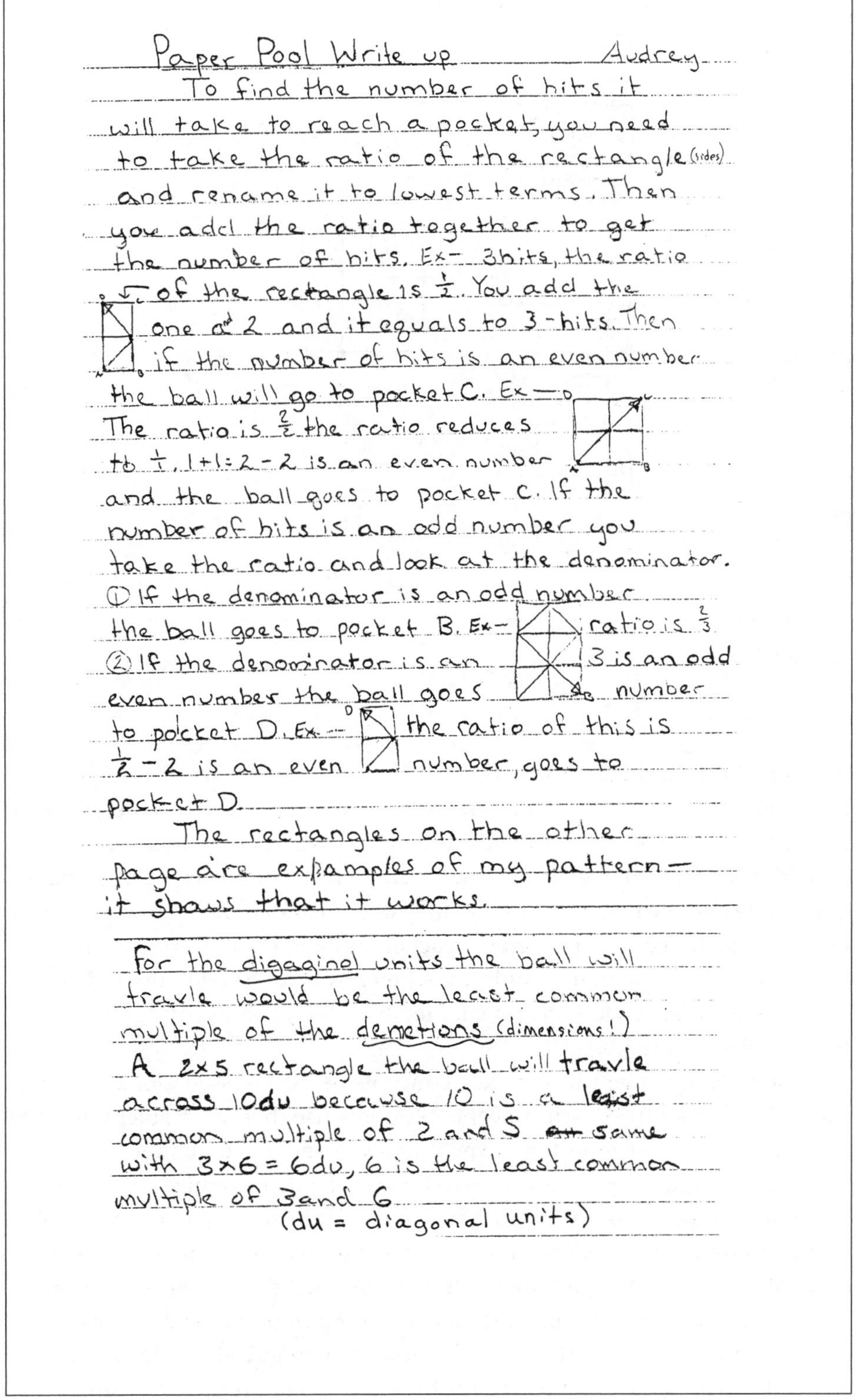

Paper Pool Write up   Audrey

To find the number of hits it will take to reach a pocket, you need to take the ratio of the rectangle (sides) and rename it to lowest terms. Then you add the ratio together to get the number of hits. Ex— 3hits, the ratio of the rectangle is $\frac{1}{2}$. You add the one & 2 and it equals to 3-hits. Then if the number of hits is an even number the ball will go to pocket C. Ex—, The ratio is $\frac{2}{2}$ the ratio reduces to $\frac{1}{1}$, 1+1=2—2 is an even number and the ball goes to pocket C. If the number of hits is an odd number you take the ratio and look at the denominator. ① If the denominator is an odd number the ball goes to pocket B. Ex— ratio is $\frac{2}{3}$ ② If the denominator is an 3 is an odd even number the ball goes number to pocket D. Ex— the ratio of this is $\frac{1}{2}$ — 2 is an even number, goes to pocket D.

The rectangles on the other page are exbamples of my pattern— it shows that it works.

For the digaginal units the ball will travle would be the least common multiple of the demetions (dimensions!) A 2x5 rectangle the ball will travle across 10du because 10 is a least common multiple of 2 and 5 same with 3x6 = 6du, 6 is the least common multiple of 3 and 6
(du = diagonal units)

FIGURE 5.7a

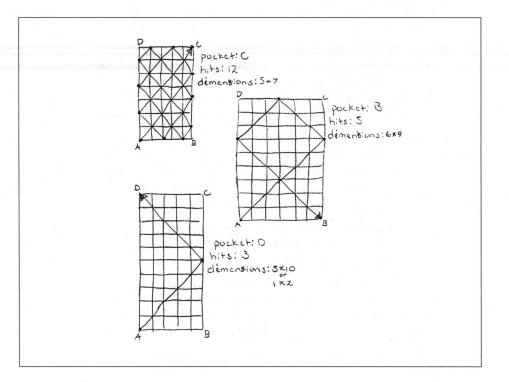

FIGURE 5.7b

Student Self-Reflection Rubric

Providing students with feedback from their work is critical to differentiating mathematics. Often when students receive an assessment with a score, they look for the score. However, we want them to focus on the types of mistakes they made and the mathematics that they demonstrated they know and understand. Barbara, a sixth-grade teacher, designed a self-reflection form for students to use with their unit test when it was returned to them. The form has since been adopted and adapted by Heather, a seventh-grade teacher. (See Figure 5.8.)

The reflection identifies the key concepts being assessed along with the questions that address each concept. Students use their assessment, teacher corrections, and self-reflection form to analyze and evaluate their performance. (See Figure 5.9.) The goal is to have students recognize their errors, know where more work is needed, and have confirmation on their demonstrated understanding. Computation is a separate item because we want students to recognize that they might have learned the concepts from the unit but that they are still making careless computation mistakes. The differentiation demonstrated with this tool is at an individual level, but when the analyses are completed for the class, small groups with similar needs emerge. As teachers, we use the completed student reflections to make decisions about next steps for students and the experiences they each

---

Comparing and Scaling Unit Assessment

Check each category based on your assessment.

---

1. Writing Comparison Statements (problems 4i, 4ii)

Does Not Meet	Partially Meets	Meets
(0 correct)	(1 correct)	(2 correct)

2. Finding unit rates for given situations (problems 1Ared, 1Ayellow, 1Ablue, 2a, 2b, 3b, 3c, 5b)

Does Not Meet	Partially Meets	Meets
(≤ 4 correct)	(5 or 6 correct)	(7 or 8 correct)

3. Working with Proportional Reasoning (problems 1b, 1c, 2d, 3a, 5a, 5c)

Does Not Meet	Partially Meets	Meets
(≤ 2 correct)	(3 or 4 correct)	(5 or 6 correct)

4. Writing Equations (problem 2c)

Does Not Meet	Partially Meets	Meets

5. Finding the scale factor (problem 6)

Does Not Meet	Partially Meets	Meets

6. Computing Accurately (no careless computation mistakes)

Does Not Meet	Partially Meets	Meets

Essential Learning for the Unit: Understands and uses ratios, fractions, differences, and percents to solve problems.

Does Not Meet	Partially Meets	Meets

FIGURE 5.8—Student self-reflection form.

need in order to meet the standard for the overall unit. For example, we can readily identify the students who need more work with scale factors or unit rates and they know who they are as well.

Comparing and Scaling Unit Assessment

Check each category based on your assessment:

1. Writing Comparison Statements (problems 4i, 4ii)

Does Not Meet (0 correct)	Partially Meets (1 correct)	Meets (2 correct)

[handwritten: It shows me I can compare things easily using fractions, ratios, percents, and differences]

2. Finding unit rates for given situations (problems 1Ared, 1Ayellow, 1Ablue, 2a, 2b, 3b, 3a, 5b)

Does Not Meet (≤ 4 correct)	Partially Meets (5 or 6 correct)	Meets (7 or 8 correct)

[handwritten: I have some computation errors, but generally, I know HOW to do it – w/ calculator on hand]

3. Working with Proportional Reasoning (problems 1b, 1c, 2d, 3a, 5a, 5c)

Does Not Meet (≤ 2 correct)	Partially Meets (3 or 4 correct)	Meets (5 or 6 correct)

[handwritten: If □ is a unit, ▭'s not similar. Easy]

4. Writing Equations (problem 2c)

Does Not Meet	Partially Meets	Meets

5. Finding the scale factor (problem 6)

Does Not Meet	Partially Meets	Meets

6. Computing Accurately (no careless computation mistakes)

Does Not Meet	Partially Meets	Meets

- -

Essential Learning for the Unit: Understands and uses ratios, fractions, differences, and percents to solve problems.

Does Not Meet	Partially Meets	Meets

[handwritten: I generally understand the unit and the steps to do that, with some computation errors.]

[handwritten:]

Math Test Studying

Abby

I started studying for math the day we started
playing the game I had someone give me a scenario
and I would provide a ratio fraction, percent I
forgot Unit Rate I did the pg. 65 + 66 I redid
one quiz and an extra problem. I did about 15
minutes a night except for the week end.
I think I will do good, like 90-97%

FIGURE 5.9—Abby: (1) how she studied and (2) reflecting on the results.

This type of reflection guide illustrates one of two other assessment characteristics at work in a differentiated math class: student self-assessment and peer assessment. Students truly are in charge of their own learning, and regular self-assessment helps them to focus on their own progress, become independent, and develop critical skills. Here, the flexibility is built into the process.

Peer assessment routines help students reflect on their own work as well. It is usually easier for students to use a rubric to assess the completeness and quality of someone else's work rather than their own. While using a rubric to assess another student's work, they can't help but think about their own product. When an exchange happens routinely before final work is submitted, peer feedback offers an important opportunity for revision. It's rubrics that make effective self- and peer assessments possible.

Summary

In this chapter, we examined how flexibility in the mathematics-teaching environment makes differentiating instruction possible. The numerous flexible options include grouping, time, content, process, product, and assessment. Underlying all of these options is the basic standard for effective differentiation: essential and appropriately challenging mathematics grounded in a well-coordinated coherent curriculum. Tasks must be worthwhile and engaging and build knowledge for all learners.

The "bottom line" for differentiating mathematics instruction is hitting the target for all students. Teachers control the bow, which must bend without breaking. Maximum control comes from the effective use of the flexible alternatives they have at their fingertips. Think of students as arrows, evolving as they learn, with mathematical proficiency as the target. Achieving success requires that as teachers we move our focus back and forth from the students to the target, selecting arrows and taking aim.

Chapter 6

Planning: A Framework for Differentiating

In planning lessons, teachers are influenced by a multitude of factors that determine what content they teach, how they teach it, and what materials they use to engage students with the content.

Iris R. Weiss and Joan D. Pasley (2004, 27)
"What Is High-Quality Instruction?"

Long Range

The planning lens provides a framework for "taming the beast"—understanding and meeting the challenges of a differentiated mathematics program. Solid long-term and short-term planning goals reduce the weightiness of the decision-making aspects of differentiating mathematics. By mapping out the curriculum for the school year in chunks aligned with the academic schedule, there is a consistent, dependable reference point for everything that follows. The major units are set down in black and white with key deadlines for beginning and ending each unit. This reference point may change, but it provides a target for moving through the year.

The following is the academic plan for the combined grades seven and eight mathematics class at the Center for Teaching and Learning in Edgecomb, Maine (Figure 6.1). The academic structure is trimesters. (All units are from the Connected Mathematics curriculum.)

The example in Figure 6.1 is an ambitious plan for an academic year, but it is for an unusual multigrade middle school class. The extensive challenges of alternating units from the grade levels gives a larger than usual number of units. Some are review from the previous year to accommodate the new seventh graders. Implementing the curriculum would be jeopardized without this plan-ahead document. Every mathematics class deserves this kind of forward thinking from the teacher.

PLAN FOR ACADEMIC YEAR – GRADES 7/8 MATH	
Fall Trimester	
1. Decimal operations and percents: relationships to fractions and place value	
Bits and Pieces III (new Connected Mathematics Project unit, 2005)	(September)
2. Integers and operations	
Accentuate the Negative	(September/October)
3. Introduction to algebra	
Variables and Patterns	(October/November)
Winter Trimester	
1. Similarity	
Stretching and Shrinking	(November/December)
2. Volume and surface area	
Filling and Wrapping	(January)
3. Algebraic relationships	
Thinking with Mathematical Models	(February/March)
Spring Trimester	
1. Algebraic relationships, irrational numbers, and symbolic manipulation	
Combination unit: *Moving Straight Ahead, Looking for Pythagoras,* and *Say It with Symbols*	(March/April)
2. Quadratic relationships	
Frogs, Fleas, and Painted Cubes	(April/May)
3. Data and statistics	
Samples and Populations	(May/June)
Other	
Daily: Mental math warm-ups; computation brush-ups; writing	
Weekly: Vocabulary	
Biweekly and monthly: Self-evaluations; problem-solving write-ups	

FIGURE 6.1

Unit Pacing

The next step in the planning process is to plan for the first unit with the school calendar in hand. We developed a simple form for this purpose. It has three columns. The first column lists the actual days/dates of the math classes during the time frame designated for the unit. The next column is for the

Unit Pacing/Planning Document		
Unit: decimals/percents (Bits and Pieces III)		**Target Date: 9/28**
Day/Date	**Problem, Assessment, or Activity**	**Progress Notes and Adjustments**
TU 9/6 W 9/7 TH 9/8 FR 9/9 M 9/12	Intro to unit/Inv 1 Problem 1.1 Inv 1 Problems 1.2/1.3 Problem 1.4 and checkup Inv 2 Problem 2.1 Problems 2.2/2.3	Started 1.2 ✓

FIGURE 6.2

portion/activity of the unit scheduled for that day. The third column is for tracking and adjusting the progress. See the example in Figure 6.2.

Weekly lesson plans develop from the pacing document, and at the end of each week (minimally) adjustments are made in order to stay within the boundaries of the yearly goals. Sometimes the teacher is actually able to improve the pace, but usually the adjustments are made to compact activities.

Weekly and Daily Planning

Once the pacing document has been adjusted for the week, the stage is set for daily planning. The details of differentiating happen here. Here is where content knowledge is combined with pedagogical training and experience to design lessons to achieve the objectives and meet student needs.

Bloom's Taxonomy Revised: *Description and Application*

Over the years Bloom's taxonomy has been helpful to educators in planning and aiming for higher-order thinking in the classroom. It's a good match for establishing high expectations—a benchmark for quality differentiation. The original taxonomy, developed in 1956, described a hierarchy of learning complexity using the labels: knowledge, comprehension, application, analysis, evaluation, and synthesis. The taxonomy was revised in 2001 with a volume edited by Lorin Anderson and David Krathwohl titled, *A Taxonomy for Learning, Teaching, and Assessing: A Revision of Bloom's Taxonomy of Educational Objectives*.

We are delighted as the new model (Figures 6.3 and 6.4) is a better match for the challenges of today's math classes and the research on learning over the past twenty years. Moreover, it is a friendly matrix model composed of four dimensions of knowledge: factual, conceptual, procedural, and metacognitive; with six levels of cognitive processing for each knowledge dimension: remember, understand, apply, analyze, evaluate, and create (Anderson and Krathwohl 2001; Cruz 2003; Conklin 2005).

Bloom's Revised Taxonomy: A Definition of Terms

Knowledge Categories or Dimensions

1. *Factual knowledge*: basic elements students must know; isolated elements or bits of information believed to have some value in the discipline, for example, the terminology and language of mathematics or the "basic arithmetic facts" (Anderson and Krathwohl 2001, 45)
2. *Conceptual knowledge*: interrelationships among basic elements; classifications, models, generalizations, for example, the relationships between the four operations or the different elements of a basic operation algorithm
3. *Procedural knowledge*: knowing algorithms, procedures, and techniques of the discipline; knowing when and how to use them
4. *Metacognitive knowledge*: knowledge of how one thinks and processes information; what one knows and doesn't know and needs to learn

Cognitive Processing Levels

Remember: recognize, recall; identify and retrieve knowledge from long-term memory (replaces Bloom's original knowledge level)

Understand: interpret, represent, summarize, predict, explain, give examples, describe, restate (replaces Bloom's original comprehension level)

Apply: adapt, revise, implement, integrate, model; for example, use the knowledge in a new situation or context (same as Bloom's original)

Analyze: classify, categorize, compare, contrast, solve, relate parts and whole; know when something does or doesn't belong (same as Bloom's original)

Evaluate: select, decide, value, justify, estimate, predict, assess; make judgments using criteria (rubrics or rules); find inconsistencies; check for accuracy and appropriateness for a given problem (same as Bloom's original)

Create: generalize, hypothesize, design, compose, invent, produce, transform; put elements together into a new pattern or structure with the end product unlike others in the person's experience (replaces Bloom's original synthesis level)

(DeVito and Grotzer 2005, 6–12)

FIGURE 6.3

It is so much more reasonable to conceive of knowledge in this context. We have always anguished over *knowledge* being defined as facts, as was true of the original taxonomy. Figure 6.4 is a graphic organizer for the revised taxonomy that can be used as a guide for the day-to-day lesson planning. It is an important reminder of the options available to the differentiating teacher. This tool is not a form "to be filled in." Nor is it a step-by-step guide. It is instead a graphic of the range of content knowledge and processes to consider while planning. It can be particularly useful in thinking through the

Knowledge Dimensions	Cognitive Processes					
	Remember	Understand	Apply	Analyze	Evaluate	Create
Factual knowledge						
Conceptual knowledge						
Procedural knowledge						
Metacognitive knowledge						

FIGURE 6.4

design of tiered activities or planning for differentiating by knowledge level and process level. For example, you can use a column to build a lesson within a cognitive process such as understanding multiplication: the facts, the concepts, the algorithms, and bringing out student ways of thinking about multiplication. On other occasions, you might focus on the row associated with a knowledge dimension and build a lesson that incorporates different cognitive processes. Or combine them as illustrated by the examples described in Figure 6.5.

Language and Conceptual Understanding

Another consideration for planning is that all mathematical concepts have three components of learning to consider: the language associated with the idea, the conceptual understanding, and the skills and procedures inherent in or connected to the concept. In the beginning of studying any new mathematical idea, language and conceptual development must have priority. Language very much controls thinking, and thinking and reasoning are major objectives for mathematics learning (Sharma 2001). These ideas are closely aligned with the revised taxonomy but add the key element of mathematical language to the mix. For example, a major goal for third-grade mathematics is developing an understanding of multiplication and mastering the basic multiplication facts. The teacher needs to sequence activities so that all students will learn the facts with deep understanding and own strategies for lifelong retrieval. Therefore, the primary goal is to develop understanding and encourage the use of all associated and appropriate language. (See examples in Figure 6.5.)

The message is that students should not be asked to memorize facts for which they don't have strong language and conceptual foundations. Students need to understand how the factors (the multiplicand and the multiplier) or

In the following examples, students learn to read and write basic multiplication facts using meaningful language while developing conceptual understanding.

Example 1

Four circles show three stars in each circle.

The associated multiplication fact is $4 \times 3 = 12$. Possible ways to read the expression include:

- Four circles with three stars each gives twelve stars
- Four groups *of* three stars are equal to twelve stars
- Four times three equals twelve
- Four threes are twelve
- Three multiplied *by* four is twelve (This is introduced only if the teacher judges appropriate student readiness.)

Example 2

A 2×3 rectangular array of tiles represents a small box of candies. The associated multiplication fact is $2 \times 3 = 6$. Possible ways to read the expression include:

- Two rows *of* three candies are six candies
- Two times three equals six
- Two threes are six

The commutative relationship can also be expressed—the power of the rectangular model—whereby $3 \times 2 = 6$, which can be read as follows:

- Three rows *of* two candies each are six candies
- Three times two equals six
- Three twos are six

Example 3

A repeated addition model shows how much five three-cent beads cost. The addition sentence is $3 + 3 + 3 + 3 + 3 = 15$. The associated multiplication fact is $5 \times 3 = 15$. Possible ways to read or interpret the expression include:

- Five threes are fifteen or five threes are equal to fifteen
- Five times three is fifteen
- Five *of* the three-cent beads cost fifteen cents
- Adding five threes is the same as multiplying three *by* five which is equal to fifteen

Paying attention to the "tiny words"—the prepositions *by* and *of* in the early interpretation of multiplication strengthens the language skills of all learners. This is especially true for English language learners whose primary language may not distinguish the subtleties they signify in our language, where these words are sometimes key to understanding directions and meaning.

FIGURE 6.5

the number representing the size of a group and the number doing the multiplying (or the number of groups) work together to form a product. The teacher wants the concept related to numerous contexts so students can conjure up a variety of models for any targeted fact. She homes in on the factual knowledge row of Bloom's matrix (Figure 6.4). The initial objectives for the unit are keyed to the understanding process level and she then considers the apply and analyze levels. All this before she sets her objectives at the recall level, remember. At the same time, students are working on conceptual knowledge at the understanding and apply process levels and using the language in meaningful contexts.

Realistically, the teacher also expects that after the initial minilesson and exploration there will be a differentiation situation that pushes her to provide challenges that reach for new levels of knowledge. She wants to accommodate that readiness and be prepared for students who need to move beyond the basic sequence. So anchor activities, additional challenges, and extension lessons are ready in folders or at stations.

For instance, the students begin the study of multiplication by brainstorming and listing things that come in groups of size two to twelve (Burns 1987, 1991) After the initial posting, the lists are word-processed and placed in a file folder. Early on, students write and illustrate multiplication problems using the lists. Then items from the lists such as "legs on spiders," "wheels on cars," "days in a week," and so on are written on 3 × 5 cards and placed in a paper bag. The folder and paper bag are now located at a workstation. Task cards (5 × 8) for the station are in an envelope. They give detailed instructions for related challenges. An abbreviated example of a task card is shown in Figure 6.6. This activity again works on both conceptual and factual knowledge across several process levels including apply, analyze, and evaluate.

Multiples: Finding Patterns

1. Draw a list item from the bag or select an item off the lists in the folder.

2. Create a table for one to twelve of the items selected. Write the multiplication sentence for each entry in the table (an example is shown on the card).

3. Color the multiples on a 0–99 chart and continue the pattern.

4. Write about the patterns seen in the list and on the chart.

5. Label your work carefully with the name of the activity, your name, and the date. Place it in your completed work folder.

6. Be prepared to share your patterns with the class.

(Adapted from Burns 1991, 127)

FIGURE 6.6

Prerequisite Support Skills for Learning Mathematics

Mahesh Sharma is the director of the Center for Teaching and Learning Mathematics in Cambridge, Massachusetts. He has studied the perplexing problems associated with children who have difficulty learning mathematics and has identified prerequisite support skills that are important to learning mathematics but not necessarily part of mathematics programs. (See Figure 6.7.) He describes them as "nonmathematical skills that are necessary for mathematics conceptualization" (Sharma 2001). These skills must also be thoughtfully incorporated into the planning process and become part of the differentiation program. Note that the multiples activity on finding patterns in Figure 6.6 works on both sequencing and patterns.

Learning Takes Time: Daily Math Class Planning

In order to get the optimal results from instructional strategies, it is important to have a well thought out basic daily routine for mathematics class. Ideally, students have mathematics for at least one hour every day. If you do not currently have such a schedule, we urge you to lobby for this critical resource for children. *Learning takes time*, so whatever time you have, use it well!

In this section, we map out a typical math class schedule as shown in Figure 6.8, describe each class segment with examples, and follow that with specific suggestions for incorporating differentiated approaches.

- **Sequencing**: following a sequence of directions; ordering and sequencing items logically
- **Classification**: sorting; Venn diagrams
- **Spatial orientation and space organization**: left to right; visual clustering
- **Estimation**: build number and measurement sense; focusing tool
- **Patterns**: recognition; extension; numerical; geometric
- **Visualization**: forming mental images; interpreting problem contexts
- **Deductive thinking**: starting with a generalization and identifying specific elements or examples
- **Inductive thinking**: starting with related specific examples and making a generalization or hypothesis

Sharma 2001

FIGURE 6.7—Prerequisite support skills for learning mathematics.

> **Outline for a Typical Mathematics Class**
>
> **Beginnings:** Students perform mental math warm-ups, skill practice, and/or estimations.
>
> **Homework processing:** Students and teacher share, review, and clarify previous day's work.
>
> **Minilesson and launch:** Teacher scaffolds, introduces and uses language, connects to prior work, sets the context, builds prerequisite skills, presents the challenge.
>
> **Exploration:** Students work on the problem of the day—partners, small groups, or individuals. Teacher observes, interacts with students, and incorporates observations into the summary.
>
> **Summary:** Teacher/students refocus on mathematical objective, share and compare strategies, justify conclusions.
>
> **Homework assignment:** Teacher explains and students record.
>
> **Daily reflection:** Students summarize mathematical aspects of class work and record questions.

FIGURE 6.8

Where and how does differentiation happen? It's the teacher's call. Attention to individual needs, interests, personalities, or learning styles can be addressed in any one of the segments of the typical math class. Some of the structural areas of the daily routines are ripe for incidental differentiation in addition to the purposeful differentiation within the major objective for the day.

Beginnings

Begin each class with warm-ups. You can jump-start the mathematical thinking and reasoning with mental math challenges. (See Figure 6.9.) Follow that with some paper/pencil or slate (see sidebar) practice drill using items appropriate to the grade level, the current unit of study, or skills that require lots of repetition over time. Better to have three or four examples daily than twenty examples once a week. Be clever with them—bury connections within the problems you select. For example: have all the answers the same so that you can ask students to think about how or why that's true and how it makes sense. One could be addition, one subtraction, and one multiplication or they could all be a single operation. Give immediate feedback. Also incorporate estimation whenever appropriate, as this is an opportunity to build number sense as well as an important prerequisite skill. All these "beginnings" should be timed carefully to occur within the first ten minutes.

Differentiating During Warm-ups and Skill Practice

Target different problems for different students; have students create and/or deliver the warm-ups; use the processing discussion to scaffold strategies for those who struggle; build language skill by having the successful students describe their strategies; and so on.

Slate Practice or White Boards

The white boards are used as a way for a teacher to quickly check in with the students. They might also be used to provide students with skill practice rather than on paper. I sometimes don't assign some recommended homework problems and save them for white board work. Students respond to a question (it might be a computation problem, a geometric sketch, and so on) by writing their answer on their individual white board and holding it up for the teacher to see. The teacher gives a nod to each child when she has seen the answer. As the students see the teacher's nod, they erase their slates and get ready for the next problem. The teacher keeps track (I use sticky notes) of students that still need help with a concept based on white board work. [State work is shown in Figure 6.11.]

Warm-up Ideas

- *Mental math problems:* Say a problem orally and students get the answer in their head and show it on their fingers in the air. For example: $4 \times 5 + 1 \div 7$ and expect kids to show three on their fingers. The string of operations can get longer and faster as kids get better at this. (Because these are given orally, i.e. "Start at four, multiply by five, add one, divide by seven," the order of operations do not apply.)

    As children get older, even longer strings are used and students are expected to keep totally silent, giving no response until the teacher poses questions, such as "Who thinks they have the solution? Did anyone get lost? If so, where?" Then different responses are honored as a way of analyzing error and making suggestions for efficient ways to work mentally with the numbers before the correct solution is acknowledged. Eventually, the students create the strings and submit them for approval. When approved, the student reads the string of operations and conducts the inquiry.

- *Skills practice problems:* these tend to be basic skills that kids are expected to retain throughout the year. For example, for eighth grade $8\frac{1}{2} \times 2\frac{1}{4}$.

- *Math Board:* A third-grade teacher uses what she calls a *math board* on which she has a problem from the district's content standards. This changes each day. For example,

    Number and operations: $45 + 67$
    Geometry: draw a rectangle and then divide in half several ways
    Algebra: 3, 5, 7, __, __, __
    Measurement: write the time on the clock
    Data: use tally marks to show the number of each coin

- *Estimation:* Once a week have a collection of objects for students to estimate such as tiles in plastic bag, beans in a jar, and so on. Also ask for preliminary estimations for board work. These can be done orally before students do the actual figuring so that strategies can be shared.

- *Sequencing:* Present a brief list of items to be sequenced by students, for example, tie laces, put on socks, put on shoes. Do these frequently so that students get in the habit of being thoughtful about procedures before beginning to work on them. Students can design these to challenge the class. Relate them directly to mathematics when possible, such as the steps for solving problems.

FIGURE 6.9

Homework Processing

Connect yesterday with today. Process the homework efficiently but do process it. Have small groups compare their work and select an item for discussion. (If your students have not worked this way in small groups, you need to provide clear expectations—for example, compare responses, explain and resolve differences, or bring up items for discussion.) The teacher selects items as well, making certain to pull out the important conceptual ideas. The work is then collected or filed as per established routine and the teacher segues into the minilesson for the day's math workshop. Keep this to five to ten minutes.

Differentiating During Homework Processing

Organize groups by differentiated homework tasks; select problems for discussion that provide intervention opportunity for identified students.

Launch

The minilesson begins the formal targeted objectives for the class period. This launch segment provides the essential scaffolding: connect to prior work, introduce or review language, and set the context. Now is also the time to remember the insights gleaned from the previous class period by way of your teacher reflection. (Reflections are discussed later in this chapter.) Is there a gap that needs to be addressed or a student who needs to be the target of a specific support or opportunity? Now is also the time to consider the prerequisite skills essential for successful mathematics learning. (See Figure 6.7.) This might be the ideal day and time to weave in some experience with patterning or sequencing. Don't miss an opportunity when it knocks!

Be careful during the launch time to not give away the challenge or close the door to student thinking and reasoning. These are hard calls but you will get better and better. Be sure the objective is clear to you and to the students, the challenge is understood, the resources are available, and the tasks are well defined. Then let the students have at it—individually or with groups. It is far better to intervene, redirect, and/or give added support during the exploration or work time than to give students too much information before they begin.

Differentiating During Minilesson and Problem Launch

Build in responses to previous reflections; select students to respond by prior experience and assessments; design participation that reflects the needs of various intelligences; embed prerequisite skills practice; utilize think-pair-share technique; introduce tiered tasks.

Exploration

During this time, students are working on the assigned tasks with partners or groups unless a specific individual task is appropriate. They are collecting data, solving problems, trying different approaches, recording and analyzing results, and communicating their mathematical ideas to one another. The teacher is moving among students, conferencing in the workshop model, observing progress, supporting and redirecting as necessary, and asking questions that probe thinking and reasoning. This is an opportunity to stretch or scaffold individual students. The teacher is also deciding the best way to have the collaborations shared in order to extract the embedded mathematics and the variety of student strategies he or she is observing. This is when we as teachers seem to spend a lot of time on our knees. While we do appreciate the wise teacher who carries a lightweight portable stool or pillow with her clipboard, we're simply grateful for the carpeting.

Some students are ready for sharing before others. They know to work quietly on anchor activities or their own individualized math challenges, such as the Menu Problems from the National Council of Teachers of Mathematics' monthly magazines *(Mathematics Teaching in the Middle School* or *Teaching Children Mathematics)*, challenge problems from a variety of resources such as Math Forum (www.mathforum.org/students/), teacher developed extensions based on current unit work, or MATHCOUNTS or Continental Math League (www.continentalmathematicsleague.com) problems. These students know to remain alert to the moment when the class reconvenes to focus on the major mathematics objectives for the day. Review Chapter 2 for the management work that prepares students for the appropriate use of anchor activities.

Differentiating During Exploration

This is the meat and potatoes of the mathematics differentiation implementation: students work with their own styles, at their readiness levels, on tasks designed to match their needs, toward important related mathematical objectives; the teacher coaches, guides, and supports with flexibility and strength of purpose—bending but not breaking. Students use anchor activities when possible and teachers work diligently to let students do the work—struggle reasonably, make mistakes, analyze errors. They are also at the ready to abate nonproductive frustration, provide scaffolding, and maintain mathematical focus.

Class Summary

The summary is the most critical part of the lesson. The purpose is to refocus everyone on the mathematics and consolidate the learning. The class meets to consider the work of the groups and connect the results to the objective for the day. The teacher facilitates the discussion, selecting the order of sharing to optimize the mathematics—asking for thinking and reasoning, questions, justifications, patterns, generalizations, and extensions. Sometimes, because of timing, the lesson is not ready to conclude at the end of the class. In this case, there needs to be a "status of the class" summary in preparation for a smooth continuation during the next class period.

Differentiating During the Summary

Results are shared, explained, and examined; this is not *all* about right answers but ideas—thinking and reasoning, making sense, communicating, showing evidence, identifying the mathematics, making connections, applying and testing new ideas, and determining next steps. It is essential that students understand the mathematical purposes of the summary. Paraphrasing practice is highly recommended during the summary to help students maintain focus. It helps them to concentrate and contribute, and as such is a powerful differentiating tool.

Homework and Reflection

The last five minutes are devoted to the homework assignment and the daily reflection. The assignment is explained and recorded (we use homework logs that are simple to monitor by both teachers and parents), and questions are answered. Students are then directed (or simply reminded) to write a summary of the mathematics they explored or accomplished during the math period and record questions they have about the work.

Gaining insight to student understanding at the end of a class is valuable information for lesson planning for the next day. Informal observation of students and anecdotal notes from a class are one way to gather this information. Some teachers use exit slips or slate work. Exit slips provide a concrete alternative. They are a quick way to survey the knowledge and understanding that students have as they prepare for the end of math class. The exit slips are generally prepared prior to class but may also be a spur of the moment decision based on the class discussion (Figure 6.10). Students complete a problem or answer a question that will provide information for the teacher as she or he reflects on the lesson and plans for the next lesson.

Here's Jenny's description of how she uses slate work (see Figure 6.11) to gather similar information:

> Knowing which students need a little more time with a concept is part of my planning process. Students use individual white boards and markers to write responses to questions. For example, I want to know if there are still any students struggling with writing the percent for a given decimal. I ask them to show me the percent for 0.35. Students write their answer on their white board and then hold it up for me to see. In this way, I can quickly see who needs more work in this area. Using the individual white boards has been a great way to quickly assess the whole class. I jot down the concept I'm checking on a sticky note and then write down the names of students who need some extra support.

Exit Slip   Name _____   Date _____

What did you learn while playing Frac–Tac–Toe? You might choose to write about fraction–decimal equivalents or a strategy that you used to win.

FIGURE 6.10

FIGURE 6.11—Slate work.

Based on the exit slips or slate work a teacher might:

■ Plan to revisit a concept the following day
■ Clarify a misunderstanding
■ Provide a comment about a common error seen in the work
■ Know that overall the class is ready to move forward
■ Plan to work with some students individually

Differentiating During the Homework Assignment
Tailor assignments to individual readiness or needs, incorporating options or choice as appropriate.

Differentiating During Daily Reflections
Individual responses within the parameters of the ritual reveal areas for concern; use suitably modified prompts when applicable; students can articulate needs through questions.

Teacher Reflection, Follow-up Planning, and Responsive Teaching

Through an introspective lens, effective teachers reflect daily upon their observations, the written work students submit, classroom interactions, and the responses of students during math class. They ponder, diagnose, and plan responses in a daily reflection ritual. Such reflective and responsive teaching is at the core of differentiating instruction in any content domain. Carol Tomlinson aptly describes a secure teacher as one who "comes away from today with important questions to puzzle about overnight and the belief that today contains the insights necessary for a more effective tomorrow" (Tomlinson 1999, 28). There is confidence to be had in the knowledge that teaching is a data-gathering and -processing profession. Good teaching evolves from keen observation and information analyses. These activities are the modus operandi for tackling the intriguing and sometimes mysterious problems associated with teaching and learning mathematics. We believe it is the very nature of effective math teachers to take on the nagging instructional problems, identify specific needs, and find creative solutions, which is why it is imperative that we differentiate our instruction.

As you enter the realm of designing a differentiated learning experience for your mathematics program, select a set of reflection questions to scaffold and support the work you must do as you expand your program.

- How did the lesson (workshop) go generally? Why?
- Who was engaged? Who was not engaged? Why?
- Who appeared to understand? Who didn't? What were they learning? What was the evidence? Do I need more evidence? What kind? How can I get it?
- What worked with the launch? Explore? Summary? What would I like changed? How?
- Was the minilesson effective? How do I know? Changes?
- Were directions clear? Materials accessible? Timing issues? Improvements?
- Groups—Were they productive? Why or why not? Interactions focused? Sizes OK? Individuals?
- What needs emerged? What startling misconceptions or perceptions did I note and what do I do about it?
- What effective interactions did I have with groups? What did I learn while monitoring groups?
- Overall, what changes might help? What minilessons are needed? For whom?
- How can I improve data-gathering and work with groups?
- What do I need to do tomorrow? Next week? Next unit?

Make notes that are easily retrievable and can be carried forward in your planning.

Also keep Mahesh Sharma's list of prerequisite skills (Figure 6.7) in mind as you reflect and diagnose the problems that emerge in your classes. The insights you have can help you plan lessons that support troubled learners. Sharma recommends that a portion of remedial/instruction time be devoted to helping children acquire these prerequisite support skills. The skills practice can be built into daily routines or become part of tiered lessons.

Summary

This chapter on planning is meant to reinforce the fact that careful planning is a crucial requisite for effectively differentiating a mathematics program. We have offered concrete support in the form of outlines, descriptions, and examples that include yearly, unit, weekly, and daily pacing and planning formats. The graphic organizer of the Bloom's revised taxonomy can help you plan for challenging students to stretch for deeper meaning. A differentiated mathematics classroom is an ideal environment for addressing this need. For additional support, we have included Mahesh Sharma's litany of prerequisite skills that need development in addition to mathematics curriculum goals. These tools can greatly enhance your ability to fulfill the promise of reaching all children with accessible opportunities to learn powerful mathematics. We believe that, along with a commitment to problem solving, flexibility, and planning, a pattern of reflective and responsive teaching is the heart and soul of differentiated mathematics instruction—observing, pondering, assessing, reflecting, predicting, and adapting.

In the next chapter, we describe four wide-ranging differentiated mathematics lessons and reflect on the strategies involved and what we learned from them.

Chapter 7

Lessons as Lenses

> *The only way to increase student achievement is to design lessons in which students will know what to do, work hard at it, and successfully complete the assignment.*
>
> Harry K. and Rosemary T. Wong (1998, 201)
> *The First Days of School*

Overview

In this chapter we offer four detailed lessons that reflect different reasons and formats for differentiating instruction along with suggestions for additional formats. These classroom exemplars offer another lens for examining what it means to differentiate instruction in mathematics. They allow us to peer inside the planning, thinking and reasoning, preparation, and implementation that we described in Chapter 6. As you read through the lessons keep Bloom's revised taxonomy matrix (Figure 6.4) in mind as a graphic tool for thinking about the types of content knowledge and cognitive processes being targeted in the differentiation.

Lesson I: The linear relationships lesson is differentiated for efficiency. There is a need to introduce five new elements related to linear relationships at the end of the seventh grade. The objective is introductory and not mastery. Small groups are assigned the task of exploring one of the five elements in depth. Each group then shares the results of their exploration with the class.

Lesson II: The two and three-dimensional shapes lesson is differentiated for student readiness and accessibility. The key challenges are identifying and relating the properties of two- and three-dimensional shapes. This lesson is tiered for a fourth-grade class.

Lesson III: The area of a circle lesson is differentiated for student interest and motivation. This sixth-grade lesson explores different ways to determine or approximate the area of a circle. It uses a menu format where process, time, and choice are the major differentiating strategies.

Lesson IV: The fraction lesson is differentiated for readiness and learning styles. The focus of this second-grade lesson is on understanding fractions. The differentiation is through a concrete, open-ended situation that provides access for all and invites students to stretch to their optimal capacity.

The Lessons

Lesson I: *Grade Seven—Linear Relationships*

For this lesson, the final mathematics unit of the school year is transformed into a modified jigsaw format because of time constraints. Thus, the lesson is differentiated for efficiency as well as interest and learning style. In jigsaw fashion, small groups investigate a single concept in depth and then present their findings to the class as a combination report and minilesson. The expected outcomes are: recognizing linear relationships in tables, graphs, and equations; familiarity with y-intercept form for a linear equation: $y = mx + b$; interpreting the point of intersection of two lines on a graph; solving linear equations; and interpreting slope and x- and y-intercepts. Prior to this lesson, the class completed investigation 1 of Moving Straight Ahead, a *Connected Mathematics* unit. In investigation 1, students collected data on dripping water and bouncing balls, made tables and graphs, and noted the patterns in both representations that confirm linear relationships. Now, groups of four or five students are assigned investigation 2, 3, 4, or 5. Group leaders are selected based upon skill level and interest relative to the goals of the specific investigation; for example, Suz is selected as group leader for the investigation using graphing calculators because of her proven facility with the technology. Students are assigned to the groups based upon a history of working well together and the number of problems in their investigation. Pertinent information from the unit teacher's guide for each investigation (a series of three to five problems) is photocopied and placed in an investigation folder for the group leader. This includes the teaching notes and portions of the answer key for the problems in their investigation. Specific roles are chosen for each member: timekeeper, materials monitor, recorder, reporter, and facilitator-pacer (leader). Students are to use their journals to record all the work they do throughout the investigation.

The investigation assignment (problems, follow-ups, and homework items) is stapled to the front of the folder with check-off space to be filled in with the date when completed. The mathematical and problem-solving goals are just inside the folder.

The groups have two additional class periods to complete their investigation and prepare a report of results for the class. They follow these steps:

- Read, discuss, and complete each problem in order; record responses in journals as usual. The homework problems can be completed for homework independently or together as a group. Plan ahead.
- Note new terminology and vocabulary to share.
- As a group, use the four-step problem-solving write-up procedure to prepare your report for each problem. The recorder can record this on chart paper or an overhead transparency.
  1. Restate the problem in your own words.
  2. Describe the work you did to solve the problem.
  3. Present and justify your solution or solutions. (Make transparency copies of graphs if helpful.)
  4. Describe generalizations or insights your group had during the problem-solving process.
- Choose one problem from the investigation for the whole class to complete; include the associated homework problems. It should be the problem you decide is most important in accomplishing the goals for the investigation.

Launch

During a whole class meeting, I introduce each group to their investigation and set the time line.

Investigation 2: Five problems are set in the context of walking rates where students determine whether a situation is linear by looking at a table of data or an equation. Students also explore how a change in one quantity affects the table, graph, or equation, for example, a change in the walking rate.

Investigation 3: Four problems explore lines on the graphing calculator in the context of walk-a-thons and party planning where students determine what a point on a graph represents and come to understand the role of the *y*-intercept and the dependent and independent variables. They also examine the common solution to two equations.

Investigation 4: Three problems are set in the context of installment buying and forensic science to develop strategies for solving equations, including the symbolic method.

Investigation 5: Three problems explore slope in the context of stairways, examining rise and run ratios and relating them to the vertical and horizontal change in a linear relationship. They also learn to use two points on a line to determine slope and *y*-intercept.

Groups have the rest of this class period and two additional class periods to complete the investigation and their reports. Then two class periods are devoted to the summary when groups share their results and challenge the class with one problem to complete. They will have approximately one-half hour for their report and challenge to the class. The following class period will be a jigsaw quiz where students work in a new group composed of at least one member from each investigation group who acts as the consultant for questions relating to their area of concentration. The total time allotted for this unit lesson is six class periods plus regular homework time. If the explorations move along quickly, the summary time will be adjusted.

Exploration

Groups collaborate for two or more days. I meet with each group in rotation—coaching, scaffolding, questioning, monitoring, clarifying, and supporting. Since the investigation 2 group has five individual problems to complete, the first consultation is with them. I suggest they work on the first problem together so that they have the basic concepts for the investigation and then assign the remaining work by partners. My next stop is with the investigation 5 group, where I first notice organization problems. The students must measure the different stairways in the school to determine the ratios for each rise and run. They need to do this by assigning partners to specific stairways. Second, I want them to measure stairways at home so that they have additional data. This group is the most challenged by the independence of the assignment and requires constant reminding to keep them focused and moving along. The other two groups work remarkably well and efficiently. Because they finish before the others, I give them the choice of practicing their presentations with each other or looking at the other investigation problems in the unit. They choose to practice and start with the graphing calculator investigation, which is great because they have time to practice window settings, tracings, interpreting equations, answering questions, and recording values.

Summary

Two days are devoted to group reports and problem solving. The report on the problem chosen for the class to complete is withheld until the class completes their work. While the class is working on the assigned problem, investigation group members visit the tables as "teachers," asking questions and making suggestions. The final portion of the summary is a jigsaw quiz that happens after the reports are complete. It is scheduled for one additional class period.

Jigsaw Quizzes

Group quizzes are completed by new groups formed with at least one person from each of the four investigation groups. They follow the procedure for partner quizzes: work individually for fifteen minutes scanning the entire quiz first; then assemble to discuss and compare responses and complete the quiz. Each student completes his or her own quiz with consultation and support from members of their jigsaw quiz group.

4. *Moving Straight Ahead* - Linear Relationships (tables, graphs, and equations)
What have you learned about linear relationships? I learned that the coefficient is also the slope. I learned how to take two coordinate points and figure out the linear equation from them. I learned the general equation for a linear relationship. I learned some new vocabulary (e.g. constant term, y- and x- intercept).

Describe how linear relationships are shown in:
    tables they change at a steady rate

    graphs They're are stright line

    equations They follow the general equation y=mx+b

Describe what each letter represents in the following basic equation for a linear relationship: y = mx + b

    y is the vertical

    m is the coefficient or the slope

    x is the Horizontal

    b is the y-intercept

Tell how you could best demonstrate what you learned and now understand about linear relationships. I would take a graph and two coordinate points then I would find the equation and make a table by just using those points.

FIGURE 7.1—A trimester three self-evaluation describing what was learned during a modified jigsaw formatted unit on linear relationships.

Lesson I Reflection

This lesson design was an act of desperation. I wanted students to experience this unit before the end of the school year, so I chose a group strategy to compact content without diminishing its potential value. *Compacting* here refers to exposure to a greater than normal volume of material in a short time span. Being able to apportion the tasks and then come together to teach each other is itself a learning experience. It was also a welcome break in the routine. The benefits included the opportunity to put students directly in charge of their learning. The sharing format (four-step problem-solving write-up) provided a good scaffold and revealed surprising results. Being asked for the group's collective insights produced the following unprompted "aha": "Solving equations is simply the reverse of the order of operations." This shared insight was helpful to the entire class with regard to thinking about and working productively through the equation-solving process.

    Three of the groups worked well together to accomplish their tasks, while the group that investigated slope required careful monitoring. Although they needed constant supervision, they did complete the work with enough understanding to help their jigsaw quiz groups. The jigsaw quiz turned out to be a good motivation for them to stay focused. However, I had to add questions during their share time such as "What if the coefficient of x is a negative number? Or what if the coefficient of x is changed from four to three? How is the graph affected? How is the table affected?"

In assessing what students learned, I found most of the students were able to describe significant learning from the unit in their year-end self-evaluations. (See Figure 7.1.) All students reached the goal of being familiar with the concepts associated with linear relationships, albeit at various levels. It's good to note that because this was a modified jigsaw format, the lesson illustrates the flexibility of this approach to differentiating.

Bloom's Revised Taxonomy

Because this lesson represents a differentiated unit, it offers a broad illustration for the use of Bloom's revised taxonomy. The four knowledge dimensions are targeted as follows:

Factual: recognizing linear relationships

Conceptual: knowing the relationships among the elements of linear relationships and linear equations

Procedural: modeling linear problem-solving situations with y-intercept form linear equations and solving the equations

Metacognitive: explaining the thinking and reasoning involved in the use of linear models and sharing that with others through the teaching process

A partial analysis of the cognitive processes involves procedural knowledge with the following objectives. Students:

- *Remember*: recognize and recall the y-intercept equation for linear relationships
- *Understand*: explain and describe each element of the equation
- *Apply*: use the y-intercept equation to model various problem-solving situations
- *Analyze*: know how to solve for various elements within a situation—either the dependent or independent variable or determine the slope
- *Evaluate*: justify a solution through a checking process
- *Create*: develop algorithm(s) or procedure(s) for solving linear equations

A complete analysis would reveal various cognitive processes associated with each of the knowledge dimensions.

Lesson II: *Grade Four—Two- and Three-Dimensional Shapes*

The motivation for differentiating this lesson is readiness. Some of the fourth graders clearly understand the attributes of and relationships between two- and three-dimensional shapes. But nearly half of the children are struggling with those ideas. The class has worked on geometry for the past week and students have experience working with Geoblocks. They also know the characteristics of two-dimensional shapes. The teacher, Mrs. Rumpf, observes that some students need more time connecting examples and language with the concept while others are ready for greater challenge. Mrs. Rumpf and Jenny, the math lead teacher, plan a tiered lesson comprised of three activities. They are targeted for students at various levels of development and understanding. Two of the activities provide basic learning experiences, and the third activity challenges the ready and eager students to apply their knowledge to creating a game.

The room is arranged for three working groups. A three-dimensional shape from a set of Geoblocks is placed at each workspace, along with directions for the group's activity—one copy for each student.

Launch

The class is asked to describe a three-dimensional shape, a hexahedron (cube), which Ms. Jorgensen (Jenny) holds up for all to see. As students give descriptions, their responses are recorded on the overhead. This helps visual learners and tracks what has been said. The introductory activity taps into prior knowledge and encourages students to use the vocabulary and attributes they have learned so far. It also models the next activity, which will be done in the small groups. The students' description of the hexahedron includes the following attributes:

- Square faces
- Eight corners (Ms. Jorgensen writes *vertices* in parentheses.)
- Parallel edges
- Twelve edges
- Three-dimensional
- Has symmetry if cut apart (This was discussed a bit by the class.)
- Polyhedron

Ms. Jorgensen then explains the lesson. The groups will be doing different but similar, related activities. They will share their work with classmates when they finish. Students are directed to their work space along with instructions to (1) describe the three-dimensional object on their work table as the whole class had done for the hexahedron, using as many different attributes and properties as they can, and (2) begin reading the directions for the activity they will be doing and be ready with any questions they have.

Exploration

Students begin work by recording their descriptions of the three-dimensional shape at their table. Jenny goes to each group to clarify the directions for their activity and talk with them about their shape. Some of the questions she asks group members are:

Petra, what is one statement you wrote about the shape?

Tim, do you have a name for this shape?

Does anyone have a different name for this shape?

Which name is the most specific name? Why?

What two-dimensional shapes do you see that are part of your Geoblock?

How many corners does your Geoblock have? What's another name for corners?

The first group follows the directions on task card one (Figure 7.2). This task is designed to give this group another opportunity to work directly with shapes and their properties. Students in the second group follow the directions on task card two (Figure 7.3). These students encounter similarities between characteristics of three-dimensional shapes and characteristics of two-dimensional shapes. The third group is asked to create a concentration game using what they know about the two- and three-dimensional shapes that they've been studying. The directions are shown on task card three (Figure 7.4). They confirm that they understand what they are to do.

Two- and Three-Dimensional Shapes I

In working with two- and three-dimensional shapes, you should be able to:

- identify, compare, and analyze attributes of two- and three-dimensional shapes and develop vocabulary to describe the attributes
- classify two- and three-dimensional shapes according to their properties and develop definitions of classes of shapes such as triangles and pyramids

<u>Materials</u>

pencil	scissors	blank paper
ruler	lined paper	

<u>Task</u>

- You will make a poster using a variety of two- and three-dimensional shapes.
- You will be given a paper with drawings of three-dimensional shapes.
- You will have to draw pictures of two-dimensional polygons. Make sure you use a ruler.
- When you have your two- and three-dimensional shapes, sort them into groups using attributes of your choice. Glue your groups onto the paper that will be provided. Below each group on your poster, write a mathematical description for each group.

FIGURE 7.2—Task card one.

Two- and Three-Dimensional Shapes II

In working with two- and three-dimensional shapes you should be able to:

- identify, compare, and analyze attributes of two- and three-dimensional shapes and develop vocabulary to describe the attributes
- classify two- and three-dimensional shapes according to their properties and develop definitions of classes of shapes such as triangles and pyramids

Materials

pencil	scissors	large poster paper
ruler	three-dimensional models	lined paper

Task

- You will be working with several different three-dimensional shapes.
- Take a three-dimensional shape; look at it and write a description of it by listing the attributes of the shape.
- Place your shape on a piece of paper and trace around the face that is touching the paper.
- Reposition your shape and trace around the new face that is touching the paper.
- Continue until you've traced all the different faces of your three-dimensional shape.
- Beside each face, write the most specific mathematical name for each face.
- Make a "flat pattern" (net) for your polyhedron.
- Glue one face of the flat pattern onto poster paper and attach your description.
- Select another three-dimensional shape and repeat.

FIGURE 7.3—Task card two.

While students work, Jenny and Mrs. Rumpf offer support, observe, and assess the knowledge that students are using.

Summary

By the end of the class, students make good progress but do not finish. Each group shares what they've done so far and what they still need to do. The group creating the concentration game talks about having a struggle to get organized. They are now organized and will finish during the next math class. Those students who finish before others have an anchor activity to complete at their desks. When all groups are ready the next day, they present their products and receive feedback from their classmates. The game was available for students to play throughout the following week as an anchor activity.

Two- and Three-Dimensional Shapes III

In working with two- and three-dimensional shapes you should be able to:

- identify, compare, and analyze attributes of two- and three-dimensional shapes and develop vocabulary to describe the attributes
- classify two- and three-dimensional shapes according to their properties and develop definitions of classes of shapes such as triangles and pyramids

Materials

pencil	scissors	index cards
glue stick	lined paper	three dimensional pictures

Task

- You are to design a geometry concentration game.
- Start by getting one of each type of polyhedron from the box.
- You will need to make two sets of cards for the game.
- One set of cards should be brief descriptions of the polyhedrons—try to use characteristics of the polyhedron in each description.
- The second set of cards should be pictures of the polyhedrons described on the first set; these will be provided for you but you could also try making sketches of the polyhedrons and use them.

FIGURE 7.4—Task card three.

Lesson II Reflection

In reflecting on the differentiated geometry lesson, it is better to begin discussing directions with the group doing the concentration game first. They finished the description of their three-dimensional shape before the other two groups and could have used the extra time to determine how they were going to work as a group. The group making the poster of sorted shapes did not use mathematical descriptions as expected. This is an indicator of the level of understanding of the students in the group. The students need more scaffolding and guidance: for example, a model of a mathematical description. To be sure, the next time we do this lesson, we will model mathematical descriptions for the entire class first, using their input. Then we will model them again with the smaller group.

Bloom's Revised Taxonomy

This lesson targeted the factual and conceptual knowledge dimensions and used the *understand, analyze,* and *create* cognitive processes as the framework for the tiering. The objectives were: to develop understanding of similar two- and three-dimensional attributes and connect them to the appropriate language; to classify pictures of shapes and use mathematical language to describe sets of objects; and to create a game using descriptions and pictures.

More About Tiering

A *tiered* format is designed for predetermined groups in response to readiness, multiple intelligences, interests, or style preferences. Jennifer Taylor-Cox urges teachers to think in thirds relative to a class profile because it's manageable and a way to begin a tier design (Taylor-Cox 2005). This works well with the Addressing Acessibility in Mathematics Project's suggestions for class profiling as described in Chapter 3. The tier design starts with a basic lesson (one tier). Add an extension as a second tier for those who need or thrive on extra challenge. Then the third tier provides scaffolds for those who need more background or support. Think about what comes before the basic concept and what comes after and you will be prepared to differentiate. This is one of the reasons it is important for teachers to have deep knowledge of mathematics and the curriculum. (See Chapter 9.) You may design as many tiers as works for your student needs.

Rebecca Pierce and Cheryl Adams of Ball State University developed an eight-step process for tiering a lesson, which we've reduced to seven (Figure 7.5).

In most cases if you are working with an organized or standards-based curriculum, steps one and two are done for you. This handy guide can get you started with the tiered approach to differentiating. Then assess, adjust, and make it fit you and your students' needs. The lesson plan that follows uses both Jennifer Taylor-Cox's advice and the steps for tiering a lesson to create a differentiated experience for fourth graders using the Array game from the *Investigations* curriculum.

Steps for Tiering a Lesson

Step one: Identify the math standard(s) associated with your objective.

Step two: Identify the big idea, key concept, or generalization.

Step three: Determine the necessary background—prior knowledge, scaffolding needs.

Step four: Determine what to tier: content, process, and/or product.

Step five: Determine whether to tier for readiness, learning style, interest, and so on

Step six: Determine the number of tiers you need.

Step seven: Develop a formative and summative assessment plan.

Adapted from Pierce and Adams (2005)

FIGURE 7.5

First the decisions are made using the Pierce and Adams guide:

Step one: (math standards) algebra; number and operations
Step two: (key concepts) properties, basic facts, and multiplication/division
Step three: (prior knowledge) understanding the meaning of multiplication; being familiar with the rectangular array model
Step four: (part of the lesson to tier) playing the Array game
Step five: (type) tier for readiness
Step six: (number of tiers) three
Step seven: (assessment component) formative: lesson products and self-evaluation
Next, describe the individual tiers. (See Figure 7.6.)

Array Game—Grades Three and Four

Three tiers
1—for kids working on learning multiplication facts
2—for kids ready to see relationships between multiplication facts
3—for kids who know their multiplication facts and are ready to make extensions

The game has students use arrays made from grid paper. The arrays have the dimensions (factors) on one side of the rectangular array, for example (3 × 4), and the product (12) on the other side. A set of arrays consists of fifty different rectangular arrays.

Tier 1. Pairs of students work with a set of arrays with the dimensions faceup. The set of arrays are shuffled and dealt out to each student. Each student then takes the top array and compares them. Whoever has the greatest product keeps the two arrays.

Tier 2. Pairs of students work with a set of arrays with the products faceup. Students will work together, taking one array and then finding two other arrays that will cover the original rectangle.

Tier 3. Pairs of students will work with a set of arrays, product faceup, and record their work. One student will take an array and then with their partner write an equation that describes how the distributive property is modeled by decomposing the product into the sum of two products for their array. For example: the array product is 18. The student would write 18 = (1 × 6) + (2 × 6). Students take turns in this process. They may even work to find several different pairs of arrays to match the product.

Extension. Students write equations that include the original factors for the array in place of the original product. For example: 3 × 6 = (1 × 6) + (2 × 6).

Adapted from *Investigations* Economopoulos et al. (1998)

FIGURE 7.6

Lesson Three: Grade Six—Area of a Circle

This sixth-grade menu of seven activities is designed to give students a variety of experiences on which to build an understanding of the area of a circle and the formula associated with its determination. *Area* is defined as the number of square units inside a figure, which is awkward for circles because circles do not share the attributes of a square unit—right angles and line segments. Furthermore, the physical acts represented by the formula for the area of a circle have eluded many a math student.

Six of the seven menu strategies are adaptations of work by Marilyn Burns and Cathy McLaughlin (Burns and McLaughlin 1990). The seventh is from the Connected Mathematics unit, Covering and Surrounding (Lappan et al. 2002). (See Figure 7.7.) They are all grounded in rich historical developments and creative problem solving.

The circle area menu differentiates for process, product, student interest, and readiness. The expectation is for students to have multiple strategies for approximating the area of a circle and be able to connect the standard formula with several of them. As they complete the menu assignment, students compare the methods, select the most accurate, justify their selection, appreciate the value of the formula, explain each of its parts, and appreciate the history of its derivation. Students have already derived formulas for the area and perimeter of basic polygons and the circumference of a circle. They have also developed an understanding of pi as "three and a little more."

The menu preparation includes copying: (1) directions for the seven strategies, (2) the menu checklist and rules for completing the assignment, (3) circles drawn on centimeter grid paper, and (4) plain centimeter grid paper. Other materials include: colored pencils, straight edges, scissors, Post-it glue, balance scales for weighing circles, cardboard circle and rectangular weights, linoleum circle and rectangular weights, beans and small plastic containers (paper cups), and drawing compasses. (The weights and circles must be cut carefully. The weights are modeled after base ten blocks—units, longs, and flats. You need only a limited number.)

Students are organized into partners with interests, strengths, learning styles, personality, and readiness characteristics in mind. Working with their partners, all students complete strategy 7; each set of partners is assigned two other strategies; students may then choose to investigate as many other strategies as time and materials allow. The sequence for exploring the specific strategies is predetermined because of time and material constraints. Materials and directions are organized in legal-size file folders with the short ends taped to make large open envelopes, one for each strategy. All materials and directions needed to complete that strategy are placed inside its folder. The envelope (folder) is then used for permanent storage and filing after the lesson is done for the year.

Menu of Strategies for Determining the Area of a Circle

1. Counting squares (Burns and McLaughlin 1990, 113)

2. Inscribing and circumscribing squares (Burns and McLaughlin 1990, 113)

3. The octagonal (or Egyptian) strategy (Burns and McLaughlin 1990, 113)

4. The simulated parallelogram—Kepler's derivation [Johannes Kepler, 1571–1630] (Burns and McLaughlin 1990, 113)

5. Finding area by weighing (Burns and McLaughlin 1990, 113)

6. Measuring area with beans (Burns and McLaughlin 1990, 113)

7. Measuring area with radius squares (Lappan et al. *Covering and Surrounding* 2002, 73)

FIGURE 7.7

Launch

Each student receives a 7-cm radius circle printed on grid paper and works with their partner to estimate its area. Students share their estimates and strategies and discuss the range of the data. Then the menu of strategies is introduced. Each student receives (1) a menu checklist that indicates his or her assigned strategies, (2) a description of all the strategies available for exploration (see list above), and (3) the expectations for the recording and reporting of the work (Figure 7.8).

Exploration

With partners, students have two class periods to complete the assigned strategies and other choices. The teacher supports students, helps with interpretations such as "measuring with beans" and "weighing," monitors the recording for the work, and directs traffic to and from the limited access area where weighing takes place. She or he also observes and identifies students who may have unique contributions for the summary.

Summary

Student partners post their circle area data on a class chart and the class gathers to compare the methods for strategies 1 through 6. Together they evaluate and make mathematical sense of the strategies. Students then select their favorite or most trusted method of the first six strategies and explain why. For strategy 7, students study the range of responses for the different circles and look for patterns. The goal is to relate the area of each circle to the number of radius squares and to the formula for the area of a circle: Area equals the square of the radius multiplied by pi or $A = \pi r^2$. "A little more

```
┌─────────────────────────────────────────────────────────────────────┐
│         Menu Directions: Determining the Area of a Circular Region    │
│                                                                       │
│  Partner Names _____ Date _____             │
│                                                                       │
│  1. Working together as partners, complete your two assigned          │
│  strategies and strategy 7. (Everyone in the class is to complete     │
│  strategy 7.)                                                         │
│                                                                       │
│     Assigned strategies: _____    _____         │
│     You will be responsible for sharing your assigned methods and     │
│     results with the whole class.                                    │
│                                                                       │
│  2. Recording your work: Once you have the result for a strategy,     │
│  analyze the mathematical connections you see in the method. Tell     │
│  why it makes sense and how accurate or reasonable you think it is.    │
│  Use the following format to record your work for each strategy:      │
│  • strategy number and title                                         │
│  • a description of what you did                                      │
│  • your result                                                       │
│  • your analysis: why the method makes mathematical sense and what     │
│    you think of its accuracy                                         │
│                                                                       │
│  3. Submitting results: When you and your partner have completed the  │
│  activities, organize your work. Make a cover sheet with your name,   │
│  date, and a table of contents for the strategies you completed.      │
│  Place it in a construction paper folder.                            │
│                                                                       │
│  4. Reflecting on the investigation: Once the class summary is        │
│  completed, you are to write an individual mathematical reflection.   │
│  In this reflection:                                                 │
│     1. Describe what you learned and/or understand about the area     │
│        of circles.                                                   │
│     2. Tell which method you trust the most and why.                 │
│     3. Tell how you relate the formula for the area of a circle to    │
│        the different methods you explored.                           │
│     4. Describe how you and your partner shared the responsibilities  │
│        for completing the investigation.                             │
│                                                                       │
│  The reflection will be judged using the class rubric for             │
│  mathematical reflections.                                           │
│                        Adapted from Burns and McLaughlin (1990, 112)  │
└─────────────────────────────────────────────────────────────────────┘
```

FIGURE 7.8

than three radius squares" is what is expected and hopefully a little more than three will connect to their discovery of pi earlier in their study of circles. They then look for the other strategies that support the derivation of the formula: (4) the simulated parallelogram; (5) finding area by weighing (see

```
              Circle Reflection and /or Write-up      Ethan

    The problem was we were to go over 4 earlier methods of finding
    the area of a circle. I got the 'Octagonal/Egyptian' and the
    'weighing' methods. Katie Perry (my partner) did the 'using
    beans' and the 'curvy parallelogram' methods.

    Some things I learned were to find the modern method A = ∏r² .
    The mathematicians did not pull ∏ out of the air. They must have
    recognized patterns between the methods, most importantly radius
    squares.

    The method I trust the most would be the 'Octagonal method.' I
    trust it because it doesn't have all the decimals ∏r² gives off:
    for ex., a circle with a radius of 3 gives you an area of ∏ · 3²
    which is 28.27433. . . .( u²).  Now using the Octagonal method it
    gives you 28 u² . It gives the same whole number. Another method
    I think is the most accurate is the weighing method. In theory
    this is the most accurate, but when you put human error into
    account, it isn't.

    In the weighing method the big circle had a radius of ten. But
    in this there were actually radius squares that you could see.
    They were 10 by 10 and with that I figured out what ∏r² actually
    meant. It meant 3.14592 . . . radius squares would fit into a
    circle.

    Katie did most of the folder work, but I let her get first
    choice on the methods.
```

FIGURE 7.9—Ethan's write-up.

Figure 7.9); and (6) measuring with beans. Finalized reports are to be submitted during the following class period.

Lesson III Reflection

This is a productive lesson. It is also complex. Students come away with a strong conceptual foundation for what it means to find the area of the circle. The weighing strategy causes disequilibrium, serving to initiate thoughtful discussion. Those who make sense of it give sound arguments for its validity; it is beneficial for the class to hear this. The proponents for weighing talk about less error because of the technology—a scale doing the work as compared to kids counting squares or stabilizing beans that wiggle. Students are amazed at the accuracy of the weighing model, as was I (Miki). Most important, a good number of the students are able to explain the connection between the radius squares and the standard formula for the area of a circle. The concept of pi is also reinforced as more than a strange number—it is an actual real-world relationship! The most significant issue during the exploration is directing traffic and monitoring the care of the equipment and materials. It was necessary to call several class meetings around the chart board to remind everyone of the procedures for handing in their work, recording data on the several different charts, and checking in on the general progress and status of the class. Calling the meetings was not part of the initial plan but worked well because the students then gave advice to those who hadn't yet tried a particular strategy. They also needed to be reminded to finish their write-ups for homework. We recorded that on the homework logs so that it was clear to parents.

Bloom's Revised Taxonomy

The differentiating in this lesson specifically targets the understand, analyze, and evaluate cognitive processes for both conceptual and metacognitive knowledge dimensions. The objectives are to: describe or explain the relationships between the different methods of representing or determining circle area; compare and contrast methods for determining circle area and relate them to the standard formula; and select and justify the most effective methods for determining circle area. Finally, students are to explain their thinking regarding the meaning and role of each element in the formula for the area of a circle, $A = \pi r^2$.

More About Menus

Menus can be tiered and/or offer an element of choice. It is a remarkably flexible format that presents a collection of activities focused on a specific concept. The activities can be introduced over a period of several days. The choice may be the sequence of doing the activities, the selection of specific activities, and/or the timing. The teacher may also assign some of the activities and leave the others to choice as I did with the circle area menu above. The menu is also an excellent format for practicing procedures, reinforcing skills, review, extension, or preparation for summative assessment.

Lesson IV: *Grade Two Fractions—Constructing Halves*

This open-ended problem is used to differentiate for readiness and learning styles. The teacher, Mrs. Redman, and the math lead teacher, Jenny, work together to help students stretch their understanding of one half and explain why part of a structure can be called one half using tangram sets. Students are familiar with the seven-piece square puzzle and know the names of its various shapes.

The lesson is designed to have students use concrete materials. Along with the tangram puzzles, triangle grid paper (the triangles are duplicates of the small tangram triangles) is prepared so that students can record their products, cut them out, and tape them to a poster to share. They will use colored markers to highlight the one half. The lesson will also reinforce the concept of symmetry.

Launch

Jenny begins a discussion of tangram pieces, reviewing the names of the polygons. She tells students the goal of the lesson is to show one half using their tangram pieces. She places two small triangles on the overhead projector and a student volunteer creates a square using the triangles. Jenny asks, "What part of the square is one of the triangles?" Many hands are raised and one student is called on to share "one half." "How do you know it's one half?" is answered by a different student: "It is the same as the other part of the square." Another student demonstrates that one triangle fits on top of the other triangle so he knows it is one half.

Students are then told to use their tangram pieces to make a shape to show one half. Once they have a shape that shows one half, they are to make a representation of the shape on the triangle grid paper and shade in the two halves using two different colors. This is modeled with the square from the initial discussion.

Exploration

Students work individually, each with their own tangram set. They are encouraged to share pieces with a neighbor if they want two different colors to make seeing the two halves easier. Jenny and Mrs. Redman move around the class observing and supporting. One student needs help drawing her shape on the grid paper. Jenny looks for typical examples of one half (bow ties, squares, rectangles, parallelograms) and examples that might be generated by students thinking outside the box (a trapezoid). When students complete a representation, they cut it out and glue it to a class poster of one half. The student making the trapezoid from the medium triangle and the parallelogram is insecure, so Jenny encourages him to use the other tangram pieces to see if he can prove that his shape shows one half. She watches from a distance as he places two small triangles on each of the pieces to be convinced that they are the same size even though they are not the same shape.

Summary

Students gather round the poster (see Figure 7.10) to think about the different representations. They come to the poster, one at a time, to point to a shape that they know shows one half and explain how they know. They also identify shapes that they are unsure of. Jenny moves these to the edge of the easel holding the poster. Students are to think about these during their recess break. They return to the carpet after recess with the poster in front of them. The trapezoid is now the topic of discussion, and its creator Tim uses his tangram pieces on the floor to show classmates his proof. The class agrees that it shows one half and the trapezoid is returned to the poster.

Lesson IV Reflection

This lesson provided students time to explore with tangram pieces and put them together to create shapes, that have two halves. Students were free to create the shape used to launch the lesson. The open-endedness provided an entry point for all students but didn't limit students who were able to take the concept of one half further. This aspect of the lesson is the differentiated

FIGURE 7.10—Samples of one half from second grade class.

component that the teacher was looking for. Tim's particular polygon is an example of a deeper understanding of one half and a use of spatial sense to create an outside-the-box solution. Jenny had watched him work through his insecurity and was confident that he could comfortably share his proof with the class.

More About Open-Ended Problems
The open-ended format matches well with the launch, explore, and summarize model and it is exactly what it says—open-ended. It's open to exploration, offers multiple solutions and approaches, and encourages students to be personally involved in extending their knowledge and understanding. Refer to Chapter 4 for more examples of this type of problem as well as suggestions for creating them.

Bloom's Revised Taxonomy

This lesson targeted the conceptual knowledge dimension with five cognitive processes—understand, apply, analyze, evaluate, and create. Students could move as far along the levels as their readiness allowed. The objectives were for students to demonstrate their understanding of one half, to apply that to various tangram pieces, to compare and evaluate the different interpretations of classmates, and to create their own accurate representations.

Reflecting on the Lessons

We've been on a virtual tour of four mathematics classrooms, peering into various types and stages of differentiation. The formats included a modified jigsaw exploring linear relationships for seventh graders, a carefully tiered readiness lesson in fourth-grade geometry, a sixth-grade menu of options for approximating the area of a circle, and an open-ended fraction challenge for second graders. Each technique was grounded in teacher assessment, reflection, and knowledge followed by thoughtful, responsive planning. In each instance, the teacher was deeply concerned that all students be able to optimize their learning of important mathematics.

These concrete examples exhibit essential components for effective differentiation in mathematics across the grade spans. The lessons provide access to all students with learning goals that are focused on significant mathematics. The teachers have high expectations, and in all cases, the students have a hand in directing their own learning with fluid support structures in place. It's a good time to take another look at Tomlinson's general differentiation principles as a cross-check for our mathematics implementation (Figure 7.11).

Key Principles of a Differentiated Classroom

1. The teacher is clear about what matters in subject matter.
2. The teacher understands, appreciates, and builds upon student differences.
3. Assessment and instruction are inseparable.
4. The teacher adjusts content, process, and product in response to student readiness, interests, and learning profile.
5. All students participate in respectful work.
6. Students and teachers are collaborators in learning.
7. Goals of a differentiated classroom are maximum growth and individual success.
8. Flexibility is the hallmark of a differentiated classroom. (Tomlinson 1999, 48)

FIGURE 7.11

It is interesting to note that in the lessons where students have the most responsibility (the jigsaw and the menu), the planning is the most intense and complex. This may not be obvious. In general, there is a broad range of complexity in the design of differentiated lessons. When you reach a stage of comfort with this kind of math instruction, some lessons will be a matter of habit while others will still require intense research and preparation. The good news is that once done, the more intense complex lessons are there for future use with ease, needing only minor adjustments for a current class, new knowledge, or up-to-date technologies.

Additional Differentiation Formats for Mathematics

Stations or centers are other options for differentiating. These are areas in the classroom where students work on various tasks at the same time. They coordinate well with flexible grouping when skills instruction or minilessons are planned for small groups.

There are a number of innovative designs for general differentiation in Tomlinson (1999, 2003) and Heacox (2002). For example, ThinkDots is an activity found in *Fulfilling the Promise of the Differentiated Classroom* (Tomlinson 2003, 151). It is designed for use after students have gained the essential knowledge of a unit or concept. The technique is useful for review, demonstration of knowledge, or extending thinking. It consists of sets of six cards, each having a task or challenge on one side and one to six dots on the other side. There are many ways to use the sets of cards: (1) for individuals or groups, (2) to assign specific tasks to specific students, or (3) using the roll of a die to determine an assignment. Selecting or designing the six related math tasks is fairly straightforward with resources like *Nimble with Numbers*, a collection of grade-level specific "engaging math experiences" (Childs, Choate, and Hill 1999). See the ThinkDots example in Figure 7.12 created for a number theory unit. Detailed directions for each activity are located in a numbered (using both die dots and the appropriate digit) file folder.

Another useful strategy for differentiating mathematics is called Pathway Plans (Heacox 2002, 101–102). It is a format for managing assignments, especially when using a looping technique where students loop in and out of small group skills instruction according to student readiness or needs. In this strategy, a checklist of skills related to a unit of work is followed by a set of five or six independent tasks, activities, or projects. This becomes a planning document for each student. The skills will be checked off when completed or crossed off because they were previously mastered. Students work on activities of choice while skill groups are having minilessons that are not part of their plans. This strategy offers a great deal of flexibility and can be adapted for a broad range of mathematics. Figure 7.13 shows the pathways for decimal operations. For this pathways unit, there is a detailed preassessment to help students and teacher determine needs and schedules.

Number Theory ThinkDots

Each activity below is on one of the six cards.

1. Play "Greatest Common Factor (GCF) Bingo." You may work alone or with a partner. [Two spinner boards randomly select composite numbers. Players identify GCF and give proof with prime factorizations.] (Childs, Choate, and Hill 1999, 29)

2. Complete at least one of the "Number Explorations: 1, 2, 3, 4, 5, or 6." [Each exploration reinforces basic number theory concepts with ten challenges plus an extension.] (Childs, Choate, and Hill 1999, 34–36).

3. Complete "Prime Target" using three (1–6) number cubes and one (4–9) number cube. Be sure to record the number sentences you use to find the 25 prime numbers. You may work alone or with a partner. [Use two or more of the rolled numbers to create an expression equal to a prime number. Reinforces prime recognition between 1 and 100.] (Childs, Choate, and Hill 1999, 40)

4. Do the "Common Factors Practice" puzzles or the "Common Factors Practice Challenge." [A set of numbers must be placed in grid so that all adjacent cells share common factors. Strengthen recognition of common factors.] (Childs, Choate, and Hill 1999, 44–5)

5. Complete Using LCM and GCF to Check Multiplication. [The multiplication of two 2-digit numbers is checked by multiplying their Least Common Multiple (LCM) and GCF. Builds and extends conceptual understanding of LCM and GCF relationships.] (Childs, Choate, and Hill 1999, 46)

6. Select a number from the "Challenge Bag" and follow the directions: show the prime factorization, all factors of the number, and prime factorizations for each factor. Use exponential notation whenever possible.

FIGURE 7.12

Finally, while the lessons we shared provide exemplars of *what* is differentiated, *why* it is differentiated, *when* and *where* the differentiation happens, and *how* the differentiation is organized at various grade levels and configurations of mathematics classrooms, they represent only the tip of the iceberg. A problem-solving platform and the flexibility within basic classroom structures offer endless opportunities for designing and organizing differentiated lessons. You'll find suggestions for additional formats for differentiating mathematics in the professional literature, especially the National Council of Teachers of Mathematics monthly journals, and on-line. There are many creative math teachers who love to share their successful strategies.

Pathways for Decimal Operations

Skill Groups:

_____1. understanding the place values of decimal mixed numbers

_____2. reading and interpreting decimal fractions

_____3. adding and subtracting decimals

_____4. multiplying decimals

_____5. dividing decimals

_____6. finding equivalent fractions, decimals, and percents

_____7. deciding when to use decimals or fractions to solve problems

_____8. solving problems involving percents

Independent Tasks

1. Create a Venn diagram showing relationships among fractions, decimals, and percents and their uses. Use examples from newspapers, magazines, advertisements, and so on.
2. Write a poem that shows what you have learned about the relationships between fractions, decimals, and percents.
3. Complete fraction rectangles using the clues on each task card for the size of rectangle and required colored portions.
4. Create Grid Designs that match the given size grids and percents.
5. Create and test a flowchart for multiplying decimals.
6. Write and solve five real-world problems that require decimal division. Show all work.
7. Complete the decimal Magic Squares (Childs, Choate, and Hill 1999, 84) or create your own decimal/fraction magic square.

FIGURE 7.13

SECTION III

The Glue: Holding It All Together

She was the polar opposite of "cool," but we hung around her classroom like it was the malt shop and she was Wolfman Jack. None of us could have articulated it then, but it was because we enjoyed being harangued by her, disciplined by her, and taught by her. She was a woman of clarity and principles in an age of uncertainty. I sit up straight just thinking about her.

Thomas L. Friedman (2005), describing the most influential person
in his life outside of family—a high school teacher.
Thomas L. Friedman (2005, 306)
The World Is Flat—A Brief History of the Twenty-First Century

Chapter 8

The Teacher: Knowing and Sharing the Self

Good teaching cannot be reduced to technique; good teaching comes from the identity and integrity of the teacher.

Parker Palmer, *The Courage to Teach*

Background and Rationale

In this chapter, we examine why teachers need to know themselves along with strategies for doing the necessary metacognitive work. The following statement from the National Council of Teachers of Mathematics *Principles and Standards for School Mathematics* (2000) is fair warning that unrecognized biases and beliefs have the potential to sabotage the good intentions of a differentiating mathematics teacher:

> To accommodate differences among students effectively and sensitively, teachers also need to understand and confront their own beliefs and biases (14).

In essence, because "we teach who we are, good teaching requires self-knowledge" (Palmer 1998 2–3). If we are cognizant of our biases and beliefs about learning and teaching mathematics, we have a firmer foundation for making the instructional decisions that will serve our students well.

Recall from our introductory chapter that differentiation expert Carol Ann Tomlinson expects teachers to create responsive classroom environments in ways that align with their own teaching styles as well as the needs of their students. An important goal is to keep a healthy balance between these two elements of instructional tension—individual teaching patterns and student needs—in the building of your differentiated mathematics scenario.

Relative to my own practice, in Chapter 1 I mentioned a deep belief that sustains my teaching: "The major work of my life commitment to teaching is to take students wherever they are and help them move as far forward as possible during our time together, doing whatever it takes." Tapping into this credo keeps me alert to the alignment or nonalignment of my belief, my current practice, what mathematics is, and what it means to do and learn mathematics—all weighty aspects of teaching the discipline. I also reflect upon how to use the energizing forces that come from the opposing and complementary styles that occur within the mathematics classroom.

The Connection Between Learning and Teaching

In math education circles, a common topic of concern is that how teachers were taught mathematics either knowingly or unwittingly influences how they teach mathematics. For that reason, it is important for mathematics teachers to reflect on their past mathematics learning experiences. When they first come to their jobs, they represent the culmination of myriad encounters as learners of mathematics from elementary school through their years of college and university (NCTM, 1991, 123). It is critical that they face their current beliefs as learners and teachers of that discipline. They also need to examine their own teaching and learning styles, multiple intelligences, talents and strengths, and thinking dispositions in order to complete self-portraits and reveal both competencies and biases. The reflective self-knowledge combined with an awareness of personal dynamics—various activity patterns, ways of processing data, and ways of interacting with people—help teachers better understand how to organize a differentiated mathematics program.

Reflecting on Yourself as a Learner

Examining how you personally learn calls for a reflective process. Think back to Chapter 3 and the learning styles used as a backdrop for observing students and getting to know them as learners. (See Figure 3.9 on page 63). Where do you fit? Maybe you see yourself reflected in elements of each learning style. Maybe you favor one of the described styles over the others. The latter is more likely. Identifying preferences in this context also reviews the range of potential learning needs in your classroom and how you relate to them. In addition, consider using some of the on-line self-analysis inventories referenced at the end of this chapter as a way to advance your self-knowledge.

Developing your own mathematics autobiography (mathography), at least informally, is another way to look inwardly to reveal attitudes as well as the foundation and generation of the attitudes.

- What positive mathematics experiences do you recall and what made them positive?
- Who were your favorite math teachers/professors and why? What specifically made the experience special?
- What struggles do you remember associated with mathematics, both academically and in real-world experiences? From your current perspective, how do you evaluate those struggles?

- In your developmental years, what did it mean for someone to be good in mathematics? Has that changed over the years for you? If so, how and why?
- How would you prefer learning about a new mathematics concept today?

Breaking Cycles and Finding Natural Teaching Pathways

Using the learning style(s) you identified for yourself along with your mathography, think about how you teach mathematics today. There is an element of truth to be found in thinking that teachers are likely to mimic ways they were taught. This may not be what is desired or what is best for you or your students. Changing undesired practices means recognizing current mathematics teaching patterns and identifying shifts that will serve students well. For an example, read Jenny's experience regarding student voice (Figure 8.1).

Teacher behaviors such as Jenny's shift to student voice are not easy to facilitate and take significant conscious effort and determination. Today, I had a conversation with a longtime professional colleague who highlighted our concern with this challenge to break the cycle of benign abuse. "It is amazing to me that we know so much about how different people learn mathematics today—the research has been so revealing in the past fifteen years—and yet schools [teachers] all over (including our local system) seem to revert back to what they've always done or what teachers seem comfortable with despite what they know about what does and doesn't work for many of their kids" (Christy Fitzpatrick 2006, personal communication). For this reason, vow to do a careful analysis of yourself, using whatever tools you can find to assist your objectivity. First, recognize your natural assets and talents for teaching mathematics. Then, especially for the purposes of differentiating, target areas for professional growth to thoughtfully increase your repertoire without sacrificing or denying your natural gifts.

Our Classroom Stories

It is straightforward and simple for me to introduce a lesson on reflective and rotational symmetry by having students read the definitions and illustrations shown in the text—that's how I learned about it as a student years ago. I do know, however, that additional illustrations will support what's being read and heard. Within the pressured context of teaching, it is easy to fall back on the pattern that matches my classroom learning history, especially if I don't take the time to think about the various needs of my students. But because I recognize and deal with the learning/teaching cycle I refer to affectionately as *benign abuse* (defined and discussed in the book's Introduction under Mathematics Classroom Issues), I do take the time. This is vividly demonstrated with the Turn symmetry lesson in Chapter 3 (Figure 3.6, page 57), where students are not only provided a visual tool but a kinesthetic experience as well. Once I began to plan and prepare in this manner, it became a habit. I

Jenny's Experience

In my teaching career, I've learned the importance of student voice in the classroom and that I have to provide opportunities for students to listen to each other. I was not always aware of how I dominated the conversation and voice in the classroom. I would regularly repeat what a student said. I think my purpose was to make sure all students heard what their classmate had said. I've since changed this undesirable practice. I learned to provide the structure and learning environment where students listen to each other. If a student says something that I'm not sure all students heard or that they might need to hear again to internalize it, I ask the student to please repeat what she said. I also learned to have other students paraphrase what they heard their classmates say—in this way I am supporting student voice. I often have to model what I'm looking for from the students until they are familiar with how our math class will function. For example:

The teacher asks a question.

Students raise hands.

The teacher gives wait time and then calls on a student.

A student (John) makes a comment.

The teacher asks the class if they agree or disagree with what John said and calls on another student, Saritta.

The teacher prompts Saritta to paraphrase what John said and then to tell why she agrees or disagrees with him.

The teacher gives John a chance to respond to what Saritta said and then asks other students if they have comments about what has been said.

If during this type of discussion a student says that they didn't hear what one of their classmates said, then he or she can ask the student to repeat what was said before they make a comment.

   The shift to student voice in my classroom was in response to the expectations and norms essential for differentiating as described in Chapter 2.

Expectation: Students understand that all members of the learning community are teachers and learners; everyone explains their thinking—orally and in writing—and makes their thinking transparent.

Norm for Classroom Conduct: Discussion/discourse: respectful interactions; listen attentively; safe environment; wait time; students formulate and answer questions; everyone contributes; share talk time; build student capacity for discourse through practice.

FIGURE 8.1—Jenny's experience developing student voice.

As a teacher, I'm aware that I am not bothered by a noisy conversation-filled atmosphere. I often have lessons that involve kids working and talking in small groups. The students will be working and exploring, fully engaged in learning mathematics. The result is a classroom filled with middle school voices. This level of noise is part of my math class; it is not something that bothers me as a teacher. But I know that as a learner there are times I need to think about a problem on my own before discussing it with others, and I like a quiet environment for this think time. I enjoy talking with others and solving problems together after *having individual* quiet *think time. Knowing myself as a learner and as a teacher, I work to make sure that I respect the students in my class who need think time and don't function well in a noisy classroom. I know my learning style supports my teaching style, but I need to plan math for a variety of styles in order to meet the needs of my students.*

found ways to use my strengths and natural inclinations to respond to the needs of my students. If I depended on following the models of my early learning experiences, I would believe such techniques to be inappropriate for mathematics classrooms. As a mathematics coordinator, I was chagrined to hear that belief expressed many times over.

In a similar fashion, Jenny, who recognizes her learning style II need for graphic organizers, always draws a picture when problem solving. She's learned to do this as an adult in her attempts to understand and relearn mathematics using practices in direct opposition to her own childhood classroom math experiences, where she was taught by practicing meaningless procedural algorithms. Her own determination to make math meaningful for herself and consequently her students keeps her from shifting back into patterns that didn't work for her. It is also her beacon for steadfastly thinking about how she can use her natural teaching assets to accommodate styles other than her own.

As teachers, Jenny and I consciously move beyond our past learning experiences and look to newly identified strengths to provide visuals, hands-on opportunities, and quiet space. While these simple gestures are essential for some students, they will not have a negative effect on others. Differentiating teachers must not only break traditional teaching patterns but also understand and implement strategies that make mathematics learning accessible to the styles and needs within their classes. To accomplish these tasks, they must first come to understand themselves, their intrinsic mental processes, and how they naturally mediate a mathematics classroom.

From Learning Styles to Teaching Styles

Gregorc Mind Styles™

In Chapter 3 we looked at the learning styles reviewed at the beginning of this chapter as they related to knowing our students. Here we examine the Mind Style work of Dr. Anthony Gregorc (1982) because of its unique relationship to teaching styles. I began using his work in my teaching in 1980 while doing graduate work with him at the University of Connecticut. I was teaching middle school mathematics at the time and found that the theory opened my practice to valuable new options. Here we summarize the salient features of the Mind Styles theory and its associated teaching styles. We also examine how this work helps teachers know themselves as practitioners and clarifies the tensions that arise naturally in the differentiating process.

Dr. Gregorc's Mind Styles represent the four possible extreme combinations for perceiving and ordering information. Everyone has characteristics of each of these four combinations "but has a natural, inherent predilection toward one or two of the combinations" (Gregorc 2006b).

1. Concrete and Sequential combination (perceive concretely and order sequentially)
2. Concrete and Random combination (perceive concretely and order randomly)
3. Abstract and Random combination (perceive abstractly and order randomly)
4. Abstract and Sequential combination (perceive abstractly and order sequentially)

Perceiving or collecting information ranges along a continuum from concrete to abstract—from using the five senses to perceiving through naturally intuitive (insightful and instinctive) ways of gathering information. Ordering the information ranges along a continuum from sequential to random—from a step-by-step linear approach to a process of chunking information in no particular order (Gregorc 1982). Most will fall somewhere on the continuums between the extremes. Profiling a Mind Style on an instrument for adults called the Gregorc Style Delineator involves ordering appropriately preferred sets of characteristics such as "objective, evaluative, sensitive, and intuitive," (www.gregorc.com) that are then mapped to the four styles: Concrete Sequential, Abstract Sequential, Abstract Random, and Concrete Random. Jenny's and my profiles are shown in Figure 8.2.

General descriptions for the Mind Styles are somewhat similar to the learning styles presented earlier, some being better matches than others. For example, Style I clearly aligns with Concrete Sequential and Style III clearly aligns with Abstract Random. Style II is quite similar to Abstract Sequential and by default we can look for the similarities between Style IV and Concrete Random. However, our major interest here is to understand our teaching style and that connection is analyzed in the next section.

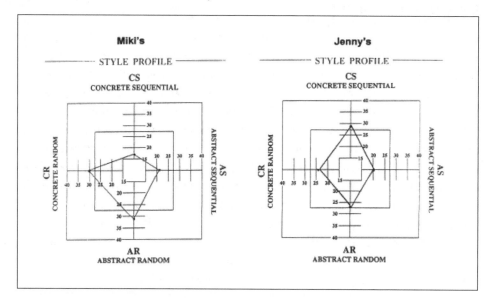

FIGURE 8.2—Gregorc Mind Styles profiles. Used with permission.

Teaching Styles

Dr. Gregorc defines teaching styles, which are of particular interest to us here, as "behaviors, characteristics and mannerisms that reflect underlying mental qualities used for presenting data in school" (Gregorc 2006, 10). The teaching styles associated with his Mind Styles were summarized in a 1998 ASCD publication written by Pat Guild and Stephen Garger. A brief description of each style follows.

Concrete Sequential. The teacher who has a preference for perceiving concretely and ordering sequentially is a naturally pragmatic hands-on practitioner who manages a highly structured logical classroom. This teacher expects students to be on-task and thorough with their work. This classroom is predictable, realistic, and secure for students.

Concrete Random. The teacher whose natural preference is to perceive concretely and order randomly is practical and realistic but exhibits originality, spontaneity, and creativity. Students in this classroom are encouraged to make choices, be active and inventive, and think for themselves. Change, a busy environment, and a variety of methods are comfortable for this teacher.

Abstract Random. The teacher whose natural mental constructs are to perceive abstractly and order randomly is enthusiastic and sensitive, designs child-centered classroom experiences, and expects students to cooperate and share. This teacher is spontaneous and responsive to the needs and interests of individual students while constantly striving personally for deeper understanding of curriculum and content.

Abstract Sequential. The teacher who prefers to perceive abstractly and order sequentially naturally provides a rich but structured environment while encouraging students to be analytical and evaluative. Students are expected to develop good work habits and support their conclusions with evidence. This teacher is always pushing for deeper understanding. (Adapted from Guild and Garger 1998)

Once teachers identify their preferred teaching styles, they can consciously develop differentiation strategies and techniques that are comfortable for them and at the same time serve the needs of the various styles represented within their classrooms. For example, a dominant concrete sequential teacher might create highly structured centers while the range of options within an individual center allows for open-ended, creative, and spontaneous responses. Menus and tiered lessons are other differentiating techniques that invite accommodation for all teaching and learning styles. In the process of identifying style(s), teachers also learn about other teaching styles and can identify areas for personal and professional growth that will add to their instructional repertoire.

The Teacher's Intelligence Strengths

You can't really know yourself as a mathematics teacher without examining your own unique intelligences through the lens of Howard Gardner's Multiple Intelligences Theory. You may be able to do this informally by simply reading through the descriptions in Chapter 3 or you may use a more objective approach by completing an inventory, such as the on-line references included at the end of the chapter. In any case, it's easy, so take the time to identify your particular intelligence preferences, which incidentally change over time (McKenzie 1999). It's also beneficial to think about how a strong preference might impact your instructional practice. Although it is possible to have a balanced profile across the eight ways to think and learn, most individuals reveal two or three strong preferences.

Classroom Application

When my students completed the multiple intelligences inventory available in Diane Heacox's book *Differentiating Instruction in the Regular Classroom* (2002), I joined them and graphed the results as shown in Figure 8.3. As a class, we focused on our three strongest areas of intelligence in order to

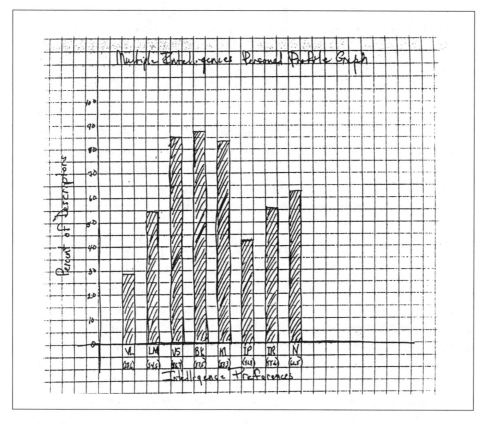

FIGURE 8.3—Miki's multiple intelligences profile.

generalize a class profile. The children appreciated knowing my preferences. [...] helped them buy into metacognitive activities such as describing [...]ng and they understood that our thinking about the same problem [...]y be different and helpful.

Self-Knowledge and Differentiating [...]atics Instruction

[...]rch by the Gallup organization confirms that top achievers in any [...]ize and develop their strengths. They then invent ways to use [...]ths to achieve desired ends (Clifton and Anderson 2004, 11–12). It [...] then, that teachers use their natural blend of style and strengths [...]udents engage in robust learning. This is an approach that [...]teacher's comfort level and reduces the stress inherent in the [...] support all styles. When teachers know their natural mediation [...]y can use them as the platform for diversifying learning opportunities. When they also know the range of style and needs in the class, planning parameters are opened up and defined.

Although it seems to be the antithesis of a learner-centered classroom, place your teacher strengths and natural styles at the center of the planning process. Visualize a core surrounded by four sections representing the major learning style needs. By targeting specific students that exemplify styles other than your own, you can plan lessons that target most students' needs. Keeping an actual student in mind for each style (see Focal Student Planner, page 58) helps to ground the planning process, as third-grade teacher Kathryn does in the model lesson that follows. Then move outward from your strengths and style to meet the needs of differing styles and invent strategies that enhance accessibility for all students. Think of eliminating potential barriers and planning for readiness levels, interests, and/or favored processes.

Model Lesson Plan

Kathryn identifies herself as a strong concrete sequential teacher. She knows her strengths and is comfortable with her carefully structured classroom environment, daily routines, and clear expectations. She sequences the mathematics curriculum thoughtfully and runs what she calls "a tight ship." She loves teaching third grade.

This week she is focusing her planning on Jonah, Kamisha, and Samantha. The content for the week is the composition and decomposition of numbers featuring addition and possible combinations of addends for sums up to twenty. It is a time she plans to cement the basic addition and subtraction facts and open the children's minds to a bigger idea of three, four, even five addends.

The three children she selected this week all seem to move to different drummers. Jonah loves to talk. He is willing to share his thinking but has difficulty decoding—his reading is labored. He is not patient with others when it comes to math. He is creative, uses pictures with his writing, and loves using formal graphic organizers. Kamisha is quiet and takes longer than most students to get started. Once she does though, she finishes her work quickly, especially if she has manipulatives—she is amazingly efficient and practical with hands-on tasks. Samantha is everywhere at once. She likes having choices and loves working in a small group. She needs definitive time limits.

Kathryn will use at least three different activities with all of the children but not at the same time. They will do small group cooperative problems using number shapes from *Get It Together* (Erickson 1989), which emphasize an algebraic approach. Another major resource is Greg Tang's delightful book *MATH-terpieces*, in which the content of famous period artwork sets the stage for adding groups of objects and considering possible addend combinations for specific sums. The children will also build trains with Cuisenaire rods as a hands-on approach to the same concept. In another activity, children will draw numbers from zero to twenty from a can of numbers and find whole number combinations with that sum.

Kathryn launches the lesson with a reading of Greg Tang's book. On chart paper, the class records groups of objects and the sum for each masterpiece. She models the process of finding combinations and the expected recording of their work using the first masterpiece painting in the book. Students will be expected to choose at least three of the paintings to complete individually, although they may work with a partner. There is an additional challenge to create their own "math-terpiece" to be shared with the class during summary. Kathryn then introduces other activities (one will be introduced the next day) and announces the carefully selected groups for the cooperative problem solving, the time schedule for working through the various activities, and the deadline for completion of the work. Students reiterate for her what they are to do and how they are to share materials, space, and time.

Kathryn checks back to her notes about the focus children. She is satisfied that she has considered their needs, built in the essential scaffolding, and in the process has prepared accommodations for the entire class. Note that she has worked with her teaching style at the core of her planning and reached out to students with different needs.

Self-Knowledge, Collegiality, and Differentiating Instruction

When you have a good working relationship with colleagues, planning and learning together, you have a wonderful resource for developing a differentiation mind-set and creating mathematics units of study. First of all, whenever possible, surround yourself with others who represent different styles and intelligences and who know this about themselves. In this way, you are in a natural environment for accepting others as they are, learning to utilize their perspectives in planning, and becoming personally broader-based.

Second, you can diminish the workload by sharing resources, ideas, and differentiated lessons. Specifically, Jenny's relationship with the special education teacher is enlightening and supportive. She learns about easy to implement techniques, which greatly benefit students with identified needs and others as well. Although they have different strengths and styles, they are able to work as co-teachers on many occasions, differentiating lessons to meet the needs of all their students.

The Value of Opposing Forces

The purpose of this chapter in a volume on differentiating mathematics instruction is to reinforce the importance of the identity and integrity of a teacher. A person's *identity* is the intersection of the inner and outer forces that structure her or his life. A person's *integrity* is a measure of his or her ability to act in ways that complement the identity. Over the years, experts who research and report on effective teachers from a student's perspective reveal that the most revered and respected teachers are those who teach from the heart, with knowledge and passion and with the need to share their passion. In *The Courage to Teach*, Parker Palmer (1998) elegantly articulates the ramifications of teacher self-knowledge. He convinces us that if teachers don't know themselves, they cannot adequately know their content, for knowledge must go deep and develop personal meaning, and the insights worthy of sharing come from deep within that personal meaning. Thus self-knowledge becomes a framework for growth and development, in the pursuit of differentiating instruction as well as deepening our appreciation for and understanding of mathematical content.

The work to develop differentiated mathematics classrooms involves tensions. *Tensions* are the invaluable opposing forces that keep us alert, support our tallest buildings, and fashion important structures in our lives. Parker Palmer offers us his principle of paradox as a model for incorporating tensions into an instructional design that acknowledges the challenges of being true to yourself and fulfilling the sometimes diametrically opposed needs of others. See Figure 8.4 for the tensions he recognizes and builds into his instructional designs.

We love these tension statements as descriptors of how a mathematics teaching and learning space will echo from within a differentiated instructional environment. These statements summarize many of the issues and challenges that we have incorporated into our scenarios and lessons. The statements also honor the challenges that mathematics teachers who know themselves and their craft are so capable of meeting.

1. The space should be bounded and open.
2. The space should be hospitable and charged.
3. The space should invite the voice of the individual and the voice of the group.
4. The space should honor the "little" stories of the students and the "big" stories of the disciplines and tradition.
5. The space should support solitude and surround it with the resources of community.
6. The space should welcome both silence and speech. (Palmer 1998, 74)

FIGURE 8.4—Classroom tensions to support differentiated instruction.

Wrapping Up Self-Knowledge

Starting with the inspirational words of Parker Palmer, the essentials of teacher self-knowledge have the power to help teachers facilitate deep mathematics learning for all kinds of students. Similarly, acknowledging tensions in a classroom environment is a way to identify opposing forces and use them to everyone's advantage using Palmer's principle of paradox. Remember also the invaluable professional community in which mathematics teachers work and learn. There are diverse groups of mathematics teachers out there who know themselves, share differentiating concerns, and are willing to contribute their individual perspectives and strengths. They can serve as a model for your classroom. You may have to go outside your immediate school or district or look for professional groups on-line. The MiddleWeb, www.middleweb.com/CurrMath.html, is one such group of dedicated middle school teachers who post amazingly helpful and supportive conversation regularly. Most of all, use the resources at hand, the most important of which is *you* for "you teach who you are."

> Great chunks of the research support a simple dictum: know yourself, know your students, believe in what both can do. Because of cognitive and learning style work we can know ourselves and our students in a way that counts—as learners and thinkers. (Gerald Kusler 1982, 14)

Internet Options for Building Self-Knowledge

Style Delineator: http://gregorc.com

Learning Style Inventory™ (Silver and Strong 2003): www.thoughtfuled.com

Clifton StrengthsFinder: http://www.StrengthsFinder.com

Multiple intelligences inventory:
   http://homepages.wmich.edu/~buckleye/miinventory.htm
   http://surfaquarium.com/MI/inventory.htm
   www.personal.psu.edu/staff/b/x/bxb11/MI/MIQuiz.htm

Chapter 9

Teacher Knowledge of Mathematics and Pedagogy

If we are to transmit a mastery of something, we need to have acquired at least enough dexterity of our own to show someone else the direction in which they can acquire "a mastery" greater than our own.

Mahesh Sharma, *Guiding Principles and Structure for a Mathematics Lesson*

Throughout this book, mathematical proficiency for all students is the driving force behind our push for differentiated instruction. It follows then that teaching for mathematical proficiency implies an analogous interwoven set of strands for all mathematics teachers.

- *Conceptual understanding* of the core knowledge of mathematics, students, and pedagogy
- *Procedural fluency* with instructional routines
- *Strategic competence* in planning and responding to problems
- *Adaptive reasoning* in justifying, explaining, and reflecting on practice
- A *productive disposition* toward mathematics, teaching, learning, and improving one's practice

(National Research Council [NRC] 2001, 10)

In this chapter, we focus on the first and last strands: the content and pedagogical knowledge necessary for differentiating mathematics instruction and the professional development needs related to both differentiated instruction and content knowledge. We look at compelling evidence for more and deeper mathematical content knowledge for teachers, we define mathematical knowledge specific to teaching, and we offer four perspectives on that special teacher knowledge: the big mathematical ideas; National Council of Teachers of Mathematics (NCTM)'s *Curriculum Focal Points*; principles for how students learn mathematics; and proven effective strategies for teaching mathematics. Finally, we consider the professional development needs regarding both differentiated instruction and content knowledge.

Scenario

We begin with a scenario to set the stage for thinking about the multiple impacts that teacher knowledge has on the processes involved with differentiating mathematics instruction.

The Need to Know

As a math coordinator in the late 1980s, I introduced my district staff to the use of manipulatives for teaching mathematics. Several days after a workshop focused on base ten blocks, Title I tutor Wilma ran up to me carrying a bag of base ten blocks and breathing heavily, saying "Miki, help!" She had just presented Tim, one of her "needy" third-grade students, with the subtraction problem 31 − 19. She had set up a display of three tens and one unit and asked Tim to use the blocks to show how he could subtract the nineteen. She expected him to use the ample supply of blocks to exchange one of the tens for ten units. Instead, he quickly and confidently said, "Oh that's easy," picked up two tens and set them aside, and grabbed one unit from the supply and put it with the remaining ten and one. (See Figure 9.1.) The action was reasonable, logical, and efficient, but neither Wilma nor the classroom teacher knew how to work with Tim's strategy. Wilma had been told he "didn't understand subtraction," meaning he didn't understand the traditional subtraction algorithm. It was abundantly clear that Tim understood subtraction but the staff (tutor and teacher) was not prepared to consider how a student might naturally think about the subtraction operation.

This brief scenario illustrates one of the reasons teachers need to continuously learn more deeply about the mathematics they teach. It also illustrates that teachers can learn from students as they teach, for the incident was the beginning of a staff exploration into alternative subtraction strategies. We studied subtractions with the same answer such as 31 − 19 and 32 − 20 where one is added to both the minuend and the subtrahend — *voilà*, no cumbersome renaming required. For a three-digit example, replace 721 − 398 with 723 − 400. Both yield the same result but the latter is simpler to complete. Counting on to the next ten or hundred is another strategy similar to Tim's. And there are more!

What the Experts Have to Say

Carol Tomlinson warns that the greatest threats to effective differentiated instruction are gaps in teacher content understanding, pedagogical skill, and/or classroom management know-how. Of these, weakness in content knowledge is the most significant barrier to reaching all students with core understandings (Tomlinson 2001).

Jenny and I both became acutely aware of this barrier when we began working with the Middle Grades Mathematics Project in the mid-1980s.

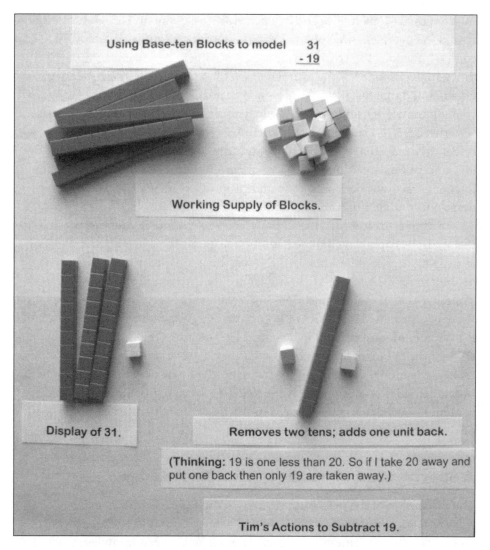

FIGURE 9.1—Tim's method for subtracting nineteen from thirty-one.

Because of our professional development experience with this program, the predecessor of *Connected Mathematics*, we discovered significant gaps in our content understanding, not from lack of course work but lack of opportunity or encouragement to explore and connect important big ideas. Our new encounters clarified for us the reasons why so many students fail to grasp relationships such as multiplication, factors, dimensions, area, and perimeter and the concepts of maximum and minimum. Uncovering the new knowledge that had hovered just below the surface for so many years opened the doors to countless new ideas for reaching all students.

There are other reasons for concern about the content knowledge of those who teach mathematics, including the results and researched analyses of recent international achievement comparisons, notably the 1995 Third

International Mathematics and Science Study assessment. U.S. eighth graders scored, on average, three points *below* the forty-one country average. In contrast, the four top scoring countries scored between twenty-four and thirty-nine points *above* the average (NRC 2001, 56). It has since been well documented that teachers in the United States differ considerably in their content knowledge and practice from teachers in high achieving countries (Charles 2005, 9–11). Another reason for concern is that "A large body of research reveals that elementary and middle school teachers hold significant misconceptions about mathematics," including multiplication and division, integers, fractions, decimals, ratio and proportion, geometric shapes, functions, and probability (Brown, McGatha, and Karp 2006, 37).

Thus, it is critical for differentiated instruction and student achievement that math teachers develop the habit of questioning, assessing, and working to deepen their content knowledge. Every time they learn something new about a math topic, there are new avenues for differentiating the new understanding as well as its connections and relationships to other math ideas. Research from the University of Wisconsin suggests that teachers need to learn mathematical content in a context that includes the different ways students might learn that content, what they call *learning trajectories* (Carpenter et al., National Center for Improving Student Learning and Achievement in Mathematics and Science [NCISLA] 2004). What a great idea! Learning content knowledge in this way is a direct model for the differentiation work of classroom teachers.

A Special Kind of Mathematical Knowledge

The discussion of the teaching principle in the *Principles and Standards for School Mathematics* (NCTM 2000, 17) makes it clear that in preparing for the work of teaching mathematics, teachers at all levels need knowledge about:

- The whole mathematics domain
- Curriculum goals and important ideas central to their grade level(s)
- Challenges students encounter in learning the ideas
- How to represent the ideas effectively
- How to assess students' understanding

The work of teaching mathematics is a complex process that goes beyond our usual understanding of what it means to know and do mathematics. It includes explaining, generalizing, analyzing errors, defining terms and symbols, connecting ideas across and within strands, and justifying processes, algorithms, and solutions (Ball 2003, Ball et al. 2005a, Ball et al. 2005b, Usiskin 2002). Competence with these processes is key to effective differentiation, as is being able to reframe concepts in less complex, learner-friendly terms or situations that maintain the integrity of the mathematics. It's what differentiating math teachers are constantly challenged to do.

It's this deep content knowledge of mathematics specifically for teachers that concerns us here. Research studies clearly indicate that greater mastery of content relates directly to higher student performance (Peske and Haycock 2006). However, mastery of content is an ill-defined concept. What we do know for certain is that teachers need to understand the big ideas of mathematics as well as its coherence and connectedness in order to differentiate effectively.

Essential Knowledge: Big Ideas and *Curriculum Focal Points*

Currently, we recommend four major sources of guidance for clarifying the content and pedagogical knowledge essential for teaching mathematics. They contain the seeds of growth for differentiated instruction:

- The standards documents of the NCTM:
  Principles and Standards for School Mathematics (2000); *Professional Standards for Teaching Mathematics* (1991); and *Assessment Standards for School Mathematics* (1995)
- Randall Charles' "Big Ideas and Understandings as the Foundation for Elementary and Middle School Mathematics" (2005)
- NCTM's *Curriculum Focal Points* (2006)
- NRC's *How Students Learn: Mathematics in the Classroom* (2005)

Clearly deep content knowledge is an important weapon in the differentiating arsenal. The snapshot in Figure 9.2 is an example of its impact in a classroom situation.

In this snapshot, the students differentiated with their approaches. It was critical for the teacher to understand that the mean represents the "even-ing out" of data and that the three very different strategies are all grounded in sound mathematics. The teacher directed the discourse to why and how the different strategies worked to solve the problem correctly and how the three methods or different representations related to each other. Together, the group created a new similar problem and tried on each other's strategies. In the differentiated classroom, the teacher sometimes needs to offer access to students through these different kinds of strategies and processes.

Big Ideas

When Randall Charles introduced his "big ideas and understandings" (see Figure 9.3) in the summer of 2005, he acknowledged, "high quality teaching begins with the teacher's deep subject matter knowledge." (9) Thus, he proposes that teachers "ground their mathematics content knowledge and practice around a set of Big Mathematical Ideas." (9) He defines a big idea as: "a statement of an idea that is central to the learning of mathematics, one that links numerous mathematical understandings into a coherent whole." (10)

> **Snapshot**
>
> Recently six middle school students were working on the following problem as one of ten problems under consideration:
>
> > Each of four test scores in Connie's class is to be weighted equally. On the first three tests Connie scored 79%, 87% and 98%. What must she score on her fourth test to have an overall average of exactly 90%? (MATHCOUNTS *School Handbook* 2006–2007, 17)
>
> After working for ten minutes on the set of problems, the students were asked to share their strategies for approaching this particular problem (not the answer).
>
> - Sixth-grader Jordan was the first to eagerly volunteer that he multiplied the ninety by four so that he knew there would have to be a 360-point total for the four test scores. He then determined the total of the three scores and subtracted that from 360.
> - Eighth-grader Anna offered her guess-and-check strategy next. She added in a score she estimated would be close and determined the average of the four scores. It was low so she went for a greater score and found it. She showed her written work to assure the group that she hadn't used a calculator.
> - Sixth grader Göran was then anxious to share his yet different strategy. He took eight points from the ninety-eight and added that to the seventy-nine for a new score of eighty-seven. Now he had to add three to both eighty-seven's to get ninety, so he needed six points in addition to another ninety.

FIGURE 9.2

Dr. Charles believes that by developing an understanding of big ideas in mathematics, elementary and middle school teachers can develop the deep, connected content knowledge they need (Charles 2005, 9–11).

In the interest of helping readers understand what is meant by big ideas of mathematics, we include Dr. Charles' list (Figure 9.3). We (and he) urge you to seek out the in-depth descriptions and discuss them with your professional community. They are available at www.ncsmonline.org/NCSMPublications/NCSMSpring05d2.pdf.

Charles is careful to explain that these are his designated big ideas in consultation with colleagues. Other mathematicians working together to do the same type of analysis would likely come up with a different set. He organizes his big ideas across mathematical content strands rather than grade levels. This presentation emphasizes the interconnectedness the big ideas represent and the depth of development across grade levels necessary to build deep understanding.

Randall Charles' Twenty-one Big Ideas of Mathematics K–8

1. **Numbers**: The set of real numbers is infinite, and each real number can be associated with a unique point on the number line.
2. **The base ten numeration system**: The base ten numeration system is a scheme for recording numbers using digits 0–9, groups of ten, and place value.
3. **Equivalence**: Any number, measure, numerical expression, algebraic expression, or equation can be represented in an infinite number of ways that have the same value.
4. **Comparison**: Numbers, expressions, and measures can be compared by their relative values.
5. **Operation meanings and relationships**: The same number sentence (e.g., $12 - 4 = 8$) can be associated with different concrete or real-world situations, and different number sentences can be associated with the same concrete or real-world situation.
6. **Properties**: For a given set of numbers, there are relationships that are always true, and these are the rules that govern arithmetic and algebra.
7. **Basic facts and algorithms**: Basic facts and algorithms for operations with rational numbers use notions of equivalence to transform calculations into simpler ones.
8. **Estimation**: Numerical calculations can be approximated by replacing numbers with other numbers that are close and easy to compute mentally. Measurements can be approximated using known referents as the unit in the measurement process.
9. **Patterns**: Relationships can be described and generalizations made for mathematical situations that have numbers or objects repeat in predictable ways.
10. **Variable**: Mathematical situations and structures can be translated and represented abstractly using variables, expressions, and equations.
11. **Proportionality**: If two quantities vary proportionally, that relationship can be represented as a linear function.
12. **Relations and functions**: Mathematical rules (relations) can be used to assign members of one set to members of another set. A special rule (function) assigns each member of one set to a unique member of the other set.
13. **Equations and inequalities**: Rules of arithmetic and algebra can be used together with notions of equivalence to transform equations and inequalities so solutions can be found.
14. **Shapes and solids**: Two- and three-dimensional objects with or without curved surfaces can be described, classified, and analyzed by their attributes.
15. **Orientation and location**: Objects in space can be oriented in an infinite number of ways, and an object's location in space can be described quantitatively.
16. **Transformations**: Objects in space can be transformed in an infinite number of ways, and those transformations can be described and analyzed mathematically.
17. **Measurement**: Some attributes of objects are measurable and can be quantified using unit amounts.
18. **Data collection**: Some questions can be answered by collecting and analyzing data; the question to be answered determines the data that need to be collected and how best to collect it.
19. **Data representation**: Data can be represented visually using tables, charts, and graphs. The type of data determines the best choice of visual representation.
20. **Data distribution**: There are special numerical measures that describe the center and spread of numerical data sets.
21. **Chance**: The chance of an event occurring can be described numerically by a number between 0 and 1 inclusive and used to make predictions about other events.

FIGURE 9.3—From Charles (2005, 12–21).

When I first introduced these big ideas to the staff of one of my consulting schools, we began processing them by exploring the meaning they had for each teacher. Beginning with numbers, three major themes and questions emerged from that one big idea: clarifying what was meant by real numbers; the concept of infiniteness and its representation by a line; and how the number line related to each of their grade levels. This discussion raised a consciousness among the teachers that changed their teaching of mathematics dramatically. None of them had valued the number line in their work previously and suddenly they were aware of its importance in articulation across the grade levels. They had an amazing conversation about how each would begin to incorporate number lines into their work. The kindergarten teacher developed a yearlong love affair, along with her children, for the number line games that permeated their classroom culture. They first had a number line on the floor of the classroom that was used daily. It was transferred to the chart board once they mastered the fundamental number relationships through role-playing. This set the stage for the seamless eight years of development yet to come. Focusing on one big idea opened up huge mathematics learning opportunities for this school community.

The NCTM Curriculum Focal Points

In September 2006, NCTM published *Curriculum Focal Points*. This document prioritizes and organizes essential mathematical content knowledge. Three key topics and their conceptual connections are designated for each grade level for grades pre-K through eight. These focal points are intended to focus the curriculum for one academic year of mathematics classroom instruction. The complete downloadable document is available on line at NCTM's website. To illustrate the value of *Curriculum Focal Points* for differentiating instruction, we trace operations through several grade levels as an example of an expected teaching/learning progression (see Figure 9.4). We use this in the section "Teacher Knowledge at Work" (page 166–68) to illustrate how a second-grade teacher uses such content knowledge in planning a differentiated unit.

The Pedagogical Perspective

How Students Learn Mathematics

From synthesized research literature on learning, the NRC identified three well-established basic "principles of learning that are particularly important for teachers to understand and be able to incorporate in their teaching" (NRC 2005, 1).

- The first principle involves the use of prior knowledge. Prior knowledge can either support new learning or form a barrier to new ideas. To assure support, it is essential to engage students' preconceptions before introducing new ideas. This is why differentiating mathematics teachers probe student understanding with some form of formal or informal preassessment.

Focal Points and Connections for Operations—Grades 1–3

Derived from NCTM *Curriculum Focal Points* (2006)

Grade One:
- Develop understanding of addition and subtraction and strategies for basic addition facts and related subtraction facts using: objects, length-based models, number lines, part-whole, adding to, taking away from, and comparing. Use commutative and associative properties and relate addition and subtraction as inverse operations.

Grade Two:
- Develop quick recall of addition and subtraction facts and fluency with multidigit addition and subtraction using relationships and properties of number and operations; develop and use efficient, accurate, and generalizable methods to add, subtract, estimate, and/or calculate mentally.
- Begin solving multiplicative problems to introduce multiplication as repeated addition.

Grade Three:
- Develop understanding of multiplication and division and strategies for basic multiplication facts and related division facts through various representations; use properties to multiply whole numbers with increasingly sophisticated strategies for solving problems involving basic facts and understanding multiplication and division as inverse operations.

FIGURE 9.4

- The second principle is that of learning concepts with understanding, which essentially has two parts: (1) creating a conceptual framework for the learning of factual knowledge and (2) using multiple representations that make the new knowledge applicable in unfamiliar situations. A good example for this principle is the preferred learning trajectory for multiplication facts: explore different models—linear, repeated addition, area and rectangular arrays, Cartesian products, and equal-size groups; connect these with symbolic representations and language interpretations; and identify and use the real-world applications.
- The third principle is the importance of self-monitoring—the metacognitive approach of putting children in control of and taking responsibility for their own learning. Providing frequent opportunities for student self-assessment and goal setting is critical to mathematics learning. Requiring explanations and justifications for the thinking and reasoning used in finding solutions is also essential in the differentiated mathematics classroom (NRC 2005, 4–12).

The pedagogical knowledge and skill of mathematics teachers is relative to how effectively they apply the three basic learning principles in their practice. Once again, the use of these principles is fundamental to differentiating instruction.

Effective Teaching Strategies

Teachers are reminded of the need to use strategies that have proven effective for teaching math. Such strategies embrace physical experience with direct concrete interaction, social interaction, and an understanding of the role of maturity. They include:

- Using visual, linguistic, and contextual supports that relate to formal math notation and language
- Encouragement for talking about mathematical thinking and reasoning
- Bridging informal math experiences to formal mathematical procedures, as with money
- Following research-based learning paths that engage children's hearts, hands, and minds
- Harnessing the power of connections within and across strands using relationships and multiple representations
- Providing multiple opportunities for skill development over time

Teacher Knowledge at Work

Planning for Success

Second-grade teacher Suzette Morrison is committed to helping her students develop quick recall of the basic addition and subtraction facts. She references big ideas 5, 6, 7, and 9, and reviews the *Focal Points* to note the first- and third-grade expectations along with the second-grade description so that as she plans her instruction, she understands the potential readiness accommodations she will need to incorporate. Key elements begin to connect to her objective, such as inverse operations, fact strategies, and the commutative and associative properties. Checking through the big ideas, she notes information about basic facts and algorithms, operation meanings, properties, patterns, and equivalence as support for the work ahead.

   She is aware of several students who have mastery over the facts as well as some that still need help with strategies. She collects a number of children's books that offer interesting contexts for addition and subtraction. Some she will read with the children; others will be used in assignments as a way to integrate math and reading. She plans a problem-solving activity to launch the unit and assembles a menu of activities to give students engaging practice opportunities over time. Some are for all students; some are assigned to students whose concepts and strategies are not fully developed and need scaffolding and support. Others are for students who are ready to move on and need appropriate challenges, such as working with repeated addition, multiplication, and more complex problem solving.

The launch problem is for the students, working in pairs, to determine how many addition and subtraction fact families there are for sums of seven through eighteen, using addends two through nine. Suzette begins by modeling the sums of seven on chart paper with the class and showing how to record the results for each sum. (For sum seven: two and five form one family; three and four form another, for a total of two families.) Once this problem is summarized, the students have the opportunity to make their own triangle fact cards on construction paper triangles cut from squares. Each addition and subtraction family is written on one fact card with the sum in the big square corner (of the isosceles right triangle) and the addends in the two smaller corners of the triangle. Students who have already mastered the facts begin alternate menu activities.

The menu options include games such as Cross Out Singles (Burns 1992, 191) and Number Ladders (Kaye 1987, 71); activities that use the triangle fact cards; hands-on materials such as number lines, cubes, Cuisenaire rods, dice, and spinners; children's literature such as Greg Tang's *MATH-terpieces*

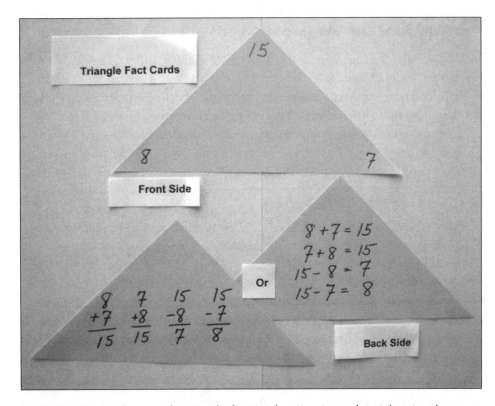

FIGURE 9.5—Student-made triangle fact cards using isosceles right triangles made from squares.

and *Math Potatoes*; textbook assignments, writing, and problem solving. Ms. Morrison increases or decreases the options or complexity of the menu as needs arise. The menu is introduced over a period of three days. Then, with partners, students work on the menu activities that alternate with minilessons and individual and small group assessments. Summary sessions ask students to share progress, game strategies, and products. Checking menu folders after each use and reading the students' reflections on the activities helps Suzette track progress; she is also assessing during the mental math and slate work challenges she uses for daily warm-ups.

In this vignette, trace the thinking and planning of teacher Suzette Morrison as she uses content knowledge (big ideas and *Focal Points*) and pedagogical knowledge and skill (learning principles and strategies) to develop her instructional plan. It is clear that this second-grade teacher understands the mathematics content she guides as well as its pedagogical requirements. She knows the connecting value of literature, continuously assesses and responds to student progress, plans for individual needs, and understands the learning conditions that help students focus and develop facility, in this case with addition and subtraction facts and beyond. She exhibits mathematical proficiency for teachers.

Professional Development Needs

In *Knowing and Teaching Elementary Mathematics* (1999), author Liping Ma awakened the mathematics education community to the professional development needs of teachers with her call for **p**rofound **u**nderstanding of **f**undamental **m**athematics (PUFM). Her reference to the big ideas is as, "the cornerstone ideas of elementary math." In an interview recorded in ENC's *Focus Magazine* (Herrera 2002), she proposes that teachers who need more content math knowledge (and who doesn't?!) should deepen their knowledge of elementary math through their own teaching, always asking themselves "Why?" with a focus on the important ideas that hold "all the pieces of a subject." Think back to the scenario at the beginning of this chapter where the entire staff learns more deeply about the thinking and reasoning related to subtraction because of a surprising student strategy. How many of us have said at one time or another, "The best way to learn something is to teach it"?

Whenever mathematics teachers take on a new initiative, such as differentiating instruction, they face a reality of professional development needs that must be met in some way. According to National Science Foundation research, they need to accomplish each of the following:

- Develop a vision and commitment
- Strengthen their knowledge of mathematics
- Understand the underlying pedagogical theories
- Learn to use effective teaching and assessment strategies

- Become familiar with associated materials and resources that are exemplary
- Understand equity issues and their implications for the classroom
- Cope with any emotional aspects of the change
- Develop an attitude of inquiry toward their practice (Borasi and Fonzi, 2002.)

No one model suffices. It takes a plethora of options to support and scaffold teachers as they learn to differentiate mathematics effectively, and since this is a relatively new endeavor, an eclectic approach is called for. Collaboration with colleagues, analysis of accessible resources, and reflection on classroom trials can form the foundation for sustained growth in the implementation of differentiated mathematics instruction. It's no further away than your computer when willing colleagues are not at hand.

Attaining a desirable depth of content knowledge is a continuous process. Follow the urgings of Liping Ma to learn from the lessons you teach, maintain an attitude of inquiry, and seek to understand big ideas. Although a number of venues are available for mathematics teachers to continue their growth, the ideal is, once again, to connect with a professional learning community, either within your own school or district or by reaching out to the larger community. Being able to discuss your own mathematics thinking and learning with colleagues and like-minded professionals is the best of all professional development worlds. In this environment, you learn about yourself as well as how others explain and understand their thinking. Bring in the work of students, sometimes puzzling and sometimes amazing, for shared analysis. There are a variety of formats as well—lesson study, action research, on-line courses, professional literature, book study, and so on. But just as children don't learn from doing but from talking about and reflecting on what they've done, this is just as true for math teachers!

One of the pitfalls of teachers attempting to design their own professional development is not being able to objectively determine their greatest content needs. There is help on the way. A series of diagnostic mathematics assessments for elementary and middle school teachers is being refined at the University of Louisville, in Louisville, Kentucky under the direction of Dr. William S. Bush. The major purpose is for planning and designing professional development that builds upon teachers' mathematics strengths and addresses mathematics weaknesses—a foundation for *differentiated* professional development. I would love this for myself because I'm always suspicious of having missed things along the way, having come from such a traditional learning environment. Teachers who use the assessments can objectively learn about the breadth and depth of their mathematics knowledge. Currently there are four diagnostic assessments for middle school teachers addressing number/computation; geometry/measurement; probability/statistics; and algebraic ideas. Similarly, there are four diagnostic assessments for elementary teachers addressing whole number/computation;

rational number/computation; geometry/measurement; and probability/ statistics/algebra. To access these materials or learn more about them, contact Dr. Bush at bill.bush@lousiville.edu. These diagnostic assessments can certainly make professional growth efforts more efficient—saving time, money, and energy.

Teachers' Perceptions

Jenny and I have asked a number of current teachers to reflect on their content knowledge: how they continue to grow and what helps them learn mathematics content. Here are some of their responses.

How do you continue to grow mathematically?

- Continue assessment scoring training
- Read as much as time allows
- Go to conferences, which I don't like because I need to be alone to think, but I like because I love to learn new ways to model mathematics!
- Understand how computers, websites, and software impact math understanding and integrating technology into math instruction
- Attend trainings and workshops
- Recognize huge growth because of classroom experience, workshops, and college classes—I'm going to keep it up!
- Note amazing professional development around college prep math
- Connect math to daily experiences, mandatory math workshops and monthly grade level discussions, learning to use manipulatives effectively with Math Their Way
- I learn from kids, talking with fellow teachers, attending math workshops

What helps you learn mathematics content?

- Applications to real-life, computer simulations
- Discussions with teachers and consultants, practice lessons with consultants, courses on how kids learn, read and reread Marilyn Burns' material and philosophy
- Experience in the classroom
- Practice with students on a daily basis
- Complete immersion—practice, problems, and studying
- Time to look at materials and plenty of examples
- Understand *why* something is used and *why* it works

These teachers' responses represent a broad spectrum of involvement in professional development, but we note that professional learning communities received little recognition. Most important is that the teachers continue to learn, for with every new understanding comes an option for differentiating a piece of mathematics for some student(s) in need.

As teachers begin or expand their practice of differentiating math instruction, it is inevitable that they will encounter elements of student reasoning that challenge their own understanding, analogous to the incident reported in the opening chapter scenario. These events should be welcomed as opportunities to grow mathematically and pedagogically. They also provide the impetus for planning and implementing sustained professional development that matches teacher needs.

Chapter 10

Putting It Together: Lessons, Anchors, and Tools

Differentiated instruction has as many faces as it has practitioners and as many outcomes as there are learners.

Kim Pettig, Pittsford, NY, Project Challenge Coordinator,
"On the Road to Differentiated Practice"

A Reminder

As the foundation for summarizing our work, we revisit what differentiated instruction in mathematics means. In various settings throughout the book it is characterized as:

- Responsive teaching
- An organized and flexible approach to teaching mathematics using a diverse collection of strategies
- The purposeful adaptation of teaching and learning processes to accommodate the different ways students learn mathematics
- All students having access to and being appropriately supported and challenged in their acquisition of important mathematical knowledge
- Teaching and learning in a problem-solving environment
- Providing all students with the opportunities they need to reach high standards, their full potential, and become mathematically proficient independent learners

We sincerely believe that differentiating mathematics instruction is all of these descriptors and more. The last bullet is particularly cogent with its embedded outcome of helping students become independent learners of mathematics. Teaching in this sort of environment calls for ready access to wisdom and a variety of tools. It is no wonder that mathematics teachers are eager for support: generative ideas, techniques, strategies, and suggestions.

The Record: Classroom Lessons and Suggestions

Table 10.1 lists the differentiated mathematics lessons and suggestions that occur throughout the text in the order of their appearance. They are coded for type and completeness, assigned appropriate grade levels, and labeled with the associated content strands from the National Council of Teachers of Mathematics (NCTM) *Principles and Standards for School Mathematics*: number and operations; algebra; geometry; measurement; data analysis and probability.

Table 10.1. Lesson and Activity Log by Chapter

Chapter	Lesson or Activity Title	Code	Grade Level	Strand
1	Place value unit	UF	3–4	Number
2	Operations with fractions	LF	7	Number
	Guess My Number	S	3–8	Number
	Mathematics survey	S	6–8	All
	Get It Together cooperative group problems	S	4–8	All
	Domino metaphor	LF	6–8	Data and number
	Graphing interests	LF	6–8	Data
	Double digit from FAMILY MATH	S	2–8	Number and probability
3	Line design	LF	6	Geometry and number
	Large numbers and the brain	S	7–8	Number
	Geometry and mozart	S	7–8	Geometry
	Median march	LF	3–8	Data
	Turn symmetry	LF	5–7	Geometry
	Graph multiple intelligences	S	7–8	Data and number
	Multiplication with multiple intelligences	S	3–5	Number
4	The Chessboard	LF	7–8	Algebra
	Petals Around the Rose	LF	4–8	Number and algebra
	All Chocolate, No Change	S	5–8	Algebra
	Blades of Grass	S	5	Measurement
	How Many Products	S	4–6	Number
	Stacking Boxes	S	5–7	Measurement

Lesson Codes: L = lesson; S = suggested lesson; F = fully developed; W = warm-up; R = reinforcement activity; U = unit

continued on following page

Table 10.1 *continued*

Chapter	Lesson or Activity Title	Code	Grade Level	Strand
	Designing Cereal Boxes	S	5–7	Measurement
	Pocket Coins	S	2–4	Number and measurement
	Four 4's	S	6–8	Number
	The Meaning of Mean	LF	5	Data
	Describe a Rectangle	S	3–4	Geometry
	Missing Digits	S	2–4	Number and algebra
	Caramel Boxes	S	6	Number and measurement
	Possible Scores	S	6	Data
	Growing Squares	S	6	Number and geometry
	Fraction Factors	S	6–7	Number
5	Matching fractions and decimals	R	6–7	Number
	Matching vocabulary and illustrations	R	3–8	All
	Matching vocabulary and definitions	R	3–8	All
	Matching computations and solutions	R	3–8	Number
	Matching mixed numbers and improper fractions	R	5–7	Number
	Multiplication with rod trains	LF	3	Number
	Weighing objects	LF	2	Measurement
	Arrays for multiplication and area	S	3–4	Number and measurement
	How Long? How Many?	S	3–4	Number
	Learning about coins	LF	K	Measurement
	Children's Theatre	LF	4	Number
	Famous mathematicians	LF	8	All
	Fraction unit pretest	US	3–4	Number
	Paper Pool	LF	7	Number and algebra
6	Writing and reading multiplication facts	LF	3	Number
	Multiples: Finding Patterns	LF	3	Number
	Mental math problems	W	3–8	Number

Lesson Codes: L = lesson; S = suggested lesson; F = fully developed; W = warm-up; R = reinforcement activity; U = unit

continued on following page

Table 10.1 *continued*

Chapter	Lesson or Activity Title	Code	Grade Level	Strand
	Skills practice	W	2–8	All
	Math board	W	3	All
	Estimation	W	K–8	Measurement and data
	Sequencing	W	K–5	Various
7	Linear relationships	LF, U	7	Algebra
	Two- and three-dimensional shapes	LF	4	Geometry
	The Array Game	LF	3	Number
	Area of a circle	LF	6	Measurement
	One Half	LF	2	Number and geometry
	Number theory ThinkDots	LF	6–7	Number
	Pathways for decimal operations	LF	6	Number
8	Composing and decomposing numbers— Kathryn's lesson	LF	3	Number
9	Alternative subtraction algorithms	S	2–4	Number
	Multiple approaches to mean	S	6–8	Data
	Kindergarten number lines	S, R	K	Number
	Developing quick recall for addition and subtraction facts—a menu	LF	2	Number
10	Farkle	LF	3–8	Number

Lesson Codes: L = lesson; S = suggested lesson; F = fully developed; W = warm-up; R = reinforcement activity; U = unit

Additional Anchor Activities and Resources

Anchor activities are critical to any differentiating program. As explained previously (Chapters 2 and 5), they are the activities that students use when they have completed their work or are waiting for help. They can also be used at the beginning of class for warm-ups as a way to introduce them. It's important to establish a routine way to store and manage anchor activities such as Jenny's crate work referenced in Chapter 5. A plastic crate of folders is Jenny's way of storing and cycling anchors. It is a management tool that also helps her keep the anchor activities current as work progresses through the year.

As indicated throughout the text, my favorite anchor activity for seventh and eighth grade is the MATHCOUNTS program materials. So much so that students have a section of their math binder devoted to MATHCOUNTS warm-ups and work-outs—sets of ten problems of increasing challenge.

Although the materials were developed for a competitive program, in reality they are simply good curriculum: engaging problems and explorations that do not need a competitive umbrella. Other contest materials like the Continental Math League problem collections for grades 2–8 are useful for students at the lower grade levels for similar anchor activities.

Next in line is the monthly menu of problems in NCTM's journal, *Mathematics in the Middle*, which Jenny also keeps in her crate work, referenced in Chapter 5. *Teaching Children Mathematics*, the elementary journal, has a similar set of anchor-type problems in its Math by the Month segment. These are conveniently categorized by grade-level bands: K–2, 3–4, and 5–6.

The books of Theoni Pappas, such as *The Joy of Mathematics* and *Math Talk: Mathematical Ideas in Poems for Two Voices*, encourage the independent exploration of intriguing mathematical ideas, especially for middle grades and up.

Jenny recommends the inexpensive Sunshine Math materials from the Greenville County Schools in South Carolina. Sunshine Math is an enrichment opportunity for students in grades K–8. The materials are specific for each grade level and offer teachers a set of ten problems each week that vary in level of difficulty. Interested teachers should contact Dr. Marjorie Claytor at 801-B Rutledge Building, 1429 Senate St., Columbia, SC 29201; (1-800-734-8372); www.greenville.k12.sc.us/mtnview/Sunshine%20Math/Sunshine%20 Math.htm.

Other challenging and engaging games and materials abound that make suitable anchoring options, including the games developed as part of your regular curriculum. Once introduced in the program, they can become part of the classroom anchor collection. In my classroom there are also Tangoes, Polydrons (the kids never have enough time with these fascinating materials that develop spatial skills), the game SET, and Geoblocks with job cards. These multigrade hands-on materials offer substantial and purposeful mathematical challenges from kindergarten through eighth grade. You need to establish firm rules for their use—they are not used as toys but mathematical tools! The rewards in spatial skill development and logical reasoning are well worth the time it takes to establish the standards for using them.

Farkle is another game that I've used as an anchor activity. It requires six dice and a list of scoring rules, which are adaptable (see Figure 10.1). Students have organized tournaments on their own time, created rules for special circumstances, and become amazingly facile with the mental manipulation of numbers. We also collected data and developed probability sense from having to make sometimes painful and costly decisions. One year the game was adapted for the holiday season and aptly titled Bah Humbug!

Recommended Resources

This is a list of additional resources we recommend for good quality anchor activities.

Marilyn Burns books (grades 1–8), Math Solutions Publications
Childs, Leigh, Laura Choate, and Polly Hill 1999–2003. *Nimble with Numbers*

Farkle Rules

You will need six dice, paper and pencil.

How to play: Each player must score 500 points in one turn to "get on the board." If a player farkles (rolls and comes up with nothing that scores) before reaching 500, their turn is over and they pass the dice to the next player. Once a player has gotten on the board, they can quit at any time during their turn, regardless of how many points they score during that turn. Play to 5,000. Once someone scores 5,000 (or more) the remaining players have one last turn.

There are ways you can vary the game at this point. If someone beats the original player who reached 5,000, they can be declared the winner, or if you want to continue playing, let all players have one more turn each time anyone beats the high scorer.

How to score: Players begin by rolling all six dice. In order not to farkle, each roll in a turn must come up with something that counts. Scoring dice are set aside and contribute their score for that turn. If a player decides to continue rolling during their turn, they use the remaining dice. If at any time all the dice produce points, the player has the option to begin again with all six dice. This still counts as one turn and should they farkle they will lose any points accumulated during that turn. Once points are recorded, they cannot be lost.

What counts:

All six dice the same	1,000	Three pair	1,000
A straight (1 through 6)	1,000	Three 1s	1,000
One 1	100	One 5	50

Three of any number equals that number times 100 (except 1s, which equal 1000)—e.g., three 2s = 200; three 3s = 300; three 4s = 400; three 5s = 500; three 6s = 600.

Have fun, play fair and take a risk now and then!

FIGURE 10.1

(*Grades 1–7*). White Plains, NY: Dale Seymour Productions.
Continental Math League Problem Collections (PO Box 2196, St. James, NY 11780; 631-584-2016 http://continentalmathleague.hostrack.com)

Hull, Henry, Joseph Quartararo, and Herman Ramakers. 1996. *The Best of CML—1990–1995 for Grades 2–3.* St. James, NY: Continental Mathematics League.

Hull, Henry, Joseph Quartararo, and Herman Ramakers. 1996. *The Best of CML—1990–1995 for Grades 4–6.* St. James, NY: Continental Mathematics League.

Teacher Tools for Differentiating Instruction

Throughout the book, we've presented numerous lists and guidelines to help facilitate the implementation of differentiated mathematics instruction. Here, we list these teacher tools by chapter for the reader's easy reference.

Chapter 6: Planning

Chapter 7: Lessons as Lenses

Chapter 8: The Teacher

Chapter 9: Teacher Knowledge of Mathematics and Pedagogy

Chapter 11: Moving Ahead

Summary

In this chapter, we reviewed the characteristics of differentiated math instruction, expanded the resource pool for anchor activities, and catalogued the lessons, activities, and tools we've used for differentiating our mathematics instruction. As you make this practice your own, pick and choose items that relate to your needs and revisit their context for additional support. Be creative, enjoy the challenge, and help kids learn and love math!

Chapter 11

Moving Ahead: Reflections and Frequently Asked Questions

Who dares to teach must never cease to learn.

John Cotton Dana, In 1912
College Motto—Kean College of New Jersey
Platt, Suzy, editor. 1993. *Respectfully Quoted: A Dictionary of Quotations.*
New York: Barnes and Noble Books (337)

The Challenge

The purposes of this chapter are to review the compelling case for differentiation in the mathematics classroom and help you move ahead from wherever you might be in the process. As indicated in the Introduction, mathematics teachers today have the exciting yet daunting challenge in the context of diverse classrooms to ensure that all students have appropriate and engaging opportunities to learn important mathematics with deep understanding. In response to that challenge, we are constantly learning, developing, and evolving as practitioners of differentiated instruction.

Growing as Practitioners

Evolution is a process of gradual change, so keep in mind the essential elements of successful change discussed in the introductory chapter: *vision, skills, incentives, resources,* and *plans.* Jenny and I developed our differentiated practices over many years beginning with the *vision* of all children learning mathematics with understanding. We've been driven by that vision and the philosophy of accepting children where they are and helping them move as far forward as possible during our time together. The *skills* for effective mathematics teaching are well defined and like any skill, are refined with practice. Celebrate the opportunity to practice and learn daily. Remember that you learn as much from mistakes as from successes as long as you use them well. In the meantime, watching a child come to understand is the powerful *incentive* that fuels our passion and probably yours as well. When you can help that happen for children who need different pathways, the reward grows exponentially. *Resources* abound: for content, lessons, techniques, strategies, formats, and so on. We've shared our favorites for now and continuously employ new ones that emerge and hold promise. We devoted Chapter 6 to *planning* because it holds the final key for unlocking the mystery to differentiating mathematics instruction. Try a simple plan to get started, and use the support available in the content and pedagogical arsenal in print, on-line, and with your colleagues. The National Council of Teachers of Mathematics (NCTM) documents are sound and substantial and the professional learning community is invaluable.

Moving Ahead: A Design Framework

If you are just getting started, think about differentiating one lesson or one activity next week. Reflect on what you learn and try again, incorporating ideas gleaned from the first of many attempts. It doesn't need to be perfect the first time nor does it need to be every lesson, every day. If you have some experience and are seeking to do more, select just one new strategy, such as a menu or pathways, for each grading period. Attempting too many elements at once may diminish the potential for your own development and make it difficult to self-assess and grow from the experience.

The following lesson design framework is a good starter. It is the outline Jenny and I use to design differentiated math experiences.

- *Essential learning*: Identify and state the mathematical ideas that are central to the experience. For an example, refer to the essential questions for the place value unit in Chapter 1.
- *Check big ideas, grade-level focal points, and NCTM standards*: Check the big ideas descriptions to confirm that this is important mathematics and appropriate focal points for grade-level development. Then ground the work with the appropriate standard(s) and expectations from *Principles and Standards for School Mathematics* (NCTM 2000). More specific information on these guidelines is found in Chapter 9.
- *Expected outcome for the lesson*: Articulate the actual change in student understanding and skill that is desired.
- *Reason for differentiating*: Articulate the basis for the differentiated experience. Be clear about why the differentiation is necessary or important. We first introduced this idea in Chapter 1 and refer to it throughout the text.

- *Format*: Select the format that best suits the essential learning, expected outcome, and student needs (tiers, menu, open-ended, and so on). For more information on different formats, see Chapter 7.
- *Prior knowledge*: Analyze what is known about various students' backgrounds regarding the mathematics and what needs to be probed further. Chapter 3 is devoted to learning about students.
- *Time frame*: Set time limits for the experience. In Chapter 6 we stress the importance of pacing as part of planning.
- *Lesson details*:
  - *Preparation*: Materials, task cards, directions, questions, and scaffolds.
  - *Launch*: Plan whole class introduction and how to weave in scaffolding.
  - *Exploration*: Plan for questions in the pocket (thoughtfully prepared questions you tuck in your pocket to challenge, redirect, or extend the work of students in the heat of the moment) and monitoring needs. Know what students will be doing and the types of support and direction they're likely to require. Be especially prepared for low status students and how they can be assigned competence.
  - *Summary*: Plan for how students will share their work or demonstrate new understandings or skills.

    For examples of these design details, see Chapter 7.
- *Assessment*: Determine evidence for student learning. You'll find examples embedded in the Chapter 7 lessons and throughout the book beginning in Chapter 1.

A routine framework like this is timesaving support—a professional scaffold that can be tailored to fit any specific situation.

Differentiating Options

Early on, we talked about the different ways differentiation can be embedded in any lesson. For example, many of the lessons or units we've shared focus the differentiation on the basic idea of varying the content, process, and/or products. In Chapter 7 the seventh-grade linear relationships unit was differentiated for content as students used a modified jigsaw model. Small groups investigated different portions of content and then taught what they learned to the rest of the class. The sixth-grade menu on finding the area of circles was differentiated for process. Students were assigned or had the option to choose how to determine or estimate the circle's area from a set of seven different processes. In both geometry lessons—the tiered fourth-grade two- and three-dimensional geometry and the open-ended second grade lesson on one half—the differentiation targeted products. Individuals or small groups were expected to create different products to show their level of understanding. From this basic structure for differentiating evolves the statement made by Kim Pettig in the Chapter 10 epigraph: "Differentiated instruction has as many faces as it has practitioners and as many outcomes as there are learners."

Reflecting on Parameters for Differentiated Mathematics Instruction

As we reflect upon lessons or whole class sessions, we find it helpful to think about *mathematical proficiency*. How did we measure up in our planning and execution? Did our processes help all our children move ahead in these intertwined strands by (1) understanding the mathematics, (2) computing fluently, (3) applying concepts to solve problems, (4) reasoning logically, and (5) seeing mathematics as sensible, useful, and doable—National Research Council's definition of a *productive disposition* (National Research Council 2002, 1). If so, we know we are measuring up to the equity, teaching, and learning principles:

- *Equity*. Excellence in mathematics education requires equity – high expectations and strong support for all students.
- *Teaching*. Effective mathematics teaching requires understanding what students know and need to learn and then challenging and supporting them to learn it well.
- *Learning*. Students must learn mathematics with understanding, actively building new knowledge from experience and prior knowledge. (NCTM 2000, 11)

It's good to revisit these succinct statements that literally guide the differentiated instruction of mathematics—simple, yet all encompassing.

Frequently Asked Questions About Differentiation in Mathematics

We close our exploration into differentiated instruction in mathematics with some questions put to us by practitioners along with our current responses.

How do you discuss homework when kids have different assignments?

It varies depending on the assignment. There are times when we discuss problems that all students completed and then the students regroup to discuss problems that were specifically assigned. Other times, I have kids start out in "like homework" small groups and have them discuss their work. I circulate during this time to make sure students are on task and to be available to answer questions or ask a probing question. There are times that I provide an answer key and students correct the problems that they were assigned. The answer key has answers to all problems assigned. When it's appropriate, I might have students who solved more challenging problems share the problem and their thinking with the whole class and then have a conversation about the problem. In this way, all students are exposed to the mathematics of the problem and the thinking of some of their classmates. And there are those times that I just collect all homework and provide written feedback to students.

How do students let you know they need something more?

I provide students weekly opportunities to complete a brief survey about the class and how things are going. I usually provide them with a couple of prompts. For example: In math I'm struggling with . . . This week I feel good about . . . I wish you'd . . . This gives me a chance to hear from the students and try to address their needs. I often will make general comments to the class about their responses, and then there are the times that I need to meet with specific students based on what they wrote. If I'm looking for a general check-in on class progress as a whole, I often don't have kids put their names on their comments. In this way, I hope to elicit feedback about class that might be considered cool feedback but important nonetheless. There are also occasions when students are completing assignments and a student may ask for help on a specific task or assignment. Students also approach me with questions during their study time, as well as before and after school. I also provide students with times that I will be available for help.

How do you build students' capacity for taking on their own learning?

I have a handout that is based on DuFour's work on professional learning communities and best practices in which I lay out the essential learning for each unit (DuFour 1998). The four questions that are addressed in the handout for the students are: What do we want you to learn? How will we know when you have learned the essential learning? What will I do if you are struggling to learn the essential learning? What can you do to increase learning? (See Figure 11.1.) I also have a variety of challenging activities (see anchor activities in Chapters 2, 5, and 10) that I expect students to work on as time permits. In other instances, I provide time for all students to have the opportunity to work on the anchor activities. There are times that students complete a self-assessment on their progress and develop a plan for how to address areas that need improvement. I collect these assessments, review them with students, and help them carry out their plan. This has been a great way for students to take charge of their learning needs.

When you differentiate instruction, how can you organize so that all groups get time to ask you questions without feeling like you should spend all of your time with one group?

I am very conscious of this because all students should have teacher attention. There are times that I provide differentiated instruction to individual students while all students are working. It might be in the form of a probing question to extend a student's thinking or a question that helps a student think about how to approach solving a problem. I have a timer that I use that helps me, as well as the students, keep track of time. This also helps me be aware of the amount of time that students work on a particular task, and it helps kids stay focused on their work. I keep written records of my work

---

> ### Data About Us
>
> *Essential learning—What we want you to learn.*
>
> - Find, use, and interpret measures of center (mean, median, mode) and spread (range).
> - Pose questions, collect and analyze data, and make interpretations to answer questions.
> - Select, create, and use appropriate graphical representations of data using line plots, bar graphs, stem and leaf plots, and coordinate graphs.
> - Use the language and concepts of statistics to express mathematical ideas.
>
> *How will we know you have learned the above concepts?*
> through daily work
> your class participation in discussions
> your homework
> assessments throughout the unit
>
> *What will I do if you are struggling to learn the essential learning?*
> I will be available to help you during class, recess, and study hall.
> If you'd like help before and/or after school, please just let me know when you will be here and I'll be available if I don't already have another meeting scheduled. You can also receive help from other sixth-grade teachers: Mr. Morse, Mrs. Ellis, or Ms. Braey.
>
> *What can you do to increase learning?*
> Participate in class—in both activities and in discussions.
> Complete all work and ask for help if you don't understand something.
> Keep your math notebook organized—this includes your daily work, homework, vocabulary, and assessments.

FIGURE 11.1—Unit overview to build student independence.

with specific groups and the members of the group. This helps me see overall trends with the times that I spend with students.

How do you have consistent expectations for all students?

There is a curriculum for all students and it's important for all students to have access to the curriculum. I hold students accountable for learning, perhaps at different paces, but I expect them all to learn the essential lessons for the year. I am consistent in my expectations that all students will complete assignments on time; the assignments may differ but are in line with the essential learning and with our district's academic expectations. As I differentiate, I have to keep good records about each student and refer to the records when planning. Having students work on different assignments does not mean that I have different expectations for them.

How do I work with those kids who are struggling?

Occasionally, students need time to work on the current concepts that they have been learning. It's class time where students have an assignment, and I use the time to conference with individual students. During this time, I am specifically interested in touching base with the students who are struggling with the current concepts. It provides me with a chance to have three to five minutes to try to understand individual students' thinking about specific problems. We might look at a recent quiz and discuss the mistakes that were made or what the student was thinking. It may prove to be a simple misconception that once discussed helps the student move forward in his or her learning. It's also a time for me to offer feedback to students who are doing fine but also need individual attention. It might be a chance to offer an extension. I also schedule time to work with students if they have a study hall. There are students who choose to meet with me before school or after school on a weekly basis. There are occasions when students ask to meet with me during their lunch break, which is fine as long they have time to eat lunch.

How and when do you provide feedback to students on the work that they do? For example, anchor activities?

I provide students with feedback on their work in a variety of ways. I sometimes have answers available for them to access when they've finished an anchor activity. They know that they are expected to complete the task, seek help if necessary, and consult with their classmates prior to checking the answers. There are other times when students will have time to get together and discuss the task they are doing and agree on their work and not need to have me see their work. In this case, I often am part of the discussion that students have together, so I also know what they've understood and where they might need something more from me as the teacher. Sometimes students seek me out to discuss an activity that they are working on. Other instances, I do collect tasks and look at them and provide students with feedback. I make decisions on the tasks to collect based on the task itself, the level of difficulty students seem to have had in completing it, or because I am looking for specific learning evidence.

What is the role of vocabulary and language in differentiating mathematics instruction?

The role of vocabulary and language in differentiated instruction is everywhere, especially if you have English language learners among your students. As TODOS (Mathematics for All) President Miriam Leiva, in her essay titled "The Problem with Words in Mathematics: A Strategy for Differentiated

Instruction," states, "The diversity of today's classrooms *mandates* that teachers address the language as well as the math concept and skills" (Leiva 2006). Language in mathematics is generally confusing because of the fact that mathematics has a language of its own. Consider all the symbols and representations that we are encouraged to use and must understand in order to do so in a meaningful way. That's what first prompted me to teach mathematics through a vocabulary lens many years ago and led to the writing of *Teaching Mathematics Vocabulary in Context: Windows, Doors, and Secret Passageways*. That book is in reality a differentiated approach to incorporating vocabulary.

Several issues emerge where language impacts our differentiated instructional model. First, with a focus on problem solving, we must be certain that problems are interpreted correctly. Always ask to have problems restated in student voice and from student perspectives using pictures, manipulatives, models, or real representations. Second, use various small group configurations so that students communicate as they work; using the language develops the language. Be sensitive to the needs of second language learners by grouping them with someone who can help with interpretation. You may have to be creative and find volunteers from the community. Finally, require students to explain their processes and justify solutions answering these three questions: What did you do? Why did you do it? and Why does the answer make sense?

How do students respond to different assignments in the classroom?

I have not had students question me about different assignments and I think this is due, in part, to the work that I do at the beginning of the year on classroom culture. (See Chapter 2.) I spend time building a learning environment in which students understand that all their classmates have something to offer and that we need to be respectful of each other. The first few weeks are spent learning about how our class will function as we are learning math. A safe environment needs to be established in order for students to work as a learning community, one where they are free to ask questions and share their ideas and know that they will be heard. I provide lots of feedback and positive reinforcement during the first few weeks regarding the learning environment. Once this has been established, then the students are part of the success. They understand that they all have different learning styles, interests, abilities, talents, and approaches to learning. It's not a question of why there are different assignments but a discussion about what students learn from their varying assignments and differentiated instruction.

How do you respond to parents who ask about their child's assignment and their neighbor's child's assignment that are not the same and yet they are in the same class?

I start by letting the parents have an opportunity to ask the question. I want to know what they've heard and what their concern is before I respond to them. I talk to parents about student learning and let them know that we do have a curriculum and essential learning for each unit of study. I provide the parents with several instances in which I have differentiated an assignment in order to help them understand that it's not necessarily the curriculum that's different—it's the assignment product that has been differentiated for student interest, learning style, or level of understanding. I also discuss equity with parents. (See Chapter 2 for the work we do to create an equitable classroom and refer to NCTM's *Equity Principle*, NCTM 2000, 12–14.) As a way to let parents know the students' perceptions about the differentiation, I share feedback that I've received from the students.

I would like to try differentiated instruction with my seventh-grade classes but I'm really nervous about it. How do I safely get started and handle student put-downs?

First of all, do the classroom culture work (Chapter 2), and deal matter-of-factly with the elements that make you nervous. Try having the students help you create the norms and expectations that address your issues. I've found that to be a first step: their behavior monitoring is so much better when they set the standards. Once that is in place, you should be able to start in small ways to differentiate. Open-ended problems are a good way to begin or a menu of activities as part of a unit wrap-up. Be sure to have some anchor activities ready as well. Take small steps and, as we said earlier, reflect on each lesson and use the results to plan for the next attempt. Then, if a put-down occurs, be calm but totally intolerant, reiterating plainly that the put-down is unacceptable. (Practice in front of the mirror—no kidding.) If possible, use the opportunity to value the person being ridiculed. In the practice of complex instruction, they delve into the process of assigning competence to low status students. (See Chapter 5 as part of the discussion of heterogeneous groups.) You might want to look into this practice. In any case, there is a learning community problem (there's a reason for everything) that needs to be solved and there may be resources in your school to help with that. I have learned over the years about the importance of maintaining neutral facial expression and response to student ideas so that the discourse remains open to the continued pondering of possibilities.

Closing

Our children's futures as well as our own depend on our ability as teachers to meet the challenge of facilitating a deep understanding of important mathematics for all students. Mathematics teachers currently have access to all that is needed to be able to respond successfully. There are concrete support tools at hand: planning guides, flexible strategies, management techniques, guidelines, superb resources, and more for just about any procedure you're willing to try. As alluded to earlier, teachers are always in the process of growth and change, and choosing to direct that process toward helping *all* children learn mathematics and learn *how* to learn mathematics best offers tremendous personal and professional rewards.

Now, go and do differentiated mathematics. Serve all your children well, learn from each experience, and celebrate your successes!

BIBLIOGRAPHY

Anderson, E. C. 2005. "Strengths-Based Educating: A Concrete Way to Bring Out the Best in Students—and Yourself." *Educational Horizons* 83(3): 180–89.

Anderson, L. W., and D. Krathwohl, eds. 2001. *A Taxonomy for Learning, Teaching, and Assessing: A Revision of Bloom's Taxonomy of Educational Objectives*. New York: Addison Wesley Longman.

Andrade, H. G. 1999. "When Assessment Is Instruction and Instruction Is Assessment: Using Rubrics to Promote Thinking and Understanding." In L. Hetland and S. Veenema, eds. *The Project Zero Classroom: Views on Understanding*. Cambridge, MA: Harvard Graduate School of Education. Available at: http://www.lookstein.org/heterogeneous/ hetero_edu_rubrics.htm.

Appelbaum, L. 2005. *Instructional Differentiation for Student Independence*. Gorham ME: Southern Maine Partnership at the University of Southern Maine.

Appleby, M. 1999. "Petals Around the Rose: Building Positive Attitudes About Problem Solving." *ENC Focus: A Magazine for Classroom Innovators* 6 (2): 26–29.

Ball, D. L. 2003. *Mathematics in the 21st Century: What Mathematical Knowledge Is Needed for Teaching Mathematics?* Prepared for the Secretary's Summit on Mathematics, U.S. Department of Education, February 6, 2003. Available at: http://ed.gov/print/rschstat/research/progs/mathscience/ ball.html.

Ball, D. L., J. Ferrini-Mundy, J. Kilpatrick, R. J. Milgram, W. Schmid and R. Schaar. 2005a. *Reaching for Common Ground in K–12 Mathematics Education*. Available at: http://www.maa.org/common-ground/cg-report2005.html.

Ball, D. L., H. C. Hill, and H. Bass. 2005b. "Knowing Mathematics for Teaching." *American Educator* Fall: 14–17+.

Boaler, J. 2006. "Opening Our Ideas: How a Detracked Mathematics Approach Promoted Respect, Responsibility, and High Achievement." *Theory into Practice* 45(1).

Boaler, J. and M. Staples. 2005. *Transforming Students' Lives Through an Equitable Mathematics Approach: The Case of Railside School.* Available at: http://www.stanford.edu/~joboaler/

Borasi, R., and J. Fonzi. 2002. *Foundations: Professional Development That Supports School Mathematics Reform.* Arlington, VA: National Science Foundation.

Borruso-Emig, V. 2000. "My Four Hats: Different Roles in the Differentiated Classroom." *ASCD Classroom Leadership,* 4(1): 6–8.

Brodesky, A., F. R. Gross, A. S. McTigue, and C. C. Tierney. 2004. "Planning Strategies for Students with Special Needs: A Professional Development Activity." *Teaching Children Mathematics,* 11(3): 146–54.

Brown, E. T., M. McGatha, and K. Karp. 2006. "Assessing Teachers' Knowledge: Diagnostic Mathematics Assessments for Elementary and Middle School Teachers." *New England Mathematics Journal* 38(2): 37–50.

Burns, M. 1987. *A Collection of Math Lessons from Grades 3–6.* Sausalito, CA: Math Solutions Publications.

———. 1991. *Math by All Means: Multiplication Grade 3.* Sausalito, CA: Math Solutions Publications.

———. 1992. *About Teaching Mathematics: A K–8 Resource.* Sausalito, CA: Math Solutions Publications.

———. 1998. *MATH: Facing an American Phobia.* Sausalito, CA: Math Solutions Publications.

Burns, M. and C. McLaughlin. 1990. *A Collection of Math Lessons from Grades 6–8.* Sausalito, CA: Math Solutions Publications.

Butler, E. and V. Robinson. 2000. "Curriculum Compacting: Recognizing Readiness and Responding." *ASCD Classroom Leadership* 4(1): 4–5.

Caine, R. N. and G. Caine. 1997. *Education on the Edge of Possibility.* Alexandria, VA: Association for Supervision and Curriculum Development.

Carpenter, T. P., M. L. Blanton, P. Cobb, M. L. Franke, J. Kaput, and K. McCain. 2004. *Scaling Up Innovative Practices in Mathematics and Science.* Madison WI: University of Wisconsin—Madison, National Center for Improving Student Learning and Achievement in Mathematics and Science (NCISLA).

Chandler, K. L., ed. 2006. *2006–2007 MATHCOUNTS School Handbook.* Alexandria, VA: MATHCOUNTS Foundation.

Chapin, S. H. and A. Johnson. 2006. *Math Matters, 2nd Edition, Grades K–8: Understanding the Math You Teach K–6.* Sausalito, CA: Math Solutions Publications.

Charles, R. I. 2005. "Big Ideas and Understandings as the Foundation for Elementary and Middle School Mathematics." *NCSM Journal of Mathematics Education Leadership,* 8 (1): 9–24.

Childs, L., L. Choate, and P. Hill. 1999. *Nimble with Numbers: Grades 6 & 7.* White Plains, NY: Dale Seymour Publications.

Checkley, K. 2000. "Serving Gifted Students in the Regular Classroom." *ASCD Curriculum Update:* winter: 5.

Clabaugh, G. K. 2005. "Strengths-Based Education: Probing Its Limits." *Educational Horizons*, 83 (3): 166–70.

Cohen, E. 1994. *Designing Groupwork: Strategies for the Heterogeneous Classroom, 2nd Edition*. New York: Teachers College Press.

Conklin, J. 2005. "Book Reviews — A Taxonomy for Learning, Teaching, and Assessing: A Revision of Bloom's Taxonomy of Educational Objectives." *Educational Horizons*, 83(3): 154–59.

Cotter, J. 2000. "Using Language and Visualization to Teach Place Value." *Teaching Children Mathematics*, 7(2): 108–14.

Cruz, E. 2003. "Bloom's Revised Taxonomy." In B. Hoffman, ed., *Encyclopedia of Educational Technology*. Available at: http://coe.sdsu.edu/eet/Articles/bloomrev/ Retrieved February 2, 2006.

Devito, B. and T. A. Grotzer. 2005. *Characterizing Discourse in Two Science Classrooms by the Cognitive Processes Demonstrated by Students and Teachers*. Presented at the National Association for Research in Science Teaching Conference. Dallas, TX. April 4–7.

Dickenson, D. J. and J. A. Butt. 1989. "The Effects of Success and Failure on High-Achieving Students." *Education and Treatment of Children* 12: 243–52.

DuFour, R., and R. Eaker. 1998. *Professional Learning Communities at Work*. Bloomington, IN: National Educational Service.

DuFour, R., R. DuFour, R. Eaker, and G. Karhanek. 2004. *Whatever It Takes: How Professional Learning Communities Respond When Kids Don't Learn*. Bloomington, IN: National Educational Service.

Eaker, R., R. DuFour, and R. DuFour. 2002. *Getting Started: Reculturing Schools to Become Professional Learning Communities*. Bloomington, IN: National Educational Service.

Economopoulos, K., S. J. Russell, and C. Tierney. 1998. "Arrays and Shares (Multiplication and Division)." In *Investigations in Number, Data, and Space*. White Plains, NY: Dale Seymour Publications.

Enterprise Management Ltd. 1987. *Managing Complex Change*. Palm Harbor, FL: Enterprise Management Ltd.

Erickson, T. 1989. *Get It Together: Math Problems for Groups, Grades 4–12*. Berkeley, CA: EQUALS, Lawrence Hall of Science.

———. 1996. *United We Solve: Math Problems for Groups*. Oakland CA: eeps media.

Friedman, T. 2005. *The World Is Flat — A Brief History of the Twenty-First Century*. New York: Farrar, Straus and Giroux.

Gardner, H. 1993. *Frames of Mind: The Theory of Multiple Intelligences*. New York: Basic Books.

———. 1999. *Intelligence Reframed: Multiple Intelligences for the 21st Century*. New York: Basic Books.

Goldsmith, L. T., J. Mark, and I. Kantrov. 1998. *Choosing a Standards-Based Mathematics Curriculum*. Newton, MA: Education Development Center, Inc.

Gregorc, A. 1982. *An Adult's Guide to Styles.* Columbia, CT: Gregorc Associates, Inc.

———. 2006a. "On Teaching Applications." *Frequently Asked Questions on Style.* Available at: http://gregorc.com/faq.html#teach

———. 2006b. Personal email communication. October 15, 2006.

Guild, P. B. and S. Garger. 1998. *Marching to Different Drummers, 2nd Edition.* Alexandria, VA: Association for Supervision and Curriculum Development.

Hart, L. 1983. *Human Brain, Human Learning.* New York: Basic Books.

Harvard-Smithsonian Center for Astrophysics. 1987. *A Private Universe.* A video documentary on education research. Available at: www.learner.org.

Heacox, D. 2002. *Differentiating Instruction in the Regular Classroom.* Minneapolis, MN: Free Spirit Publishing, Inc.

Herrera, T. 2002. "An Interview with Liping Ma: Do not forget yourself as a teacher of yourself." *ENC Focus* 9(3): 16–20.

Heuser, D. 2000a. "Mathematics Workshop: Mathematics Class Becomes Learner-Centered." *Teaching Children Mathematics* 6(5): 288–95.

———. 2000b. "Reworking the Workshop for Math and Science." *Educational Leadership* 58(1): 34–37.

Hill, H. C., S. G. Schilling, and D. L. Ball. 2004. "Developing Measures of Teachers' Mathematical Knowledge." *Elementary School Journal,* 105 (1): 11–30.

Hodges, T. D., and J. K. Harter. 2005. "A Review of the Theory and Research Underlying the StrengthsQuest Program for Students." *Educational Horizons* 83(3): 190–201.

Hooper, M. 2000. "Starting Up the Differentiated Classroom." *ASCD Classroom Leadership* 4(1): 1–3.

Hyde, A., K. George, S. Mynard, C. Hull, S. Watson, and P. Watson. 2006. "Creating Multiple Representations in Algebra: All Chocolate, No Change." *Mathematics Teaching in the Middle* 11(6): 262–68.

Jensen, E. 1998. *Teaching with the Brain in Mind.* Alexandria, VA: Association for Supervision and Curriculum Development.

Johanning, D. I. and T. Keusch. 2004. "Teaching to Develop Students as Learners." In R. Rubenstein, ed., *Perspectives on the Teaching of Mathematics,* 107–16. Reston, VA: National Council of Teachers of Mathematics.

Kansky, R. 2005. *Getting Smarter, Becoming Fairer: A Progressive Education Agenda for a Stronger Nation—A Summary.* Available from: robt@trib.com.

Kaye, P. 1987. *Games for Math: Playful Ways to Help Your Child Learn Math from Kindergarten to Third Grade.* New York: Pantheon Books.

Kitchen, R. S., and J. Depree. 2005. "Closing the Gap through an Explicit Focus on Learning and Teaching." *NCSM Journal of Mathematics Education Leadership,* 8(1): 3–8.

Kusler, G. 1982. "Getting to Know You." In National Association of Secondary Principals, ed., *Student Learning Styles and Brain Behavior: Programs,*

Instrumentation, Research, 11-14. Reston, VA: National Association of Secondary Principals.

Lappan, G., J. Fey, W. M. Fitzgerald, S. N. Friel, and E. D. Phillips. 2006. "Comparing and Scaling Teacher's Guide." *Connected Mathematics*. Upper Saddle River, NJ: Pearson Prentice Hall.

———. 2002. "Covering and Surrounding." *Connected Mathematics*. Upper Saddle River, NJ: Prentice Hall.

———. 2002. "Moving Straight Ahead." *Connected Mathematics*. Upper Saddle River, NJ: Prentice Hall.

Lappan, G. and E. Phillips. 1998. "Teaching and Learning in the Connected Mathematics Project." In R. Rubenstein, ed., *Mathematics in the Middle*. Reston, VA: National Council of Teachers of Mathematics.

Leiva, M. 2006. *The Problem with Words in Mathematics: A Strategy for Differentiated Instruction*. Available at: http://www.beyond-the-book.com/strategies/strategies_092006.html.

Ma, L. 1999. *Knowing and Teaching Elementary Mathematics*. Mahwah, NJ: Lawrence Erlbaum Associates, Inc.

Mathematical Sciences Education Board. 1993. *Measuring What Counts: A Conceptual Guide for Mathematics Assessment*. Washington, DC: The National Academies Press.

McKenzie, W. 1999. *Multiple Intelligences Inventory*. Available at: http://surfaquarium.com/MI/inventory.htm

Mokros, J., S. J. Russell, and K. Economopoulos. 1995. *Beyond Arithmetic: Changing Mathematics in the Elementary Classroom*. Palo Alto, CA: Dale Seymour Publications.

Murray, M. 2004. *Teaching Mathematics Vocabulary in Context: Windows, Doors, and Secret Passageways*. Portsmouth NH: Heinemann.

National Council of Teachers of Mathematics. 1989. *Curriculum and Evaluation Standards for School Mathematics*. Reston, VA: National Council of Teachers of Mathematics.

———. 1991. *Professional Standards for Teaching Mathematics*. Reston, VA: National Council of Teachers of Mathematics.

———. 1995. *Assessment Standards for School Mathematics*. Reston VA: National Council of Teachers of Mathematics.

———. 2000. *Principles and Standards for School Mathematics*. Reston, VA: National Council of Teachers of Mathematics.

———. 2006. *Curriculum Focal Points for Prekindergarten through Grade 8 Mathematics: A Quest for Coherence*. Reston VA: National Council of Teachers of Mathematics.

National Research Council. 2000. *How People Learn: Brain, Mind, Experience, and School*. Expanded Edition. J. Bransfold, A. Brown, and R. Cocking, eds. Division of Behavioral and Social Sciences and Education. Washington, DC: The National Academies Press.

———. 2001. *Adding It Up: Helping Children Learn Mathematics*. J. Kilpatrick, J. Swafford, and B. Findell, eds. Mathematics Learning Committee,

Center for Education, Division of Behavioral and Social Sciences and Education. Washington, DC: The National Academies Press.

———. 2002. *Helping Children Learn Mathematics*. Mathematics Learning Study Committee, J. Kilpatrick and J. Swafford, eds. Center for Education, Division of Behavioral and Social Sciences and Education. Washington, DC: The National Academies Press.

———. 2005. *How Students Learn: Mathematics in the Classroom*. Committee on *How People Learn*, A Targeted report for Teachers, M.S. Donovan and J.D. Bransford, eds. Division of Behavioral and Social Sciences and Education. Washington, DC: The National Academies Press.

Nugent, C. 2006. "How Many Blades of Grass Are on a Football Field?" *Teaching Children Mathematics* 12(6): 282–88.

O'Connell, S. 2005. *Now I Get It: Strategies for Building Confident and Competent Mathematicians, K–6*. Portsmouth, NH: Heinemann.

Palmer, P. 1998. *The Courage to Teach: Exploring the Inner Landscape of a Teacher's Life*. San Francisco: Jossey-Bass.

Pappas, T. 1993. *The Joy of Mathematics*, Second Edition. San Carlos, CA: Wide World Publishing/Tetra.

———. 1991. *Math Talk: Mathematical Ideas in Poems for Two Voices*. San Carlos, CA: Wide World Publishing/Tetra.

Peske, H. G. and K. Haycock. 2006. *Teaching Inequality: How Poor and Minority Students Are Shortchanged on Teacher Quality*. The Education Trust. Available at: http://www2.edtrust.org/EdTrust/Product+Catalog/alpha.htm.

Pettig, K. L. 2000. "On the Road to Differentiated Practice." *Educational Leadership* 57(1):14–18.

Pierce, R. and C. Adams. 2005. "Using Tiered Lessons in Mathematics." *Mathematics Teaching in the Middle School* 11(3): 144–49.

Platt, S., ed. 1993. *Respectfully Quoted: A Dictionary of Quotations*. New York: Barnes and Noble Books.

Purcell, J. H. 2005. *Differentiating the Pre-K–2 Mathematics Curriculum*. PowerPoint Presentation, National Council of Teachers of Mathematics Regional Conference. Hartford, CT. October 2005.

Quigley, K. and C. Gomez. 2006. "Becoming 'Highly Qualified'." *Teaching Children Mathematics*, 13(4): 232–35.

Ritchhart, R. 1999. "Generative Topics: Building a Curriculum Around Big Ideas." *Teaching Children Mathematics* 5: 462–68.

———. 2002. *Intellectual Character: What It Is, Why It Matters, and How to Get It*. San Francisco: Jossey-Bass.

Rogers, S., J. Ludington, and L. Renard. 2000. "Learning to Be Flexible: When Quality Counts More Than Timeliness." *ASCD Classroom Leadership* 4(1): 3, 6.

Schniedewind, N. and E. Davidson. 2000. "Differentiating Cooperative Learning." *Educational Leadership*, 57(1): 24–27.

Seagal, S. and D. Horne. 1997. *Human Dynamics: A New Framework for Understanding People and Realizing the Potential in Our Organizations*. Cambridge, MA: Pegasus Communications.

Sharma, M. C. 2001. "Improving Mathematics Instruction." In Math Curriculum Revision Committee, ed., *Addison Central Supervisory Union K–12 Mathematics Curriculum*. Available at: http://www.acsu.k12.vt.us/curriculum/Math.htm.

———. 2003. *Guiding Principles and Structure for a Mathematics Lesson*. Framingham, MA: Center for Teaching/Learning of Mathematics.

Shreffler, M. 2002. "A Deeper Look at Elementary Mathematics." *ENC Focus* 9(3): 16+.

Silver, H. E. and R. W. Strong. 2003. *Learning Style Inventory*. Ho-Ho-Kus, NJ: Thoughtful Education Press. Available at: www.thoughtfuled.com

Sowder, J. T. 2000. *Mathematics in the Middle Grades: Linking Research and Practice*. Invited Plenary Address. National Conference on Curriculum, Instruction, and Assessment in the Middle Grades: Linking Research and Practice. Sponsored by the National Educational Research Policy and Priorities Board, U. S. Department of Education, July 2000.

Stenmark, J. K., ed. 1991. *Mathematics Assessment: Myths, Models, Good Questions, and Practical Suggestions*. Reston, VA: NCTM.

Strong, R., E. Thomas, M. Perini, and H. Silver. 2004. "Creating a Differentiated Mathematics Classroom." *Educational Leadership* 61(5): 63–78.

Sullivan, P., and P. Lilburn. 2002. *Good Questions for Math Teaching: Why Ask Them and What to Ask, K–6*. Sausalito, CA: Math Solutions Publications.

Sutton, J. and A. Krueger, eds. 2002. *EDThoughts: What We Know About Mathematics Teaching and Learning*. Aurora, CO: Mid-continent Research for Education and Learning.

Tang, G. 2003. *Math-terpieces*. New York: Scholastic Press.

———. 2005. *Math Potatoes: Mind Stretching Brain Food*. New York: Scholastic Press.

Taylor-Cox, J. 2005. *Empowering Students and Teachers: Differentiating Instruction in Mathematics*. PowerPoint presentation, National Council of Supervisors of Mathematics Conference. Anaheim, CA. April 2005.

Tomlinson, C. A. 1999. *The Differentiated Classroom: Responding to the Needs of All Learners*. Alexandria, VA: Association for Supervision and Curriculum Development.

———. 2001. *How to Differentiate Instruction in Mixed-Ability Classrooms*, Second Edition. Alexandria, VA: Association for Supervision and Curriculum Development.

———. 2003. *Fulfilling the Promise of the Differentiated Classroom: Strategies and Tools for Responsive Teaching*. Alexandria, VA: Association for Supervision and Curriculum Development.

Trubowitz, S. 2005. "On Balance: Creating a Culture for Learning." *Educational Horizons* 83(3): 171–76.

Usiskin, Z. 2002. "Teachers Need a Special Type of Content Knowledge." *ENC Focus* 9(3): 14–15.

Walsh, J. A. and B. D. Sattes. 2005. *Quality Questioning: Research-Based Practice to Engage Every Learner*. Thousand Oaks, CA: Corwin Press.

Weeks, D. J. 2002. "Targeted Learning with Differentiated Instruction: Designs of Difference." *Northwest Teacher*. Mathematics and Science Education Center. Available at: www.nwrel.org/msec/nwteacher/spring2002/designs.html.

Wehrmann, K. S. 2000. "Baby Steps: A Beginner's Guide." *Educational Leadership* 57(1): 20–23.

Weiss, I. R. and J. D. Pasley. 2004. "What Is High-Quality Instruction?" *Educational Leadership* 61(5): 22–28.

Willis, J. K. and A. N. Johnson. 2001. "Multiply with MI: Using Multiple Intelligences to Master Multiplication." *Teaching Children Mathematics* 7(5): 260–69.

Willis, S. and L. Mann. 2000. "Differentiating Instruction: Finding Manageable Ways to Meet Individual Needs." *ASCD Curriculum Update* winter: 1–3+.

Wisconsin Center for Education Research. 2005. *What 'Travels' in Mathematics Reform?* Available at: www.wcer.wisc.edu/news/coverStories/what_travels_in_math_reform.php.

Wlodkowski, R. 1978. *Student Motivation Information Form*. Milwaukee, WI: University of Wisconsin—Milwaukee.

Wong, H. K. and R. T. Wong. 1998. *The First Days of School: How to Be an Effective Teacher*. Mountain View, CA: Harry K. Wong Publications.

Zemelman, S., H. Daniels, and A. Hyde. 2005. *Best Practice: Today's Standards for Teaching and Learning in America's Schools*. Portsmouth, NH: Heinemann.

INDEX